Trout, Salmon
& Sea Trout Fishing

Charles Bingham

Trout, Salmon & Sea Trout Fishing

The Concise Guide

BLANDFORD

A Blandford Book

First published in the UK
1994 by Blandford, a Cassell imprint
Villiers House
41/47 Strand
London WC2N 5JE

Copyright © 1994

Distributed in the United States
by Sterling Publishing Co, Inc
387 Park Avenue South, New York, NY 10016-8810

Distributed in Australia
by Capricorn Link (Australia) Pty Ltd
2/13 Carrington Road, Castle Hill, NSW 2154

British Library Cataloguing-in-Publication Data
A catalogue record for this book
is available from the British Library

ISBN 0-7137-2359-9

Typeset by Litho Link Ltd, Welshpool, Powys, Wales

Printed in Great Britain by The Bath Press. Avon

Contents

Introduction

Looking back over 50 years of fishing, from the age of 12 years until this spring, I am amazed, not by my initial ignorance of the sport, but by the many years I spent 'finding out'. The quarry at first was chub and pike, the former caught on bees, grasshoppers and buzzy artificial flies, the latter on a jointed wooden plug. Those were the baits used by a school gardener whose example I followed, without much thought, in Northamptonshire. It did not occur to me to examine the mouths of the two fish to confirm that nature had adapted them to eat these foods: insects and other invertebrates; fish, frogs and other worthwhile mouthfuls. Small mouths for chub, wide jaws for pike; fat ambling feeders, fast-streamlined predators.

Trout followed in Anglesey in my 'teens. These, sometimes, fell to wet flies: Peter Ross, Black Pennell and others of that type. I did not question why trout attempted to eat those lifeless lures, or what they thought they were. Trout were hooked. The results sufficed.

At the age of 21 years, I visited Scotland to fish for sea trout on loch Maree. They took wet flies and dapped flies, despite the fact that they were not thought to feed. Their supposed lack of appetite was not questioned; neither was the fact that they were not present in the loch before the end of June. In August they were there. That was enough, together with the sight of many on the hotel plate. Their life-cycle, where they came from, or were going to, was submerged beneath the beauty of the waves and the bend of the rod.

In the 1950s I caught trout on the rivers Exe and Dart. They fell to dry flies – Blue Uprights, dressed from the hackles of ancient cockerels by two old ladies in Tiverton. The Blue Upright did not imitate a particular insect, which was just as well for I knew nothing of the naturals: the iron blue, hawthorn, and sedges of the summer months.

Chalk streams followed, with mayfly at the appointed time. Mayfly appeared miraculously, sat on the water, drifted along and then took flight. What they hatched from, and to where they flew, was the business of the keeper.

By 1960 I had caught several salmon on fly, following the instructions of a friend or a gillie, but there is the memory of asking, in June, on a Highland river, whether there were any kelts which ought to be returned. I was not aware that all spawned fish had long since died or departed to the sea. In the same decade, in March, there was a protracted struggle with a black and sunken something in the river Torridge. I was fearful, in my ignorance, that it was a kelt – the tailer drew out a sodden gatepost.

Slowly, over the years, awareness was acquired: the life-cycles of insects and fish, categories of waters, tackle knowledge and a library of fishing books in which to delve. Spate rivers, chalk streams, lochs, loughs and lakes were fished. Trout, sea trout, grayling and salmon graced my table, from Sutherland to Cornwall and from Kent to Anglesey. In 1976 the hobby became a livelihood in the establishment of a game-fishing school in Devon. Sets of instructions are written for pupils; books on rivers and fish for publishers. Now, to shorten for others the years of angling education, I set myself to write a concise book of practical information on game angling. Within these pages is the knowledge imparted to pupils on my instruction days. I have not included details and photographs on how to execute overhead, double-haul, roll and Spey casts. Books are a poor medium for imparting these physical accomplishments. Go to a qualified game-angling instructor; there is a list at the back of the book.

Charles Bingham

Part 1

Trout fishing in still waters

1 Trout and trout still waters

The two trout with which we are mainly concerned are the brown and the rainbow. Both fish are spawned and raised artificially in hatcheries. In addition, and to a greater extent in suitable areas, the spawning of brown trout occurs widely in many rivers and streams, whilst the rainbow spawns naturally in few British rivers and has a shorter life-span. Fast-flowing streams with beds of gravel and small stones are most suitable for the cutting of the redds in which the hen deposits her eggs. Such streams are more common in the west of the British Isles; chalk streams of the south and the rivers of East Anglia are slower-moving. The waters of the western streams tend to be acidic, whilst chalk streams are alkaline; the former produce less trout food than the latter. The consequence of these physical conditions is that one usually finds many small wild trout in the West Country and smaller numbers of larger trout in the chalk streams.

Of course, trout populations rise and fall in response to angling pressures. A heavy demand by anglers on the chalk streams is often beyond the fish-producing and fish-feeding capacity of the river, which, to meet the demand, has to be stocked with fish from hatcheries. Trout of takable size could also be stocked into acid upland rivers, but such a practice would be unwise because of loss of weight by the trout through lack of food. I once made the mistake of stocking 1 lb brown trout into the river Lyd in Devon. The water of the Lyd is slightly acid and only small wild brown live therein, in addition to non-feeding migratory fish. Within 3 months my 1 lb browns had reduced in weight to 12 oz – those which were not eaten by the herons.

Life history of the trout

During the summer months the ovaries of hen fish enlarge until, by October, they fill the body cavity. This will be obvious to any angler who has caught and cleaned a hen brown trout in the final days of September. Such trout should be returned unharmed to the river.

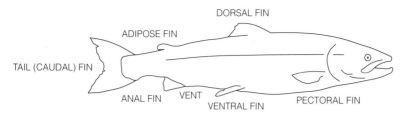

DORSAL FIN

ADIPOSE FIN

TAIL (CAUDAL) FIN

ANAL FIN   VENT

VENTRAL FIN   PECTORAL FIN

1 Fins of trout, salmon and sea trout (also grayling).

The testes of male trout also increase in size during the summer months, but do not fill the body cavity to its entirety. The testes produce white sperm containing milt, and reach their maximum size by the end of October. The ova of hen fish, and the milt of the cock, are extruded through the urino-genital pore behind the anus.

Spawning usually takes place in November, but may be delayed in some rivers until after Christmas. I have observed trout redds in the brooks of Dartmoor in November, and on the upper waters of the river Test in the same month. Trout in the river Wylye in Wiltshire spawn later, in December, and, as in many rivers, move up side streams to cut redds, in this case the Till and the Chitterne brook. On the upper Itchen, at Martyr Worthy, spawning peaks in the final week of December and the first week of January. Brown trout in lakes and reservoirs also spawn if there are suitable feeder streams. The trout congregate at the mouths of these rivulets in autumn and move upstream when there is a rise in water level.

Spawning takes place usually at the rising tail of a pool where gravel has been washed clear of silt. The redd in which the eggs are laid is usually about 3 in. deep and 1 ft in length for a 1 lb trout. The hen cuts the redd by turning on her side and flapping her tail. Suction, as the tail lifts, raises stones and gravel which the water current deposits in a bank below the depression. When the depression has been suitably shaped the female depresses her vent into the redd, raises her head and, with open mouth, extrudes the eggs.

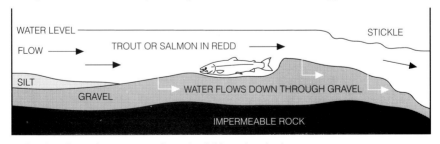

WATER LEVEL   STICKLE

FLOW   TROUT OR SALMON IN REDD

SILT

GRAVEL   WATER FLOWS DOWN THROUGH GRAVEL

IMPERMEABLE ROCK

2 Section through a trout or salmon 'redd' in a river bed.

The male positions himself alongside the hen, quivers, and releases sperm in a white cloud of milt. One sperm will enter and fertilize the egg through the micropyle, a tiny pore in the egg membrane. When the sperm nucleus has fused with that of the egg, fertilization has taken place and the membrane closes and becomes impermeable.

The egg is heavier than water, sinks into the redd and is covered with gravel, sometimes by the hen cutting a further redd above the original depression. If the gravel is clean, oxygenated water will reach the eggs by downward currents through the river bed. If the redd becomes silted, due to lack of water flow and the ploughing-up of filtering water meadows, the eggs will be deprived of oxygen and will atrophy. In a trout hatchery, ripe hens are stripped of eggs into a bowl or bucket by running the thumb down the belly of the trout towards the vent. Cock fish receive similar treatment into the same container. The eggs are then stirred with a feather to assist fertilization before being placed on trays in running water.

Hatching may take place in about 40 days for brown trout, and less than this for rainbow, if water rising from a spring at 50°F flows over the eggs. Between 70 and 90 days may be required in a river or hatchery if the water is at 41 or 42°F as is the case in natural upland waters in winter.

The eggs hatch soon after becoming 'eyed', and an alevin emerges with a sustaining yolk sac beneath its chin. The yolk is absorbed over 2 or 3 weeks, when the fishlets become known as *fry* and commence feeding, taking up station facing the current in a stream.

Subsequent trout growth depends upon the environment, which governs the availability of food. Temperature, hardness and the stability of flow of the water, and competition from other fish, all bear upon the prosperity of the troutlet. A wild brown trout in the Cherrybrook on Dartmoor may take 3 years to reach a length of 6 in.; a stew-fed brown may reach 12 in. in 2 years and a rainbow in half that time.

Types of still-water fisheries

The demand for trout fishing by a growing number of fly fishermen has increased dramatically since the end of World War 2. The length of river suitable for trout fishing is reduced and increased following pollution and subsequent cleansing; it is also reduced by long-term water abstraction. Some brooks and small rivers have disappeared into the earth, their water pumped away to the pipes of distant towns. River spawning areas become barren due to acidity following the planting of new softwood forests and, in the chalk streams, the silting of redding areas due to low water flow and the ploughing-up of adjacent filtering water meadows. Concisely, fishable trout-river mileage has probably reduced over the last half-century; certainly, it has not increased.

Additional demand for trout fishing has been met by stocking long-established reservoirs, the creation of new reservoirs to store water which, as a by-product, provide trout fishing and other recreations, and the excavation of small man-made lakes.

In addition to these artificial waters there are the natural lochs of Scotland and the lakes of England and Wales, the majority of which rely, in the provision of sport, on the presence of wild trout.

Which of these waters should be chosen by the beginner? Which are suited to the gregarious angler, the competitive personality, the filler of the deep-freeze, and the fishers to whom the chance to stretch their eyes to the distant hills is of more importance than a heavy creel?

The small stocked lake

Privately owned, regularly stocked with rainbow trout of 1 lb and above, widespread geographically and numerous, these waters have satisfied increased angling demand. They may be fished by day, half-day or evening ticket. The cost usually allows one to take six, four or two trout within the price of the ticket, or there may be a cover fee and the angler pays a charge for each pound of fish extracted. These lakes are not for the person who likes to fish the lonely wilds, but much will be learned around their edges by a beginner. The tackle to be used will be described in Chapter 2, but, even properly equipped, the new man would do well to take a fish on the first day. Nevertheless, he will see many rainbows landed. Diffidence should then be overcome and successful anglers questioned. A man who has just netted a trout is joyous, pleased with his skill and at once talkative. Approach him for information at that moment: pattern and size of fly, where he cast and why, depth of fishing and speed of retrieve. A 10-minute conversation will provide a fund of knowledge.

The small lake is the place to go to make a start. The owner wants you to catch fish, for on satisfaction and fish sales depends his living. At the time of writing, rainbows may be purchased from a trout farm for about £1.50 a pound for the table. Many trout farms have adjacent fishing lakes, which they stock, and where an angler may pay £5 to fish and £1.50 a pound for his catch. Clearly, the more fish that are caught the happier the owner, and his rod, who is able to stop when financial prudence dictates – if his skill is of that level! To assist success, stocking may take place either weekly or daily. The tyro's first trout will not be delayed and long-distance casting is not a priority. Much will be learned about attracting, hooking, playing and netting trout, but conditions are a trifle cramped where a dozen anglers fish a 4 acre lake and a visit must usually be booked in advance.

The stocked reservoir

This should be the second stage in the advancement of the still-water trout angler, for longer casts are usually required. From the bank, to reach that rising fish, which is usually just beyond the range of those making a start, calls for casting skills and the correct tackle, or the use of a boat. Water-supply reservoirs vary in size from 20 or 30 acres to over 3000 acres and range from the unstocked, where reliance is on natural spawning in feeder streams, to those where the annual catch is several thousand hatchery-bred trout, or 'stockies' as they are called. Personally, I would rather fish a stocked reservoir, where the fish per acre are fewer, than a small, heavily stocked

Fernworthy Reservoir, Dartmoor. Lara Bingham with a 3 lb 12 oz brown trout taken on a 5x leader with a No 18 Black Gnat.

lake. The preference is based upon my wish to fish in uncrowded circumstances, and to take trout which have, usually, had a longer spell of freedom in which to develop their natural feeding habits and instincts for preservation.

It does not take long to learn the 'hot spots' on a small lake but it does require many visits to acquire knowledge of the underwater bed contours of a large reservoir and the best areas in which to catch trout. Wind direction, depth, weed growth, the incidence of feeder streams and the presence of bankside bushes all play a part in making portions of the reservoir attractive to the occupants. Underwater walls harbour trout and trout food; the stumps of below-surface felled trees are a safe refuge for hooked fish; the cool deep channels of original, but now flooded, streams provide refuge for fish in heatwaves – the whereabouts of these must be learned over many visits.

Boats are usually available, but I advise the beginner to fish from the bank in the first season, there being sufficient to learn without the added worry of handling a boat and evading the casting of a companion in the bows or stern. Unlike fishing a small lake, one does not normally need to book in advance to fish a reservoir, although boats usually have to be reserved. Tickets are available at self-service kiosks and return cards must be completed before leaving the water.

The Welsh lakes and Scottish lochs

Remoteness does not guarantee anything in the way of heavy trout baskets, but often ensures the taking of much exercise. The lakes of Wales, the lochs of Scotland and the loughs of Ireland are so varied, between highland and lowland, deep and shallow, acid and alkaline, that there cannot be a general description of their characteristics. Some are stocked, some entirely barren, some so deep that the fringes produce 4 oz dark-coloured trout and the depths are inhabited by cannibal ferox trout.

The most noticeable common feature of these waters in wild places is their beauty. Those which I have fished in Wales, Ireland, the Isle of Mull, Inverness-shire and the far north of Scotland have all refreshed the soul, but few have provided much food for the family. If asked to categorize them I would do so by depth and pH (hydrogen ion concentration, i.e. acid/alkaline level) of the water. Some are shallow, with vast areas at an average depth of 12 or 15 ft, such as loch Leven. These provide excellent food for trout growth and thus good fishing for anglers. One of the smallest lakes, which I visited many years ago, was llyn Llygarian on the island of Anglesey. It was a shallow

water, 100 ft above sea level, with a plentiful supply of weed and brown
trout of 1 lb or more in weight. The owner, a Mr Mounfield, had a 14 in.
mark scraped on the thwart in his boat and a small wooden club to hand.
Both were in regular use. Another was loch Flemington, just off the Nairn/
Inverness road – a fine shallow lowland loch, close to the Moray Firth. In
such lochs, large or small, the environment encourages fish growth unless
there is too much interference or pollution by man. Those which are
unproductive are often found at considerable heights above sea level and,
the higher they are, the lower is the average water temperature. Many are in
steep valleys and are of great depth. Some are planted around with conifers or
have formed naturally in areas of peat and heather – these lochs are usually
acid and inhabited, if at all, by quantities of small thin trout and a few large
ugly cannibals. Many lochs are fished from boats. Bank fishing may be
difficult and dangerous in places due to soft edges or precipitous banks of
loose stones – once in, it is hard to climb out!

My advice is to make enquiries in advance. Do not imagine that a 10 mile
uphill trudge over midge-infested heather will be rewarded because the water
is unfished – it is probably unfished for valid reasons, of which the most
common is lack of takable trout. The fishing is often free, and that is an
indication of poor quality fish.

2 Fly-fishing tackle

Standing on the bank of a reservoir or hill loch, or wading, you cannot move closer to a rising trout than the tops of your thigh boots allow. It can only be caught if it is within your casting range. In addition, the trout may move off in any direction, of which yours is not likely to be chosen. Other unseen trout may be in the vicinity. The ability to cast up to 25 yd is essential to cover fish. On a river a trout tends to remain in one position, feeding on morsels brought to it by the flowing water. Such a fish may be approached by creeping along the bank until a short accurate cast places the fly within its circle of vision. The distance casting necessity on still waters calls for a different rod than the river situation, which will be discussed in Chapter 7.

Rods and fly lines

These should be considered together since the weight of the line per unit of length outside the rod tip must match the power of the rod to cope with that weight. For example, a 14 ft salmon rod would not throw a line as light as a

The rod should be held high to act as a spring.

length of thin string, since the rod would not be flexed, whilst a 7 ft trout brook rod would break if called upon to cast a line suitable for the 14 ft rod. These matters are taken into account by the manufacturers of fly lines, who rate their products on the AFTM Scale (Association of Fishing Tackle Manufacturers). Scale categories are the weight in grains of the first 30 ft of the fly line, excluding the thin level tip which may be 1 ft in length or thereabouts. It is not necessary for the angler to know the grain weight of a line but the AFTM number must be taken into account when purchasing both a rod and the line to match that rod. The 30 ft of the forward end of a fly line is used for the calculated weight because it is considered to be the average length false cast outside the rod tip by the average angler.

Examine the tube of a fly rod just above the butt. There, you will find one of the following marks: AFTM No 6, AFTM No 7 or AFTM No 7/8, according to the ability of the rod to cast these lines; this varies, in this example, from medium weight No 6 to a heavier No 8. You would be likely to find an 8 ft brook rod rated at AFTM No 5, whilst a 9 ft rod for distance casting on a reservoir or Highland loch would be AFTM No 8. Knowing that the line has to match the rod, let us choose suitable equipment for still waters.

Rods

The materials of which fly rods are made today are: split cane, fibreglass, carbon fibre and boron. Split cane is not suited to still-water fly fishing because a rod of sufficient power to cast the required distance would be too heavy for comfort.

Fibreglass is inexpensive and light in weight. It is suitable except in one respect – the tube diameter is greater than that of carbon-fibre rods. This makes it more tiring to use, particularly when casting against the wind, because of the greater air resistance, or drag, of the fatter tube.

Boron is excellent but expensive. I doubt that the extra cost is warranted for those making a start and therefore suggest, in this case, that the best material is carbon fibre.

Some carbon rods are stiff, bending little in casting except towards the tip, these are called *tip action*. Others are softer, bending almost the whole way from tip to butt, and these are known as *all-through* or *easy* action. Two rods, both of 9 ft in length, may be rated AFTM No 6 in one case and AFTM No 8 in the other. The former is likely to be a rod of easy action and the latter of tip action. The tip-action rod, being stiff, will handle the heavier line and move it at a fast speed through the air. Now, momentum, being the product of

The strap prevents the wrist 'breaking' on the back cast.

velocity and weight, will be greater in the tip-action/heavy-line combination than in the easy-action/light-line outfit. The greater momentum will carry the line a greater distance; this is particularly so against the wind because the tip-action rod casts a tighter, narrower loop of line. The wider line loop of the easy-action rod will tend to be blown about by the wind.

It is not the case that a 10 ft rod will, due to extra length, always cast further than a 9 ft rod. If the 10 ft rod is of tip action it may well cast further, but extra effort will be needed from the angler. Is there a case for a 10 ft easy-action rod which casts almost as far as a tip-action 9 ft weapon? There is such a case when fishing a dry fly off fine nylon. The fly itself has a delicate lightweight hook in order not to sink it and the nylon may have a breaking strain of 3 lb; such a combination is likely to snap, or the hook may bend, following the take of a heavy trout when the angler is using a tip-action rod, but an easy-action rod will bend and accommodate the stress. Wet flies, being sub-surface, may be fished off heavier nylon without risk of breakage by the tip-action rod.

I take two rods to a reservoir or loch: a 9 ft tip-action AFTM No 8, and a 9½ ft easy-action AFTM No 6. The former is for wet flies and lures on floating and sinking lines, and the latter for floating lines and dry flies. If fishing from a boat, in which one ought to sit rather than stand, a longer rod will compensate to some extent for loss of height. In this situation a 10 or

11 ft easy-action rod is desirable, unless one wishes to cast a long way with a
fast-sinking line, in which case a tip-action rod is required.

Correct choice of rod is important. It is almost impossible to cast into a strong
wind with an 8½ ft easy-action rod. The power is not available to put
sufficient momentum into the line, whilst the vicious action of an AFTM No
8 rod will send the line cutting through the air 1 ft above the waves.

The maintenance requirement of a carbon-fibre rod is minimal. Inspect the
silk bindings of the line guides each winter and dab with varnish where
necessary. During the season, each month if fishing weekly, rub the joint
spigots with a candle – the wax protects the fibres of the tube and stops the
sections working loose. If two sections of a carbon rod cannot be pulled apart,
do not hold them in a vice or pliers which will crush the tube. Just immerse
the joint in cold water for a couple of minutes and, in four out of five cases,
the joint will come apart.

Fly lines

Having learned the weight of line needed to match the rod, the line *profile* has
to be decided to cater for fishing circumstances.

1.

| 6 IN | 8 FT | 73 FT BODY | 8 FT | 6 IN |

2.

| 6 IN | 12 FT | 24 FT BODY | 6 FT | 62 FT 6 IN THIN LINE |

3 Fly-line profiles.

(1) Double taper. Traditionally preferred by trout and salmon fishermen and
particularly useful where roll casting is required. Can also be reversed once the
used end begins to show signs of wear. Available in floating, sinking and sink-tip.
Total length 30 yd.

(2) Weight forward. Features a long, slender front taper which is ideal for delicate
work with small and medium-sized flies yet allows the long cast for extra distance
with very little effort. Cannot be reversed. Available in floating, sinking and sink-
tip. Total length 35 yd.

Fly lines are tapered towards the point, sometimes at one end only and
sometimes at both ends. The line tapered at both ends has a profile known as
double taper; other profiles are *weight forward* and *shooting head*. A level line is
uncommon. As will be seen, the fly is attached to a *leader*, a length of
monofilament which is usually 9 ft long and tapered from a thin diameter at
the fly end, or point, to its thickest at the butt, which is the end joined to the

fly line. This taper is continued in the line itself until a uniform maximum thickness is reached at the length described as the body of the line. This gradual tapering of line and leader, all the way to the fly, assists 'turn-over' so that the fly alights at the extremity of the cast.

Double taper

Fly lines for trout and sea-trout fishing are usually 27 or 30 yd in length. The profile may be as follows: 6 in. level tip, 8 ft taper, 73 ft body, 8 ft taper and 6 in. level tip – total length 30 yd.

When one end is worn and cracked, the line may be reversed and another year or two of use obtained. Roll and overhead casts may be executed with this line, but it is not the most suitable for distance casting.

Only a certain length of any line may be false cast outside the rod tip; extra distance beyond this is obtained by *shooting* additional line forward through the rod rings. The extra line is pulled out by the momentum of the line outside the rod tip as the cast straightens and extends over the water. It follows that the lighter the weight of the line to be shot, and the thinner and more slippery it is, in order to pass through the rod rings, the further it will be pulled. The double-taper body is the thickest and heaviest part of the line and will not readily shoot long distances. Such a line is better suited to shorter casts on a river.

Weight forward

This is the best line for the reservoir and loch angler. The profile may be as follows: 6 in. level tip, 12 ft taper, 24 ft body, 6 ft reverse taper and 62½ ft thin running line for shooting – total length 35 yd. The running line is light in weight and, being thin, produces low friction on the rod line guides; thus considerable lengths may be shot.

When purchasing both types of line, be sure that the surface is smooth by running it through the fingers – a rough-surfaced line will not shoot far.

Shooting head

This is a variation of the weight-forward line. About 30 ft is cut from the foreward end of a weight-forward line or from either end of a double-tapered line. To this is joined flat or round monofilament, or braided backing line. The backing, being extremely light and so fine that it is almost frictionless, may be shot further than any other line. Whilst considerable distances may be achieved, as often as not none is shot at all, because you have put your foot on the coils on the ground, or they have tangled in a bramble.

Density

Until about 1960 fly lines were made of silk; they were all heavier than water (i.e. of greater density) and thus sank. If the line was required to float for dry-fly fishing or greased-line salmon fishing, it was greased with solid Mucilin, Cerolene or a similar product. Modern lines have a braided core covered with plastic. If the plastic contains minute air bubbles, the line will float and should not be greased, for the floatant may damage the plastic, causing it to crack, let in water and sink. If such a line does not float well it is probably dirty and should be cleaned by washing in soapy water or drawing through a wet cloth at the waterside. Such a floating line will have a density that is less than water.

If the density of the line exceeds that of water it will sink. The greater the density, the faster will be the rate of descent to the required depth. We thus have slow-, fast- and extra-fast-sinking fly lines, the very fastest being lead-cored. It is normal for an angler to carry floating and fast-sinking lines. Also available are intermediate, or neutral, lines which fish *in*, rather than on or under, the water surface, and sink-tip lines where the body floats and 3 or 4 yd at the tip sink.

Lines in a tackle shop are identified on the package. For example:

*DT*8F Double-tapered AFTM No 8 floating line.

*DT*8S Double-tapered AFTM No 8 sinking line, with rate of sinking described.

*DT*8F/S Double-tapered AFTM No 8 sink-tip line.

Colour

My preferred colour for a floating line is green. White lines flash in the sky and are more visible, both on the water surface and in the air, when seen from under the water. I prefer a white fly line for fishing in the dark (see Chapter 19). Sinking lines should be dark in colour.

Backing

You can run up and down the bank of a river after an athletic fish, but you cannot run out over a still water. A large rainbow or heavy brown may pull out all the dressed line on the reel, but behind this should be 70 or 80 yards of backing. This will be 20 or 30 lb BS monofilament, joined to the fly line by a needle knot, or braided backing joined by the Albright knot or a whipping.

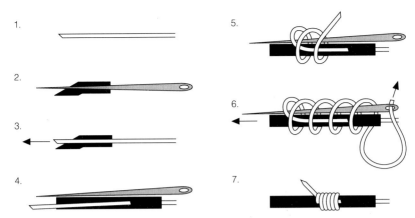

4 Needle knot. Used to join monofilament backing to fly line. Also used to join 1 ft of 20 lb BS monofilament to the forward end of a fly line; the butt of the leader is joined to this with a blood knot.

(1) Cut the fly-line end square and the nylon end at a sharp angle.

(2) Push a stout darning needle 3/8 in. up the fly-line core and out through the wall. Carefully heat the needle eye. This keeps the hole open when the needle is withdrawn.

(3) Thread 6 in. of monofilament through the fly line.

(4) Lay the needle parallel to the fly line.

(5) With the spare end, take four or five turns around the needle and fly line.

(6) Thread the nylon end through the needle eye and carefully pull it through under the turns.

(7) Moisten the turns. Pull both ends, keeping the turns neatly side by side. Snip off the waste end.

There should always be sufficient backing to fill the spool of the reel; this allows each turn of the reel to recover the maximum length of line. To ensure that the spool is filled, wind on the fly line first, follow this with backing to capacity, then draw off and reverse the line and backing.

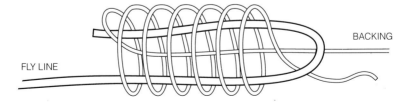

BACKING

FLY LINE

5 Albright knot. Used to join braided backing to fly line.

Reels

It is better to have a large, simple, reliable centre-pin reel than a small multiplier. It is also less expensive. The reason behind this statement is that the less complicated the reel, the less likely it is to go wrong. If you place your reel absentmindedly on the sand at the edge of a loch in heavy rain it will be splashed with sand grains. It is an easy matter to wash out a simple reel in the loch, but a multiplier might need the attentions of a screwdriver.

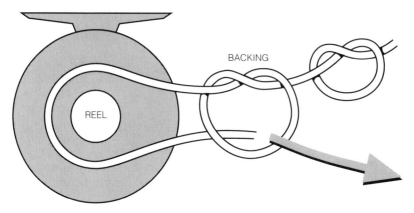

6 Arbor knot. Used to join backing to a reel.

Fly reels have their capacities, AFTM line number and length of backing displayed on the box by the manufacturer. Buy a slightly larger reel than one of the exact capacity required, e.g. a No 7 reel for a No 6 rod and No 6 line. The diameter of such a reel will be slightly greater and it will need a little more backing to fill the spool, but it will recover line, per turn of the spool, faster than a No 6 capacity reel. The reel will be a trifle heavier but, in carbon-fibre or aluminium alloys, the difference will be barely noticeable.

I would not like to claim that the products of one manufacturer are better than another, for price and purpose render comparisons valueless, but these are the reels I use:

Leeda Dragonfly 100 For my AFTM No 8 still-water fly lines and for sea-trout – inexpensive.

Hardy Marquis No 7 For river trout and AFTM No 6 lines – expensive.

Both reels are excellent and both may be purchased with spare spools to accommodate the different types of line. Over the years neither of these has let me down, but one day, may be, something may go wrong! If you have one reel and two spools you cannot fish if the reel breaks – take two!

Both reels have adjustable drag. Do not buy a reel without this facility, for a reel which cannot be altered may have the 'pull-off' set too hard, resulting in the breakage of fine tippets when playing trout. In all game fishing by fly I tend to control the drag on a fish by a light setting on the reel and then use my fingers to provide infinitely variable pressure. This resistance may be applied either by a finger placed on the rim of an exposed reel spool or, if the spool is enclosed, by running the line between the forefinger of the hand on the rod and the cork butt. If the drag on a reel is not adjustable, but can be changed from right- to left-hand wind, or vice versa, it may still be set light. If winding with the right hand, turn the right-hand wind-cam inside the reel to the inoperative position and bring the cam for left-hand wind into use, and vice versa. The angler will then wind in at a greater resistance than will be applied to the trout pulling out line.

Leaders

The length of a leader, which joins the fly line to the fly, is variable, and so is the strength of the nylon, which should be related to the weight of the fly. As already noted, the leader is tapered down from butt to point. I use two types: home-made for wet-fly and lure fishing sub-surface; manufactured knotless tapered for dry-fly fishing. Leaders for still-water wet fly may be made from many different brands of nylon; Maxima Chameleon is one of the best.

A tapered leader for a water holding trout up to 3 or 4 lb could be:

2 ft of 20 lb BS.
2 ft of 15 lb BS.
2 ft of 10 lb BS.
3 ft of 6 lb BS, which is of 0.009 in. diameter.

Such a leader will 'turn over' against the wind and present flies to a hook size of No 10. If large No 8 weighted flies are in use, the strength of the point section should be increased. A No 14 wet fly would fish better, with a freer action in the water, off a 4 lb point, and so on.

The sections should be joined together with a blood knot, and an eyed fly tied to the point with a two-turn Turle knot. To join the leader to the fly line I have 1 ft of 20 lb BS nylon permanently needle-knotted into the point of the fly line and I join the 20 lb BS, 2 ft butt section to this with a blood knot. Such a junction will wind in and out of the rod tip without jamming and the fly is unlikely to catch upon the smooth joint when casting.

It is common to fish more than one wet fly on the same leader, although the novice may find this produces more tangles than extra fish! If three flies are to be fished, the top one, at the 20/15 lb BS junction, would be called the *top dropper* or *bob fly*; the second, at the 15/10 lb BS junction, the *dropper* or *first dropper*; at the leader end is the *point fly*. Attach droppers by taking a length of 6 or 8 lb BS nylon and tying this onto a main section of the leader with a tucked half blood knot, and then sliding it down to rest against the blood knot joining the two main sections. The fly is then attached at a dropper length of 4 in. with a tucked half blood knot. Whilst two-turn Turle knots are best for the attachment of eyed trout flies, one cannot be used in the dropper situation

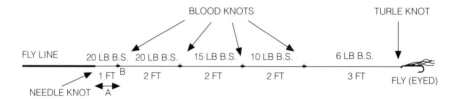

7 Home-made leader for still-water trout fishing. Section A is permanently inserted into the fly line by a needle knot. The leader is replaced by cutting at point B. If the fly line terminates in a braided loop connector, a blood-bight loop would be tied in the end of the leader at point B.

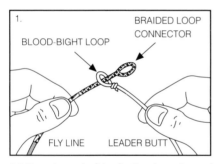

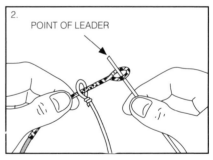

(1) Pass the end of the fly-line loop through the larger end of the leader butt loop.

(2) Pass the small end of the leader through the fly-line loop.

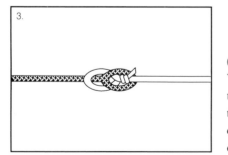

(3) Tighten by pulling in opposite directions. You can disconnect the loops by pushing them towards each other and reversing the process. A correct loop-to-loop connection looks like a square knot when complete.

8 Joining the blood-bight loop on the butt of a leader to a braided loop connector.

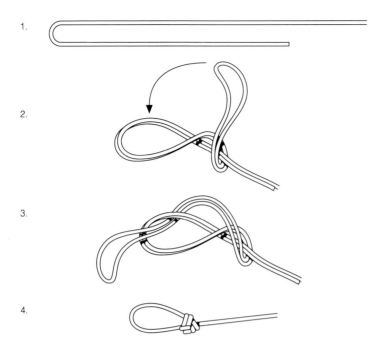

9 Blood-bight loop. Used to form a loop in the end of a nylon leader.

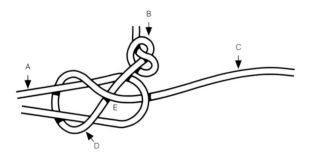

10 Sheet bend. Used to join the fly line to a salmon leader when a long rod is in use.
Tie a knot at point B in the fly line, which is threaded through the leader loop (A).
Loop D is tightened by pulling on end C. To release, push end C towards loop A.
For extra security, knot B may be passed a second time around loop A before
being tucked, as shown, beneath end C at point E.

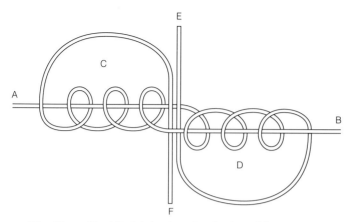

11 Blood knot. Used for joining lengths of nylon of the same, or not too dissimilar, diameter. To tighten pull A and B, then snip off E and F. A dropper may be formed by leaving E or F long, about 4 in., but the end which is left long ought to be a continuation of the length closest to the leader butt.

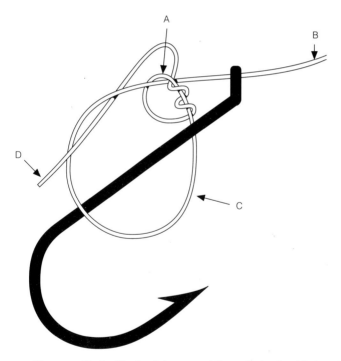

12 Two-turn Turle. Used to join an eyed fly to the leader. Tighten knot A on the leader (B), then pass end D inside loop C. Tighten loop C behind the eye of the fly. End D, about ⅛ in. long, will lie along the shank of the hook.

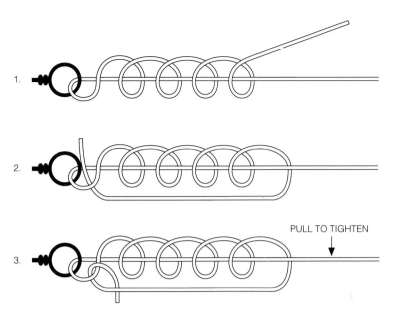

PULL TO TIGHTEN

13 Tucked half blood knot. Used to join nylon to swivel, Wye-weight loop, eye of
treble hook etc., but not correct for eyed flies as they can turn sideways.

due to insufficient length of nylon. If dropper lengths are long, tangles are
more likely to result.

For dry-fly fishing the best results are obtained by the use of manufactured
knotless tapered leaders. This is because one does not want knots joining
sections of nylon to show on the water surface and, when moving, to produce
a wake. I use packaged, Leeda, knotless tapered leaders in the range, shown
in the table below, which is denoted by an 'x' number identifying the
thickness of the point.

Range of knotless tapered leaders

Number	Tip diameter (in.)	Breaking Strain	Loop colour
6x	0.005	2 lb	Natural
5x	0.006	3 lb	Green
4x	0.007	4 lb	Yellow
3x	0.008	5 lb	Blue
2x	0.009	6 lb	Lilac

6x and 5x are for my smallest flies on No 16 or No 18 hooks, 4x for No 14 and No 12 hooks, and 3x for mayflies, on No 10 hooks. This is a rough guide which must be adapted according to the clarity of the water, the presence of weed and the size of the fish. It would be unwise to fish 5x nylon in the presence of heavy fish; 4x would be safer. On an acid Highland loch, over-populated with 4 oz or 6 oz trout, a 6x leader could be used, unless one wished to deter the hungry masses! The loop colours vary and identify the diameter of the nylon and the 'x' rating, it being beyond the capacity of the human eye to note a difference of one thousandth.

Pre-stretched nylons, such as Drennan Double Strength and Orvis Super Strong, have reduced diameters whilst retaining full pull strength. For example, the Orvis nylon at 0.005 in diameter has a breaking strain of $3\frac{1}{2}$ lb instead of the 2 lb, shown above, for the Platil leader. I advise the beginner to avoid pre-stretched nylons at the start of an angling career, for they do not always withstand shocks. Progress to these fine nylons, particularly for dry fly in clear water, but rods must be of an easy action.

Braided leader butts are available which float, or sink, at variable rates. They are attached very simply at one end to the fly line, whilst 3 or 4 ft of monofilament forms the tippet at the other. Fishing depths may be altered whilst using a floating fly line. Braided leader butts are expensive and it would be best for the novice to progress to these. Short, braided loop connectors are also available to join line and leader.

Nets

When fishing from the bank it is as well to have a net clipped to the trouser belt. This enables one to be mobile as long as the handle is not too long. From a boat a longer shaft enables one to reach out to a fish. A telescopic shaft meets these two requirements. The frame should be of rigid metal in order that a trout balanced on the edge may be shaken into the net; if made of two folding arms, joined at the front by a cord, the cord may sag and the fish slide away. An additional risk in the folding-arms, cord-joined net is that the points of the arms may catch in the net mesh and fail to open.

If a net has a metal bowframe 20 in. wide and hinged at the handle, it will serve for all reservoir and loch trout fishing and also for fishing at night in a river for sea trout. When wading a river at night, I place my hand on the hinge of the net to probe the river bed, using the net handle as a short wading staff. The length of the shaft is such that, if my hand touches the water surface, I know the river is just about to overflow the tops of my thigh boots.

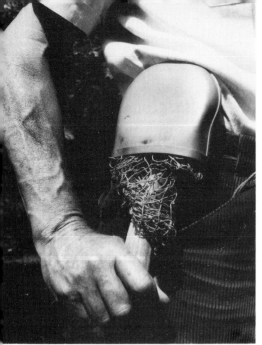

The emergency net.   The emergency net extended.

A smaller net is suitable and more convenient for wading below the bank of a moorland or upland limestone brook or stream. The Hardy Favourite Trout Fisher's net has a bowframe of 14½ by 14½ in. and a handle 21 in. long. The handle is also telescopic with an overall extended length of 49½ in. It is available with a knotted or knotless net.

Net attachment to belt. The cord leads to a priest in the trouser pocket.

The Orvis Co. of Stockbridge stock a 'Hang-All Belt Loop' – a leather loop with swivel and brass clip that is ideal for net suspension.

Clothing and boots

Clothing requiremens vary with the season and also depend on whether one is fishing from the bank or a boat. Take early spring and autumn first. Most brown trout seasons start in mid-March or early April and finish at the end of September or during the first week of October. Rainbows are in season for the whole year in some places. Cold weather will be encountered and is best warded off with three or four layers of wool: vest, shirt and sweater, with Long Johns if wading. A waxed jacket covers all and must be of sufficient length to extend over the tops of thigh boots. A waxed hat with a brim to tip the water over the back of the coat is better than a detachable hood which limits side vision and hearing – fish movement and a splash may be missed. Mittens should also be worn at this time of year – Orvis stock polypropylene mitts which may be squeezed out when wet.

Feet are catered for by oversized pairs of thigh boots or, for boat fishing, gum boots. The extra foot room allows two pairs of socks to be worn. The boat angler will need a pair of waxed overtrousers to keep his bottom dry. In summer I purchase a pair of cheap thigh boots and cut them off behind the knees. This gives 6 in. more depth than a gum boot and is cooler than a thigh boot when much walking has to be done.

In mid-season one needs to keep cool and the fishing waistcoat becomes a 'must'. Not only will this hold fly boxes, nylon, floatant and other items, but the large back pocket can take a thin plastic raincoat as well as a small salmon. Worn over a sweater, the waistcoat ensures cool arms and free movement.

Other equipment

NRA (National Rivers Authority) rod licence

The regulations covering rod licences were changed in 1992 and are to be altered again in 1994. A licence entitles the holder to use two rods in England and Wales, and is required by anyone of 12 years or greater age. There are concessions for registered disabled persons, juniors aged 12–16 years and those aged 60 years and over. Current regulations must be ascertained. The licence does not entitle one to fish without permission; it just entitles the angler to carry and use two rods. A rod licence, at present, is not required in Scotland.

Polarized spectacles

These protect the eyes from glare and the risk of damage by a hook when
casting. They are of greatest use for spotting fish in a river, but do not enable
much to be seen below the surface of still waters. They are available with grey
and yellow lenses, of which I prefer grey. Those made by Optix are excellent,
particularly their HLT (High Light Transmission) types, for the lenses
should not be dark, but let through as much light as possible.

Fly boxes

There are three useful designs. For wet flies the box may have clips, or clips
on one side and a foam lining on the other, or just foam-lined sides. These are
not suitable for dry flies because the hackles would be flattened and dry fly
hooks, being small and fine, may be damaged by the clips. Dry flies should
be stored in compartment boxes. Leeda Tackle, House of Hardy and Richard
Wheatley Ltd produce a wide range.

Floatants

For dry flies the best floatants in my opinion are Gink Fly Float and
Supafloat, both of which come in small bottles. Silicon Mucilin is one of the
best solid pastes to make a leader float and Mucilin Quick Sink will do the
opposite. To make my leader sink I dampen a small piece of cloth in the
kitchen sink, sprinkle on Fuller's Earth (from the chemist) and a few drops of
Fairy Liquid. Stored in a 35 mm film cassette and rubbed down the nylon, it
makes a leader sink at once.

Tippet spools

Carry 50 m spools of 4, 6 and 8 lb BS Maxima Chameleon to make droppers
and replace tippets. Spare leaders should also be carried.

Priest and scissors

I carry a 6 in. length of ½ in. metal pipe as a priest in my right trouser
pocket, secured to me by a cord carried under the coat or waistcoat and
passed around my neck. A trout may then be knocked on the head whilst
I am wading without risk of dropping the priest in the water. A pair of
scissors or nail clippers for cutting nylon, and a pair of artery forceps for the
removal of hooks from the mouths of trout, are also looped on ribbon around
my neck.

The author's priest.

Fish bass

A wet fish bass hung in a breeze will keep trout cool by evaporation of water.
I carry a sharp knife and, if circumstances permit, clean fish soon after
capture, particularly in hot weather.

Midge cream

Anyone who has fished a heather- or bog-surrounded Highland loch on a
damp warm day in August will know why this is essential.

Sharpening stone

This will keen the point of a wet fly or lure hook. Dry-fly hooks are small and
it is better to replace the fly than attempt to sharpen a blunted point.

Tackle bag

Mine has a larger compartment at the back and two small ones at the front to
accommodate most of the tackle items mentioned, spare reels and spools. If in
a boat, I take the bag with me. If fishing a river or covering a long length of
bank in a still water, selected items are placed in the pockets of my waxed
jacket, in winter, or fishing waistcoat, in summer.

3 Natural insects and artificial flies

Trout feed daily. It is thus rational to study trout food: beetles, nymphs, fish fry, flies, shrimps etc. These are imitated in order to catch trout.

The season for the river angler burgeons with the advent of warm weather in May; natural flies can be observed and representations of those flies, knotted to the point of the leader, have a chance of success. Perplexity may arise in early spring or later autumn when you are confronted with a cold reservoir, the wind tugging at your coat and not a natural fly in sight. In such a bleak situation I once sought the advice of a fishery warden who told me:

'Tie on something large, black and white. Cast out as far as possible and retrieve at speed. These trout are newly stocked rainbows; they don't know the difference between a loaf of bread and a midge pupa. In addition, they won't have time to find out before they are caught.'

Well, that was what the locals were doing. The evidence was there: long gaudy flies, curved rods bent into trout, wet nets, happy smiles and plastic bags of fish. It worked for them, why not me? I joined their ranks and my bag, if not full, did not remain completely empty. Those trout, clearly, wanted to eat; they were hungry. Whilst a river trout in adverse conditions of scanty food supply, perhaps in winter, finds little to digest, here it was different. Lures 'large, black and white' were drawn through the water, sometimes at great speed. Might not these things, to the trouty mind, be eatable? Pursue, catch, taste and see. Result – into the plastic bag!

There are two distinct branches of still-water trout fishing: imitating natural insects at various stages in their life-cycles; and enticing trout to take a wet fly or lure, usually sub-surface, through hunger, curiosity or aggression. The latter branch accounts for more trout than the imitiative method and may be practised throughout the year, rainbows in many waters having no close season. Imitative fishing – using bugs, beetles, nymphs and natural flies – is restricted to the weeks and months when those naturals are evident, in the warmer periods of late spring, summer and early autumn.

For each of these methods, hooks of different sizes are required. The smallest in general use for dry flies is the No 18 on the Redditch Scale and the largest the No 8 for large wet flies and lures. Dry-fly hooks, in order not to sink the fly, are of fine, lightweight wire with upturned eyes. Wet-fly and nymph hooks may be of heavier wire with downturned eyes, whilst lure and streamer flies are the same but with longer shanks. Whether the eye is turned up or down for dry and wet flies is a matter of tradition and is not critical to their performance.

Some hooks are made without barbs to facilitate the release of fish which are undersized and young salmon (parr) in migratory fish rivers. Use of barbless hooks may be obligatory in some waters, or the angler may be required to press in the barb with snipe-nosed pliers. The wire of hooks may be round in cross-section, or flattened (forged) at the bend for increased resistance to bending open.

Barbless flies are not always obtainable.
Artery forceps and a file can be used
to remove the barb at the river.

Dry flies are usually tied with hackles from the cape (neck feathers) of a cockerel, preferably an ancient, stiff-feathered farmyard fowl, or from deer hair, with other animal furs for the body. They may be dressed with hackles and wings (winged artificials) or without wings (hackled). Wet flies, winged or hackled, are tied with the feather of a hen; if winged, the wings slope back along the body. Such is a very brief description of fly-dressing materials and styles – the traditional styles of dry and wet flies. Today, modern plastic and metal materials, often in fluorescent colours, widen the scope of the fly-dresser to startle both trout and angler.

Imitative fishing – the dry fly

There are four orders of insects which are important to the trout angler: Ephemeroptera, Plecoptera, Trichoptera and Diptera. Of these, all are of interest to the river fly fisherman and the final two mentioned bring dry-fly opportunities to the still-water man. I shall discuss Diptera and Trichoptera in this still-water section and Ephemeroptera, Trichoptera and Plecoptera in the study of river fishing (Chapter 7), with passing reference, again, to Diptera.

Diptera

These are insects with two flat wings and no tails. Of this order, the following members bring exciting dry-fly days to the lake and reservoir angler: the midges, hawthorn fly, crane fly (daddy-long-legs) and black gnat. Reed smuts which are also dipterans, are very small, but of concern only to the river scene as the larvae prefer running water.

The midges

The life-cycle commences with an egg which hatches into a tiny red or green worm in the mud of the lake bed, at which stage it is known as a bloodworm. The worm pupates and the pupa swims to the water surface, below which it hangs, breathing through tiny tubes which pierce the water film. At this point it may be imitated by fishing a No 18 midge pupa, usually in black, green or amber, commonly known as a *buzzer*. Trout taking buzzers stroll along just beneath the water surface, their dorsal fins often being visible. The pupa breaks through the water film, the fly emerges, dries its wings in a matter of seconds and flies away, leaving behind the grey lifeless pupal case – a process clearly visible to the watcher.

The aerial stage may be represented by the smallest dry fly I use – the No 18 Black Gnat. Although this artificial is larger than the natural, I find it takes trout and has the merit of a better hold on the fish than a smaller hook of size No 20 or No 22.

The black gnat

This is a general name for a number of land-breeding species. Some may be present throughout the fishing season, being blown by the wind from bushes and bankside vegetation on to the water. They may often be seen mating.

Again, I use the No 18 hackled Black Gnat which should be knotted to
a 5x leader.

The hawthorn

This large, black, land-based fly has two prominent back legs. Hatches may
be observed for about 2 weeks at the end of April and in May, although I have
seen this fly as late as July by waters at high altitude. The flies are seen over
land in groups and small swarms, and are readily identifiable by the drooping
hind legs as they rise and fall in flight. If blown upon the water, they are taken
by trout and they may be imitated by the artificial Hawthorn on a No 12
hook. Once fallen upon the water, the natural rarely manages to become
airborn again, but slowly sinks under its own weight – in such a state trout
fall to a wet No 14 Black & Peacock Spider. At times, trout seem scared of so
large an insect and reject the No 12 artificial in favour of the No 18 Black
Gnat.

The crane fly

Commonly known as the daddy-long-legs (or father-long-legs by the Rev.
Richard Durnford of Wherwell, on the river Test, in the nineteenth century),
this land-breeding insect may be blown upon the water in late summer and
autumn. If it falls upon the surface it provides a substantial meal for a trout,
but it usually wafts along in the air, legs trailing, to arrive safely on the far
bank. It is imitated by the artificial Daddy-long-legs on a No 10 hook, or by
dapping two naturals using a long rod and an undressed, fluffy blow line.

Trichoptera

Commonly known as sedge, or caddis, flies, trichopterans have two pairs of
wings which fold back in a ridge or roof shape over the body, the wings being
covered with tiny hairs. The insects have no tails but possess two antennae
which may be as long as their bodies. The caddis life-cycle is similar to that of
moths kept by school children: egg, caterpillar, chrysalis and then the adult
winged insect. The female lays her eggs on the water, or below the surface by
crawling under water. Sometimes eggs are laid on waterside vegetation.

The eggs hatch after about 2 weeks into caddis larvae, which at once
commence constructing a case of particles of sand, vegetable matter and tiny
stones. These cases are sometimes attached to short sticks and may be 0.2–1.2
in. in length. The case is open at one end, from which the head and legs
emerge as the larvae moves and feeds.

Sedge flies emerge from caddis cases found on the river bed.

When picked out of the water, it retreats into its case but, if held still, the head emerges with caution after 1 or 2 minutes.

Ultimately, the larva pupates inside the case, undergoing metamorphosis, it then swims or crawls to the water surface to emerge as a mature sedge fly. In rivers and lakes, where sun-warmed boulders or posts rise above the level of the water, empty caddis cases may often be seen on these projections, their occupants having crawled up the boulder from the bed of the lake or river to hatch above the surface. Some caddis swim to the surface and may be seen skittering about, or whirling in circles on the water, as they try to divest themselves of the case and become airborne.

Imitating sedge (caddis) flies

Three stages in the life-cycle may be imitated: the larva in pupal case, the emerging fly, and the emerged fly.

The larvae I usually imitate these with a green-and-buff coloured dressing on a No 10 long-shank hook.

The emerging fly As already stated, some sedge flies, at the termination of the pupal stage, swim to the water surface, struggle through it and become airborne. The moment of eclosion, when the fly is wet and not yet able to take off, may be imitated by the Invicta wet fly with wings sloping back along the body. The size of hook should be about a No 12 or No 14.

The emerged fly There are in the region of 20 recognizable sedge flies (out of a total of 200) of interest to the angler. Many are confined to rivers, including the earliest to appear, in April, the grannom, of which more in Chapter 7.

It is possible to study the fly lists of tackle merchants and to acquire many unnecessary patterns. For still-water fishing I rely on two: a No 12 Red Sedge and a No 14 Brown Sedge.

It does not seem to be a matter of any moment whether the Red Sedge is winged or hackled; both kill, but the little Brown Sedge does well, with wings sloping back over the body.

Sedge flies hatch throughout the day and into the night, but the most prolific appearances are in late afternoon and until dusk from June until September.

Other forms of life

There are other forms of life which form part of the trout diet and which may be copied for still-water use.

Damselfly nymphs (*Odonata*)

On long-shank No 8 hooks, preferably with added weight, these account for many trout in the summer months, whether or not damselflies are present. Mayflies are of minor importance on still waters but hatches occur on some lakes.

The weighted mayfly nymph takes many trout and may be fished in addition to the fly, a procedure precluded by the rules on many dry-fly rivers. The nymph dressing should be on No 8 or No 10 long-shank hooks.

Freshwater shrimps (*Gammarus pulex*)

These are present in lakes, reservoirs and rivers. They may be observed in summer in shallow water, scuttling about in short darting movements. The natural shrimp is small, being about 0.2–0.3 in. in length; the artificial should match the natural size.

The alder fly (*Sialis*)

A dark-coloured fly of medium size, this resembles a sedge fly in shape. Part of the life-cycle is spent on land, part under water, and some as a winged insect; it may therefore be fished by wet-and-dry patterns of that name on No 12 hooks. The fly is widespread on rivers and lakes, appearing in May and June.

Coch-y-bonddu beetle (*Phyllopertha horticola*)

Common in Wales, this beetle is blown on to the water in summer. Fish a dry imitation on a No 14 hook or use a wet Black & Peacock Spider of the same size.

Trout fry

At times, trout are seen slashing through the shallows. These fish, usually large, may be chasing their own fry. If that fluffy white lure, the Appetizer, is slicked down by the angler's tongue, the dark squirrel hair along the top resembles the steel-blue back of a fish fry and the pink throat hackle the gills. Many and many are the trout I have taken on this lure close to the bed of a lake.

Non-imitative fishing – wet flies and lures

Trout see in colour. It has been established that the greatest visual impact is made by the colours red, orange and yellow, in that order. They also see stripes clearly, whether in the form of silver or gold tinsel wound around the black body of a lure or as the natural stripes on some feathers. Visual awareness does not guarantee that a trout will take a wet fly or lure sporting these colours, but if the lure were not noticed it could not be taken.

To these colours one would not go far wrong by adding black. A small black fly, fished just beneath the surface, must present a dense silhouette against the sky; a long black lure, ribbed silver and fished deep, is readily seen due to the contrast between the silver ribbing stripes and the black body. If allowed only two colours for all my game fishing – trout, sea trout and salmon – they would be black and orange. Visual attraction by colour is, perhaps, half the battle, the second half being concerned with stimulating a 'take' of the noticed fly by fishing method, as will be discussed.

Traditional wet flies

From the end of the last century until about 1960, fishing was by wet fly, the patterns being formulated by trial and error without much knowledge of fish vision. An increase in the stocking of rainbow trout, to cater for the growing numbers of anglers, coincided with the establishment of the fact that trout see in colour (as do sea trout and salmon).

Advantage of this knowledge was taken in the design of new trout lures, mainly on long-shank hooks, the new anglers being uninhibited by tradition. Let us look, first, at traditional wet flies. Listed are those which find a clip in my box.

Peter Ross

As a boy this was one of the first wet flies to find a place in my box in the 1940s, the fly being given to me when fishing a brown-trout lake in north

Wales. One has only to study the fly, armed with today's knowledge of fish vision, to see why it was an immediate success and still takes many trout – the dressing incorporates all the visual attractors the scientists recommend.

Hook Usual trout sizes are fished with No 12 and No 10.
Body Red.
Rib Silver.
Throat hackle Black.
Wing Striped teal flank feathers.
Tail Whisks of golden-pheasant tippets, themselves yellow and tipped with black.

Black Pennell

This fly was the invention of H. Cholmondeley-Pennell, a fisherman and author. Again, by chance or by trial, probably more of the latter, he pre-empted the scientists.

Hook No 12 and No 10.
Body Black.
Rib Fine silver thread.
Hackle Black.
Tail Golden-pheasant tippet and a yellow golden-pheasant crest feather.

Mallard & Claret

This is a superb trout and sea-trout fly for loch, lake, reservoir and river.

Hook No 10 to No 14.
Body Claret.
Rib Oval gold tinsel.
Hackle Red cock.
Wing Speckled bronze mallard flank feathers.
Tail Golden-pheasant tippet fibres.

Dunkeld

Better known as a salmon fly, this pattern is the only one in my short list for trout to incorporate two small jungle-cock feathers as 'eyes'. The feather is a remarkable attractor, being striped along its length in black, yellow and white. Jungle-cock cheeks are incorporated in the two salmon flies and in one sea-trout fly I designed for my own use.

Hook No 10 and No 12.
Body Flat gold tinsel.
Rib Gold wire.
Hackle Orange.

Cheeks Jungle cock.
Wings Bronze mallard.
Tail Golden-pheasant crest.

Black & Peacock Spider

The body of this fly is of bronze peacock herl and the hackle is soft black hen. Appearing entirely black at a cursory glance, it resembles a little beetle. On small-sized hooks, No 12 or No 14, fished off a floating line and thus moving just beneath the surface, it accounts for many trout in warm summer months.

The Invicta

A remarkable trout wet fly, this is never missing from my outfit. It is remarkable because, with the stiff hackle resembling legs and rear sloping wings over the body, it is both imitative of a surface-hatching sedge and, in the yellow of the body and the golden-pheasant-crest tail, it impinges upon the colour reactions of a trout.

Hook No 12 or No 14.
Body Yellow seal's fur.
Rib Gold tinsel.
Head hackle Striped jay.
Wing Hen pheasant tail
Tail Golden-pheasant crest.

Fished just beneath the surface, or in the water film where sedges hatch, it usually takes half of my summer still-water trout if on wet fly or lure.

Lures

Lures are large wet flies, usually dressed on long-shank No 8 or No 10 hooks. They are numerous in pattern and account for many rainbow trout, particularly in those cold months from October to the end of April, when natural insect activity is at a low level and rainbows remain in season. They are also taken by brown trout in their open season, but rainbows, costing less than brown, tend to be the major, and sometimes only, stocked trout in still waters. Lures may be fished off floating, sink-tip and sinking fly lines, but much of their success comes when fished close to the lake bed in cold water.

Many are of colours that are unrelated to rational thought – they achieve limited success and are amongst the hundreds of designs which are soon discarded. Some achieve distinction, mainly those incorporating colours at the red end of the spectrum, black, white and stripes, just as in the best traditional wet flies.

Sweeney Todd

This, one of the earliest arrivals on the lure scene, was Richard Walker's invention.

Hook Long-shank No 8 or No 10.
Body Black floss silk.
Rib Silver tinsel.
Throat Fluorescent magenta wool.
Hackle Magenta cock or hen (underneath the body only).
Wing Black squirrel.

Simple to dress, slim in outline and correct in colour, it is often on my leader point, particularly in the smaller size in clear water.

Whisky

An entry for this fly in my Purchase Day Book has troubled my accountant. Instead of putting this Whisky in soda it should be employed in water where the visibility is poor due to algae, mud or stirred-up peat. It is the most visible and startling lure in my collection, being almost entirely hot orange in colour.

Hook Long-shank No 8 or No 10.
Body Scarlet floss silk.
Rib Gold tinsel.
Hackle Hot orange.
Wing Hot-orange calf-tail hair or hot-orange hackle.

Black Lure

Apart from the ribbing, this lure is entirely black.

Hook Long-shank No 8.
Body Black floss silk.
Rib Oval silver tinsel.
Head Black tying silk and black varnish.
Wing Two black cock hackles.

On a long-shank No 8 hook it is a great lure to fish close to the bed of a lake in clear, cold, winter water or when trout seek the chilly refreshing depths in a heatwave. It is also a first-class sea-trout fly.

Black Muddler Minnow

This lure, like most, does not resemble anything natural that I have observed on or in the water! Nevertheless it takes many trout, at varied depths and even when floating on the surface.

Hook Long-shank No 8.
Body Black floss silk.
Rib Fine silver tinsel.

Head Bulky, of spun, natural brown bucktail.
Wing Black squirrel tail.
Silk Black.

This lure may be dressed in other colours, of which orange would be my second choice. Deer hair is hollow and consequently floats. If this lure is greased, cast out and left to float, stationary, on a calm still water (the angler dozing the while in otherwise hopeless conditions), it will take inquisitive trout.

Montana nymph

Why this is called a *nymph* I cannot explain. It resembles a green and black or yellow and black striped football jersey. All the same, this North American pattern is a killer of rainbow trout. Usually weighted to fish off a floating line, but at some depth, the striping effect of the black ostrich herl, yellow chenille and black cock hackle may be the triggering factors.

Worm fly

This lure does not resemble a worm. It is two flies tied in tandem (one behind the other). Both flies have identical dressing.

Hook No 12, two flies tied in tandem.
Tag The rear fly only, red floss silk.
Body Bronze peacock herl.
Hackle Dark red cock or hen.

When all else fails, creep this outfit over the mud at the lake bottom and beside those beds of weed.

Baby Doll

Although my emphasis is on the colours red and black, one ought to have a white lure in the box for a fast retrieve close to the water surface. Perhaps the speed of movement attracts trout; perhaps they imagine this lure is a minnow, escaping, and the only way to taste is to catch and grab. One cannot tell what makes them take, but take they do – at speed.

Hook No 10 not necessarily with a long shank.
Body White wool teased out at the end to form a stumpy tail.
Head Varnished black silk.

★

The techniques of fishing insect imitators, wet flies and lures will be considered in subsequent chapters.

4 Dry-fly fishing on still waters

This is the cream of the lake and reservoir trout fishing. To arrive after breakfast and to see the surface ringed by the rises of fish taking natural flies; to identify the natural, knot-on an artificial of the right size, cast out and see it taken – that is the peak. Such satisfactions are experienced only in late spring, summer and early autumn, when the days are warm and fruitful. Fishing a floating fly is a waste of time in winter when naturals keep their heads down. So, from May to October, fish dry fly whenever conditions allow – you may not catch as many as the wet-fly angler but each achievement will be memorable.

The normal method of fishing dry fly is with the standard outfit of 9 or 10 ft easy-action rod, floating line and tapered leader. In addition there is *dapping*. This entails the use of a long rod of about 18 ft in length, a fluffy, undressed blow line, short length of untapered nylon and a natural or artificial fly. This method is practised to a greater extent in loch sea-trout fishing (see Chapter 20) than in still-water trout fishing, although the system is commonly used with natural 'daddies' in Ireland.

Preparation of tackle

As noted in Chapter 3 there is a variety of land- and water-bred flies which appear from beneath, or are blown on to, the water. The technique of leader and dry-fly preparation is the same in both cases and a floating fly line is always used.

The first step is to identify the natural fly and select the correct imitation. If a replica is not available, a fly of the same size will be almost as effective, even if not of the same colour. Size is important.

Now the knotless tapered leader: should one use 5x of 3 lb BS, 4x of 4 lb BS, or stronger? Consider the size of fly. A small No 18 hook fishes freely off a thin, almost invisible, 5x leader but, if there are large trout and weed beds, 4x is safer. A 4x is more visible. There are conflicting factors and you will have to weigh them in your mind and decide. In order to cast a fat mayfly on a No 10 hook a 2x or 3x leader is necessary, because the weight of the fly may crack-off 5x nylon and the leader may not have the resilience to 'turn over' and extend the fly. A No 12 sedge fly fishes well on a 4x leader. The leader must match the fly.

Knot on the fly with the two-turn Turle, passing the point of the leader through the hook eye from front to back. With the Turle, the nylon passes straight through the hook eye to tighten in a loop around the neck; thus the fly will never alight on its head, but always be in line with the leader. Do not use the tucked half blood, this knot is free to move around on the perimeter of the hook eye and the fly may alight on its head or at right angles to the leader.

Knot the leader loop to the fly line by the double sheet bend. If there is a length of 20 lb BS nylon permanently needle-knotted to the end of the fly line, cut off the loop of the knotless tapered leader and join it to the 20 lb BS line extension with a blood knot. This arrangement eliminates the fly catching on the line/leader junction knot when casting and allows the junction to pass freely through the top ring of the rod when playing a fish. The needle-knot junction is almost essential when fishing in the dark. An excellent method of joining the leader to the fly line is to thread the end of the fly line into a 6 in. braided loop connector. Line and leader are then joined 'loop to loop'. Dip the fly in the Permafloat bottle, shake it and allow it to dry in the breeze. Rub your thumb and forefinger in the solid Mucilin and grease the 2 yd of leader closest to the fly line. Ideally the final 2 or 3 ft of the leader point should sink beneath the surface, where the monofilament will be almost invisible – only the 6 ft of nylon closest to the fly line being on the surface. This is rarely achieved unless the final 3 ft are wiped with 'sink mix'. To make your own de-greasing, surface-tension-destroying-preparation take a few inches of wet cloth, add some drops of Fairy Liquid and sprinkle with Fuller's Earth. The piece of soggy material may be stored in the container used to hold 35mm film spools.

All is now ready, but be sure the fly has fully dried before using it. To be certain, brush the hackles against your lips; if the fly is cold to this touch, the fly is still wet.

Fishing conditions

Time of day and year

Trout do not eat and flies do not hatch throughout the hours of daylight. In May a rise to hatching flies may take place from mid-morning until tea-time, following the warming and before the cooling of surface water. There is likely to be reduced activity in the middle of the day.

In June the mid-day reduction may deteriorate into a standstill in bright conditions; the rise being from 9 am until 11 am and from 4 pm until the chill of evening at 8 pm or thereabouts. July is the least attractive fishing month; heatwaves are experienced and conditions can be hot and bright. The water may be too warm at the surface for the comfort of trout, which sink to the depths where all is cool and restful. In such conditions fly still hatch and trout rise, but only for an hour or two following the dawn and in the hour of dusk.

The first half of August may be as bad as July, but the last 2 weeks are better. In this month the dawn and dusk taking periods lengthen and the mid-day standstill shortens. September is very good indeed, as productive as the last 2 weeks of May and the first fortnight of June. You may succeed throughout the day, although activity, as usual, slackens between noon and 3 pm.

October can be good in the first half, but cold weather may arrive at any time to bring dry-fly fishing to an end. Brown trout will be out of season by the end of September or in the early days of October on some waters.

Weather

The best days are warm, drizzly and overcast. The worst are cold, when the air is at a lower temperature than the water. Look at these statements in greater detail. For good fishing, the air should be warmer than the water but, by mid-summer, if this condition prevailed every day, the water would become too warm and trout would descend to the depths. When this happens, dry-fly fishing, except at dawn and dusk, comes to a halt. There may then follow 2 or 3 chilly days with north or north-easterly winds cooling the water and few rises at the surface. If this is followed by a warm southerly or south-westerly wind, once again warmer than the water, good fishing will be experienced.

A gentle breeze is a great help; ruffling the water, disguising the leader, drifting the fly, blowing land insects over the lake. A strong wind will blow any fly clean off the water if it is brave enough to hatch; one's only dry-fly hope in wavy situations is a large, buzzy, buoyant offering, preferably dressed almost entirely of deer hair.

A cold dry wind from the north or east usually produces poor fishing. Not only is the air colder than the water, but evaporation cooling the water surface inhibits natural flies from hatching. Warm southerly or westerly winds are best. A wet day is good; not a violent storm when the rain sheets down by the bucketful, but a drizzly day. Flies hatch and trout feed in these conditions. Even a very wet period can change for the better, the rain cease, the sun come out, warmth return and rises appear.

High, bright, cotton-wool clouds in a blue sky signal poor results. Your only chance with dry fly may come when the sun is hidden, passing behind a cloud. Certainly no more than one or two trout will be taken, particularly if the water surface is disturbed by casting and retrieving fly line and leader. There is a chance: cast out a fat, greased Black Muddler and let it rest. Lie down, cross your legs, doze and watch from the corner of one eye – after half an hour a passing trout, all being quiet and still, may take.

Do not fish during a thunderstorm whilst holding your personal lightning conductor, a carbon-fibre rod. When the storm has moved away you may have great sport.

The fishing

Where to fish from the bank

I rarely fish dry fly from a boat. If you know where to go on a lake or reservoir it is almost always possible to find trout rising within easy casting distance of the bank. Furthermore, because the dry-fly fisher casts infrequently, there is less water disturbance than is made by the constantly casting and retrieving wet-fly man and trout swim closer to the angler.

In May, at hawthorn-emergence time, I like to fish with the wind at my back, blowing on to the water. It does not matter if the first few yards of the surface are unruffled; the breeze will stir up ripples 15 yd from the bank and windborne flies will fall there. Your fly will remain extended at the extremity of the leader, held there by the breeze, and sooner or later a trout will take. The same thinking applies to gnat and midge fishing; the windward side will be reasonably calm and suited to fishing tiny flies.

For sedge flies and daddy-long-legs, both of which may be fished in rougher water than a No 18 Black Gnat, choose a bank along which the wind is blowing. Cast out at right angles; the floating fly line will soon form into a curve and the fly will swing in at the line extremity towards the bank, sweeping a wide arc of water. As the fly swings, give it a wake-creating 6 in. tweak every 2 or 3 yd. Sedges sometimes create a wake as they try to become airborne and your tweak may attract attention.

It is not satisfactory to fish into the wind from the leeward shore with a dry fly. It is true that *drowned* food will arrive there, but we are imitating living

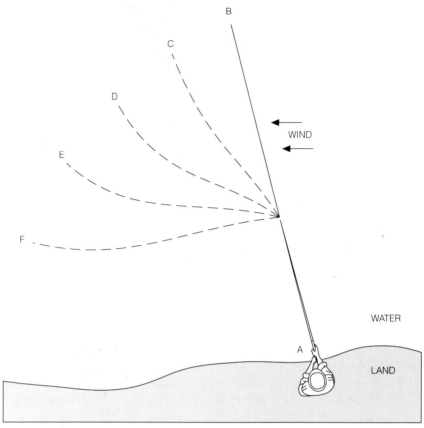

14　Searching an area of water in a lake by dry fly with the help of a wind parallel to the bank. The angler at point A casts a floating fly to point B. He does not retrieve the line or move his feet. The wind pushes the water and floating line into a curve, moving the fly to points C, D, E and F. The angler repeats this in the same place or he may move.

flies, newly emerged or just alighted on the surface. In addition, a dry fly has little weight, and thus little momentum, and it is also wind-resistant; these two factors make it hard to cast against the wind. The lee shore is the place for a nymph, as will be seen in the section below.

Many still waters have feeder streams. Attention should be paid to those areas into which they flow, for trout are attracted to these places, not only for food but also for oxygen in hot weather.

Nymph fishing

If trout are strolling along just beneath the water surface, apparently rising but showing dorsal fins in a luxurious roll, they are probably taking nymphs rising to the water film to emerge. This does not stop you fishing a floating fly for the trout are there, clearly, feeding. If the dry fly fails, try a nymph just below the surface. Black Buzzers, representing midge pupae, are effective if fished very slowly in the surface film.

Although olives (Ephemeroptera) are not of major importance on many still waters and have still to be discussed (page 72), the Pheasant Tail nymph, representing this order, hooks many trout. The sedge pupa also takes its share.

Buzzers should be fished on 5x nylon and Pheasant Tail on 4x, but sedge pupae are safest on a 3x leader as they sometimes tempt trout to smashing takes at dusk.

Standard 9 ft leaders may be used, but if one wishes to fish a weighted nymph at some depth off a floating fly line, a longer leader is required. It should be remembered that, whilst it is hard to cast a dry fly against the wind, a nymph, being slim and less wind-resistant, and having a trifle more weight, is readily cast from a lee shore.

Hooking the risen trout

It is more difficult to hook a trout taking a dry fly on still water than in a river. In a stream a trout faces into the current, takes the fly and again heads into the flow. Therefore, if the angler tightens after a slight pause following the rise, he is likely to draw the fly, from behind, into the scissors of the mouth of the fish if his cast has been upstream. In a still water, there being no current, the trout may come from, and depart in, any direction. When the angler strikes, the fish may be facing the rod. There is then the possibility that the fly will be pulled out of its mouth. Thus, you are less likely to hook a trout taking a floating fly on a lake than in a river.

What may be done to increase the chance of establishling a firm hook hold? Very little! But many of the fish will be stocked trout, usually of 1 lb or more in weight. Unlike a 6 oz wild brown in a river, they do not take and eject a fly at speed. Give still-water trout 2 seconds to turn down; at the worst, when facing the rod, the fish will by then be at an angle to the floating leader.

Hooking trout on the sub-surface nymph is much easier – just watch the floating portion of the leader. When the leader tweaks or slides away, the trout has the nymph in its mouth, the leader is passing backwards down the side of the body, and you should raise your rod.

It must be appreciated that dry-fly and nymph fishing require concentration and, for dry fly, good eyesight. If attention wanders a rise may be missed and the draw on the nymph leader remain unnoticed. If an angler suffers from poor eyesight it may be impossible or very tiring to concentrate for long periods on a small floating fly 15 yd distant. He may fail to spot a rise to his fly, or strike at the rise of a trout to a natural close to his artificial. This causes a disturbance. Such an angler is well advised to fish the nymph; on many occasions he will not even have to note leader movement, for the trout will hook itself.

Playing and netting

Great skill is not necessary in playing still-water trout in most lakes and reservoirs. Rivers are a different matter but this will be discussed in Chapter 8.

It is likely that, when a trout has been hooked, the angler will have beside him loops of retrieved line, probably resting on the ground, or floating on the water if he is wading. The line will be trapped beneath the forefinger of the hand on the rod. The strike (which should not be violent, but a decided lift) will have raised the rod near to the vertical. Keep it in this position to act as a spring to absorb shock. Keeping the rod close to the vertical will also hold line out of the water; much sunken line puts a heavy strain on the leader and hook hold. Throughout the battle to tire the trout the rod should be kept at between 45 and 90° to the water. Now, the trout has two options: to move away from the angler or towards him. If it moves away, let it go, the line loops sliding up and out over the forefinger; if towards, draw in the line over the forefinger and let it fall at your feet.

One of those courses is the first immediate move. Action will soon settle down at a fairly constant distance for a minute or two. Now is the chance to recover all the slack line on to the reel. Once this has been done the trout may be played 'off the reel', the handle of which should not be gripped, other than when being grasped to turn the spool and recover line. The fish will then pull against the reel drag, which should have been set to a resistance that will give line at violent moments. Do not hold the handle other than to recover line – you may be broken by the fish if the rod is low and the reel cannot unwind.

Many anglers do not trouble to recover excess line on to the reel. They may not suffer mishap on a still water, but this is a slack habit. Once the trout has been landed they may tread on the line; if in a river the loops of line will wash downstream and may become tangled in the fish if it swims in that direction; if the angler has to run along the river bank after a large trout or salmon, slack line may catch in vegetation, become tangled in his feet and the fish lost.

Rainbow trout on a spring balance.

Slowly the fish will tire and be drawn towards the net. If this is clipped to the belt, unclip it, extend it by flipping it open and place the net ring in the water, the shaft resting against your thigh boots if you are wading. If the net has a small stone in the bag, or a small piece of lead or copper strip crimped on the bottom meshes, the net bag will sink rather than floating inconveniently on the surface. With net extended in one hand and the line trapped beneath the rod forefinger, the rod may be raised to the rear of the head and the trout netted. The length of line and leader outside the rod tip must not be too short in order to accomplish this movement.

The fish should at once be killed by a blow to the top of the head with the priest. If the trout is to be returned to the water it should be held still on the ground with a wet hand, through the meshes of the net, whilst the hook is removed. The net may then be placed in the water and turned inside out to release the fish.

It must be remembered that to play and net a 3 lb trout on a 5x leader of 3 lb BS (reduced to 2½ lb BS by the strength reduction of the Turle knot) is a more skilled and tender operation, than when finishing with wet flies and leaders of 6 and 8 lb B.S.

5 Wet-fly and lure fishing on still waters

There is no doubt that, on still waters, more anglers fish wet flies and lures than dry fly. Moving a wet fly through the water and casting in an arc covers a wider area and thus more fish, than a static dry fly. The system works throughout the year and is not limited to warm months. These facts result in the majority of the annual catch on a still water being taken sub-surface. This is not to say that dry-fly fishing is more skilful than wet on still waters; the results do not support that argument if the weight of fish caught is used as the measure of competence. Wet fly is skilled; awareness of size of fly, colour, depth of fishing, speed of retrieve and where to cast all add up to ability.

If one accepts that both methods require knowledge and experience, on which should the beginner concentrate at the start of his angling career? In my opinion the answer must be wet fly and lure because weather and water conditions almost always give a chance if the angler chooses the correct method of fishing: large fly or small, fished shallow or deep etc. In addition, the tackle is stronger. Hook and leader will suffer the ham-handed manner in which the first two or three trout are played. When the first trout takes a tyro's fly all the instructions given are forgotten, mistakes are made and stress is placed upon the fly and leader. I have seen a 1 lb trout pulled in to within 1 ft of the tip of a horizontal rod and then, like a carrot in front of a donkey, swung ashore! Playing a trout on a fine-hooked dry fly and 5x leader calls for delicacy and here, perhaps, the method calls for greater skill.

Preparation

Tackle

Assume that the beginner has a 9 ft tip-action rod and three weight-forward fly lines: fast-sinking, sink-tip and floating. Start with the floating line, even if conditions are unsuitable and trout are deep in the water. Nothing will be caught if conditions are adverse, but casting, shooting a greater length of line through the rod rings, and lifting-off into the back cast are more readily accomplished if the length of line outside the rod tip is visible and not sunk beneath the surface. When competence has been achieved the line may be changed to a sink-tip, if conditions dictate, or to a fast-sinking line.

Now, take one of your home-made four-section leaders tapered to 8, 6 or 4 lb BS, depending on the clarity of the water, the brightness of the day and the size of trout. Attach the loop of the leader to the fly line by a double sheet bend or by a blood knot to a needle-knotted line extension, as noted in Chapter 4, or by a braided loop connector. Attach the fly to the leader point with a two-turn Turle. Wipe the leader with your wet 'sink-mix' cloth to ensure its immediate submersion when cast upon the water.

Depth of fishing and choice of line

Observation is one of the keys to success. The first action on arrival at the water is to look at the surface. If trout are feeding there, as evidenced by rises, fish the floating line. If there are no rises, then trout are either not feeding, feeding elsewhere or foraging at some depth. Investigate the lower depths by changing to the sink-tip or the fast-sinking line.

The easiest sinking line for a beginner to handle is a sink-tip. This statement is based upon observation of the many people I have taught to fish. When they have cast out a sinking line and retrieved a few yards, they don't know the length which remains beneath the water. This leads to attemps to 'lift off' a greater length of line than can be raised from beneath the surface or, conversely, to the line being retrieved to within 2 or 3 ft of the rod tip before the line/leader junction becomes visible. In the latter case much false casting then takes place to re-extend the line.

Neither of these situations arise with a sink-tip line because the colour changes from the lighter shaded floating line to the dark tip about 10 ft from the point. If the line is retrieved until the beginning of the dark length just reaches the rod tip, the sunk section is then of a length which is readily lifted from the water into the back cast.

So far, with floating and sink-tip lines, we have been able to cover depths from a couple of inches to 3 or 4 ft below the surface. Greater depth may be required and, for this, the fast-sinking line must be used. Once full casting competence has been achieved there is no need to go through these stages; a fast-sinking line may be the one with which to start the day. On the other hand, the sink-tip may place the fly at the required depth for the prevailing conditions.

How is the correct depth ascertained? Well, if there is no surface activity and the fast-sinking line is on the rod, cast out about 20 yd, count to five, to give the line time to sink, and retrieve. With a pause of five, cast half-a-dozen times in an arc. Now increase the count to 10, again covering an arc of water, then 15 and so on. Ultimately the bottom will be touched – reduce the count by five. If a trout takes at a count of 10, continue at that depth.

It will be found that the density of the fly line to be used is usually dictated by weather and water conditions, which themselves tend to follow the months of the year. Thus, winter fishing in cold water is usually by sinking line while, in summer, when there is surface insect life, the floater predominates. The use of the floater in summer may be forced upon the angler by weed growth rising from the bottom; this would clog the hook of a fly fished off a sinking line.

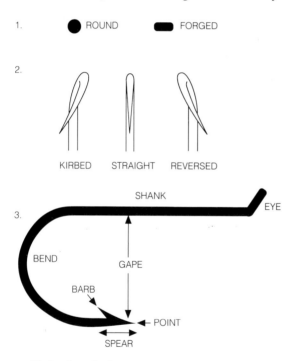

15 Fly hooks – single.
   (1) Cross-section. Fly hooks are formed of wire, either in its normal round section or flattened by forging. Forged wire is considered less likely to bend.
   (2) Spear of the hook. This may be turned to one side or the other. I have not noticed any advantage in the offset spear.
   (3) The hook. The eye of a dry fly, and of salmon flies, is usually 'up'; that of wet flies and lures is 'down'.

There is a situation in summer when the use of a sinking line is rewarded – a heatwave. If surface water becomes too hot for trout, perhaps at 70°F, they seek the cooler depths and there a sinking line will find them. This is particularly the case if a sinking line is used in a heatwave to fish close to the bed of a feeder stream where it enters a lake or reservoir.

Size of wet fly or lure

In cold water (below about 50°F at the surface), cloudy water and rough water, use a large No 8 or No 10 fly. In warm water (late spring, summer and early autumn), clear water and water with a gently rippled surface, try a small fly of hook size No 12 or No 14.

These are generalities. Usually it will be found that large lures fished deep are the order of the day in winter and smaller flies fished off floating lines bring success in summer. Such guidelines follow common sense: a No 18 fly is unlikely to be seen in the opaque water stirred up by a gale; a No 8 Whisky lure is hardly the thing to use in gin-clear water, at the surface, when trout are feeding on midge pupae.

A maximum size of hook is sometimes stipulated on a still water by the controlling authority. The rules should be studied.

Fishing conditions

Time of day and the weather

When considering the time of day to fish wet fly in late spring, summer and early autumn, the suggestions in Chapter 4 on dry fly apply. In winter I am not worried if there is little response to a sunk fly early in the morning when the air may be colder than the water. If the atmosphere has warmed by 10 am there may be a taking period of an hour or so, followed by a quiet spell around mid-day. The hour of tea-time may produce trout but, as soon as the air cools, they become unresponsive. The weather notes on page 48 also apply to sub-surface fishing, but rough weather with rolling waves suits wet fly rather than dry.

The fishing

Where to fish from the bank

The choice usually depends on wind direction and water depth. It is hard for a beginner to cast against the wind. A stiff breeze blowing parallel to the bank is a considerable help for it conceals angler, leader outline and the disturbance of casting. If possible, choose a situation where the wind blows from left to right if you are right-handed and from right to left if you are casting from the left hand. In each of these cases the fly line and hook will be downwind of the angler as he casts and the fly will be unlikely to contact his ear!

As in dry fly, if wind is blowing insects off the bank or off trees on to the water, and trout are feeding, fish with the wind at your back. In such a situation a calm area extends outwards from the bank. This calm band has to be cast across, creating some disturbance, but if the fly reaches rippled water beyond the flat band the leader outline will be broken and takes are likely.

To cast against the wind calls for a considerable degree of skill. It requires a tip-action rod casting a narrow loop of heavy fast-moving line; the line will thus have considerable momentum. Such casting is more effective with a sinking fly line, which is thinner, and thus has less wind resistance, than a floater. A wet fly or lure is better than a wind-resistant dry fly. The practice is usually productive, for trout food is swept close to the bank and trout feed within 10 or 15 ft of the shore if there is sufficient depth.

Water depth also plays a part in deciding where to fish. Trout do not like to follow a fly into shallow places only 2 or 3 ft deep. If you do not know the lake and are unaware of deep and shallow areas, look at the slope of the bank. A gentle slope is likely to lead into shallow water where a cast of 20 yd may be needed to reach trout. In such a case, if trout are deep, the area in which they are to be found on a sinking line may be beyond casting distance. Conversely, a bank which slopes steeply down to water level is likely to continue thus beneath the surface, providing deep water within casting range.

If you arrive at a water where you have not fished before, study the bank and the wind. Try to choose a place or bay into which the wind is blowing, and has been blowing for a day or two, and where there is a fairly steep bank. Warm surface water will have been pushed into this bay, as well as trout food, and fish have usually followed. I sometimes think that trout arrive at such places by being carried along, like drifting logs, in the wind-pushed water close to the surface.

Having chosen a position from which to cast on to rippled water, make the first throw to a distance of perhaps 10 yd straight ahead, then to the right and the left. Next, lengthen the cast by a yard or two and repeat. The retrieve of the fly has to be almost straight back to the angler if he remains rooted to one spot. A straight return is not as attractive to a trout as a fly moving in a curved path.

A curve may be created by taking two steps along the bank as soon as the cast has been made and then retrieving from the new position. If the wind is blowing along the bank the curve will be enhanced if the steps are made upwind. Such a movement emulates the cast made at right angles to the path of a boat being rowed slowly into the wind – trout usually take as the fly whips around in a curve behind the boat. It is also similar to the system known as *backing-up* in salmon fly fishing, which will be described on page 155.

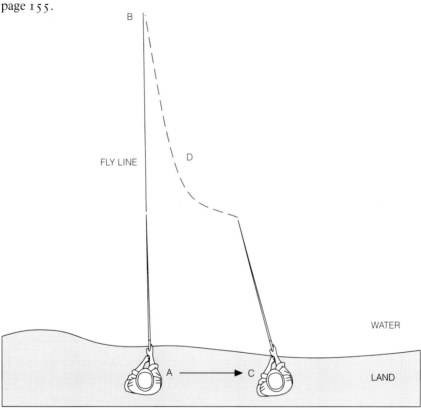

16 Retrieving a wet fly in a curve in a lake. The angler at point A casts the fly to point B, takes two steps to point C and retrieves the fly in a curve (D).

Use of droppers

The fly at the end of a leader is known as the 'point' fly. It is common practice to fish one or two additional flies, known as droppers. These are positioned at intervals on the leader. If the tapered leader is home-made the dropper flies would usually hang down from the blood-knot junctions. A dropper is usually 3 or 4 in in length; if longer it tends to tangle with the main leader.

I make these short protrusions by taking 9 or 10 in of nylon of the same diameter as the point section or a trifle thicker and, with this, tying a tucked half blood knot against one of the main leader sections. This half blood is then slid down the main section to rest against the chosen blood knot. The fly is then attached.

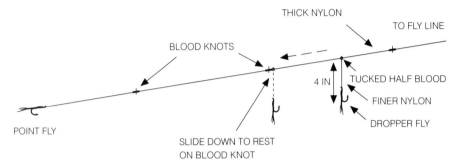

17 Dropper attachment. Nylon near the butt of a sectional tapered trout leader is usually too thick for a blood knot, joining two sections, to make a satisfactory dropper by leaving one end of the knot long whilst clipping off the other. Instead, take a length of finer nylon, tie a tucked half blood against the leader just above the chosen position and slide it down against the blood knot.

If an untapered leader is in use, not my practice other than in salmon fishing, dropper attachment is simple. Cut the leader at the chosen position and re-join with a blood knot, but leave one of the knot ends protruding to the required dropper length, cutting off the other close to the knot. The end which is left protruding, and to which the fly is to be attached, should be the continuation of the top section closest to the fly line; if the knot comes undone the fish would remain attached.

The other method of making a dropper is to use a water knot. When this is tightened, one of the ends points up the leader towards the fly line; this end should be cut to the required length to form the dropper, whilst the downward-pointing end is cut off short.

If two droppers are added, the one closest to the point is known as the 'first dropper' and the one positioned one yard below the fly line/leader junction as the 'bob'. It is unwise for the beginner to fish more than one fly if tangles are to be avoided. Once competence has been achieved, droppers and the bob fly may be fished as follows and a choice of fly offered. Cast out this 'team' of flies as usual and retrieve in the normal manner, but when it is sufficiently close to the angler, raise the rod tip to scuttle the bob fly across the surface.

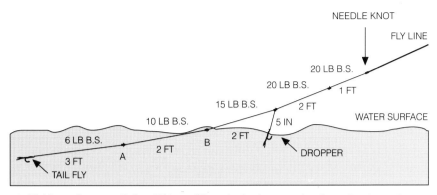

18 Fishing a dropper. Before lifting off into the back cast, raise the rod point and
scuttle the dropper (if at the top of a leader, it may be called a 'bob') across the
water surface. Note: a third fly could be added at points A or B.

The bob produces a small wake which is most attractive to fish: trout, sea
trout and salmon. As this scuttling takes place not more than three or four rod
lengths from the angler, it should be practised in rough water which masks
his outline against the sky whilst standing on the bank. If the angler chooses a
place where deep water is close to the bank, this allows trout to follow the
dragging bob and take without coming into shallow water and losing their
confidence.

The minimum length of rod for fishing droppers and lifting them to drag
across the surface is about 9 ft. A 10 ft rod is a better length.

Speed of retrieve and hooking trout

It is impossible to put forward specific instructions on the speed with which a
wet fly should be drawn through the water. Each angler follows those
personal methods which have brought him success. For myself, when fishing
a floating line, I tend to move small wet flies and nymphs slowly and impart
more speed to larger lures, such as Muddlers. A No 18 Black Buzzer should
be tweaked along 2 or 3 in. at a time in, or just under, the surface film. A No
10 Sweeney Todd, fished through rough water, might be recovered by pulls
of 6 or 9 in. with as short a pause as possible between each pull. A large,
greased Muddler, fished on the surface as a wake-creator, should be moved
really fast. In all of these movements, the fly line should be trapped under the
forefinger of the hand on the rod between pulls, to set the hook if a trout
takes.

The retrieval of a large No 8 Black Lure, or a tandem-hooked Worm Fly,
fished close to the bottom on a sinking line, may be either fast or slow.

I prefer slow but, if a snail-like pace, is adopted the fly will become snagged on the bottom. One has to experiment. On the whole it is probably best to impart rapid movement to large non-imitative brightly coloured lures – they do not stand close inspection!

There is little one can do to ensure a firm hook-hold when fishing sunk fly, other than to point the rod straight down the line with the tip almost touching the water. In this way any tweak at the fly will be felt at once and the rod raised. One usually just finds that the trout has hooked itself. If the rod tip is held 1 ft above the water surface, movement of the line indicates a take, to which one must respond like lightning.

Some assistance can be given to the surface-taking trout. A boil at the fly means that the trout has or has not taken the fly. If raising the rod does not establish contact, continue the retrieve for the trout may make a second attempt. If the boil was at the bob, continue to scuttle the first dropper; it may take that or the point fly if they remain in the water. I have often found that a large lure, such as a No 10 Black Muddler, fished as the only dropper, attracts trout, which make a visual inspection, reject, but turn and take a smaller point fly, such as a No 14 Black & Peacock Spider.

Boat fishing

One has to be careful not to spend more time rowing from place to place than fishing. I rarely take out a boat because the ancillary equipment – drogue, anchors, ropes, life-jackets, cushions and so on – encumber the expedition.

Some of the Devon reservoirs close to my home are small, being in the region of 50 or 80 acres. In these places it is easier to catch sufficient trout from the bank – and less expensive. The only time I use a boat on such small waters is in a heatwave. At such times trout retreat to deep water in the centre of the expanse and may be caught there on a fast sinking line from an anchored boat. It must be granted that, on a large water of 1000 acres or more, a boat confers mobility and saves much walking to productive areas. Even so, having reached a fishy area, I often beach the boat and cast from the bank.

Loch-style boat fishing is the commonest method by which two anglers may fish, one at each end of the boat. A drogue, a canvas sea anchor resembling a large wide-mouthed bucket with a hole in the bottom, is streamed out from a rowlock placed mid-way along the length of the gunwale. The boat then drifts slowly broadside to the wind and the two anglers cast ahead.

Fishing should be done whilst sitting; in fact, in some waters it is against the rules to cast whilst standing because of the danger of falling overboard.

A long easy-action rod of 10 or 11 ft, probably taking a No 6 line, is the most useful weapon. The extra length of such a rod enables the angler to fish a team of three flies. Of these, the bob and first dropper may be scuttled across the water surface, one after the other as the rod is raised, before going into the back cast. In rough weather trout will often follow these dibbled flies and take within a few feet of the boat. Many trout rise, bulge the surface water – and miss. Try them again at once.

If one wishes to fish lures at considerable depth, and still fish loch-style whilst drifting, a very fast-sinking line is necessary. If a slow-sinking line is used the boat will have drifted over the flies before they have reached the required depth and the angler has had time to make a retrieve. A most successful and enjoyable style calls for a boatman and for one angler, who sits in the stern. The boat is rowed very slowly upwind, preferably, if allowed, about 30 yd from a bank. The angler casts at right angles directly to the shore; the line swings in a curve (curves entice) and, just before it straightens behind the boat, trout take. This course may raise a protest – keep clear of bank anglers. Two anchors are necessary if two anglers wish to cast downwind from a stationary boat. The anchors, being at bow and stern, hold the boat broadside to the wind. Such a stationary platform enables one to fish dry fly downwind when anchored off a lee shore.

Cleaning and keeping trout

On a hot day trout should not be kept in a plastic bag placed in water at the edge of a lake. Such shallow places are warm, the water temperature often

Trout should be cleaned as soon as possible in hot weather.

Trout stomach and contents.   The gill filaments should be removed
                                            when cleaning trout.

reaching 75°F. The fish should be placed in a wet cloth bag or fish bass.
This should be suspended from a bush or tree in a breezy shady place where
evaporation will keep the contents cool. The bass must be wetted at intervals
throughout the day.

Clean trout as soon as possible. If they are to be frozen, cut out the gill
filaments, clean, clear the blood from the backbone and pack individually in
polythene bags. I purchase 18 × 12 in., 100 gauge polythene bags in lots of
1000. Such a consignment is bought at the same time as a bulk purchase of
bin bags for house refuse, and for holding salmon in the back of my car and in
the deep-freeze.

Part 2
Trout fishing in rivers

6 Trout streams

The quality of *wild* brown-trout fishing depends upon the suitability of the river bed for trout spawning and the availability of trout food. Food, in addition to that which falls upon the water, consists of shrimps, nymphs, caddis larvae, molluscs, and other invertebrates, all living beneath the water. These trout foods are, in the main, themselves dependent for their sustenance on algae. In their turn, algae need the sanctuary of water weeds and stones on which to live or they will be swept away and the river will become barren. Weeds need a stable water flow and, for generous growth, alkaline conditions.

Grayling are present in many rivers. Note the large dorsal fin.

Types of trout stream

Consider the types of streams where the requirements for trout spawning and sustenance are, and are not, met. They may be divided into those fed directly by rain and those which are sustained by springs, breaking out from chalk and limestone rock. In both cases the water must be reasonably free of pollution, have a good oxygen content and, preferably, be neutral or slightly alkaline. A water which is slightly acid is a poor producer of fat trout.

Rain-fed streams

Spate

A spate is the rise and fall of water level in a river following rainfall in surrounding hills or moors. In effect a bulge of water rushes down the valley, the speed of flow increases dramatically and then, slowly, flow and water level return to normal before the next rainstorm, which might take place after an interval of days, weeks or even months. Such a river has a bed which is washed clear of mud and sand, but on which gravel and boulders remain. The gravel and small stones provide suitable areas on which trout can cut their spawning redds and the production of trout alevins is prolific. There is little weed growth, for the speed of water flow in a spate washes away the mud in which a water plant will thrive. In addition the water itself is usually acid, a factor discouraging plant growth. Algae, therefore, have the availability of secure environments reduced to those provided by the surfaces of boulders and small stones. We thus have a river where spawning is good and food supply poor; this is a water of many small trout, usually to be found in the western side of the British Isles.

A rain-fed stream of this category is often narrow and constricted. In those lengths the bed is of boulders and small stones. In places the river broadens and thus, in spate, the rate of flow is reduced over the wider area and there sand settles. These wide flat areas are usually devoid of trout and the unrippled surface makes every cast by a fly rod a visual disturbance.

Mud-bottomed

These usually have a gentle rate of fall from source to sea level. As a consequence the speed of water flow is insufficient to wash away mud. This settles, water weeds grow, further holding back flow, and algae flourish.

All is thus set for trout-food growth, provided that there is no pollution, there is sufficient aeration and the river does not overheat. Such rivers are not prolific trout streams because they lack mud-free spawning areas.

Sandy-bottomed

These usually have a featureless river bed. Lack of boulders, small stones and anchorage for weed growth means little cover for algae, and thus trout-sustaining invertebrates are scarce. Not only is there little to eat, but the bed is unsuitable for spawning. If fish cut a redd and deposit ova, the sand soon covers the ova, which atrophy due to lack of oxygen; alevins thus fail to hatch.

Spring-fed stream

Rain falling on chalk downs or limestone hills filters below the surface into the underlying porous rock, or aquifer, which resembles a sponge. If there is good rainfall in winter, up to the middle of April, the sponge fills and water is released upwards into the river valley through springs. If there is insufficient rain in winter the sponge is not replenished and the flow of the river is reduced. Rain falling after mid-April is taken up by vegetation and trees, and fails to replenish the sponge. There has been a reduction in rainfall in recent years in the south of England; flow has been reduced and silt has settled and clogged the gravel beds of the chalk-stream trout and salmon-spawning areas.

The deposition of silt has also increased due to the ploughing and cultivation of the old water-meadow systems of the river valleys. These meadows filtered surface-water flow into the rivers but, now that large areas have been ploughed, much soil is carried into the waterway. Some estates have narrowed the river by pushing the bank forwards; by halving the width of a river the flow is doubled over that section of the river bed and the gravel is swept clean.

Before the recent period of reduced rainfall which, as I write, has lasted for 6 years, the flow of alkaline water in a spring-fed stream was stable. The water environment favoured prolific weed growths which had to be cut to be kept in check; algae and all forms of trout food flourished and wild trout, if not caught, grew to considerable weights. The bed of gravel was clean and trout spawned successfully. The satisfactory river conditions of the 1970s and early 1980s has not been maintained; rivers are over-abstracted of water for human needs, undernourished by rain and many have become clogged by mud and excessive weed growth.

Stocking policies

Spring-fed rivers have the potential to produce considerably weights of wild brown trout. In general they no longer generate quantities of fish in the 1–3 lb category. This deterioration is due to the physical matters referred to above and excessive angling pressure. The chalk streams are more heavily fished today by rods than at any time in their history and wild trout do not have time to grow, even if they are able to spawn. Rods expect to catch fish in return for their fees; river-owners need these fees as a return on the capital locked up in the river. To keep the rods happy and willing to pay, hatchery-bred trout are stocked. These introductions may be of fry, to grow-on in the river, or of takable trout, or both.

Chalk-stream levels are controlled by hatches. These artificial barriers may be raised, lowered, opened or closed to control flows and levels. They also inhibit the movement of stocked trout, enabling an estate to retain the fish it has introduced in its section of the river.

The stocking of takable brown and rainbow trout takes place throughout the season. Where fishing commences on 1 May, a stocking is likely to take place in April, followed by a top-up after the mayfly period and a further addition following a June weed cut. There may be four weed cuts during the season and perhaps half-a-dozen stockings.

It is not normal to stock a spate river with takable trout. To control trout movement may not be possible, because of lack of weirs and hatches, and fish food is likely to be scarce. Lack of food will reduce the weight of a 1 lb hatchery trout to 12 oz in 3 months in an acid moorland stream.

Open seasons

The open season for brown-trout fishing in rivers is usually from mid-March to the end of September. This is regionally variable and dates should be checked. In Scotland the season continues into the first week of October. Whilst the NRA controls statutory close seasons, riparian owners may vary opening dates within the statutory open season, e.g. a chalk stream estate may commence fishing on 1 May although entitled to open on 1 April.

7 Dry-fly fishing – tackle, natural insects and artificial flies, the senses of the trout

Rods, lines and leaders

The general principles governing fly-line AFTM ratings, rod actions (tip and easy), reels, backing, leaders and other items of equipment have been described in Chapter 2. The following additional matters should be considered when fishing dry fly for trout in rivers.

Rods

A rod must not be soft and without character; neither should it be stiff or fine leaders may snap when a heavy trout is hooked. Distance casting is not a necessity; few trout rivers are wider than the Test and, if they are, one would only wish to cover one side or accuracy of fly presentation would be lost. In addition, one may usually stalk closer to a rising fish by creeping along the bank.

Look for a rod that is firm rather than soft or stiff, is in the region of 9 ft in length and rated for a No 6 line. For reasons which will be seen, a 9 ft rod rather than a 7 ft weapon is of help in presenting the fly and playing trout on a brook, unless the stream is overhung by trees. My own choice is a 9 ft Bruce & Walker carbon rod rated at AFTM No 6/7, on which is mounted a No 6, green, Air Cel, double-tapered floating line and Hardy Marquis No 7 reel. The House of Hardy produce superb river trout rods in carbon fibre and will still make a split-cane rod to your personal requirements. Sometimes, if feeling old-fashioned and on an élite river, I take down an almost new split cane, the England's Favourite by Fosters of Ashbourne. This is the top-quality trout rod made by that ancient firm.

This rod does not have the power and lightness of the Hardy and the Bruce & Walker carbon rods, but it casts well, with a lazy action, and plays trout with authority. The same Hardy Marquis No 7 reel and Air Cel line mentioned above are suitable.

My daughter's favourite river trout rod is an 8 ft Sharpe's resin-impregnated split cane. This little rod is firm in action, casts a No 5 double-tapered line on a Marquis No 6 reel and sends the fly skimming up the river as far as she and the trout require. As Lara usually catches more than I do on the chalk streams, her outfit must suit the situation when coupled to female wiles. Fishing with her on the Test (on 9 June 1992) she took two brown trout of nearly 3 lb each on a No 18 Black Gnat and 5x leader.

River trout fishing is about the only situation in which split cane is now used. The cane rod ought to be no more than 9 ft in length or it will be too heavy by the standards of today. I sometimes use a 12 ft, double-handed, Sharpe's spliced impregnated, split-cane salmon fly rod for nostalgic reasons – but it is double-handed!

Lines

For river dry-fly fishing only one line is needed, a floating double taper, usually rated at AFTM No 5 or No 6. Line colour is a matter of preference – my own is for light green. A white fly line in the air against a background of trees is clearly discerned, and underwater photography has shown it to be more visible on the water surface when viewed from below. If looking for an angler at a distance of 100–200 yd, I am often attracted to his position by the flashing of a white line as he casts. It is a mistake to purchase a cheap line with a rough surface; it will not shoot out through the line guides unless much effort is applied. When buying a line, run it between the fingers – it should be smooth.

Leaders

For both river and still-water dry-fly fishing, Leeda, knotless tapered leaders are excellent. On an acid moorland brook, where trout weigh a few ounces, a 6x is suitable for the smallest flies, or 5x if casting a No 14 fly. 4x might be needed to turn over a large fly, but really large flies, such as the mayfly, are few on the acid streams.

On the chalk streams the following matters have to be considered before making a choice on leader diameter and strength: weight of individual trout (large fish may be stocked), size of fly, brightness of the day and clarity of the water, and the presence of river weed. Even in the most risky situation of heavy trout and much weed, it is rarely necessary to go thicker than 4x. In June 1992, on the river Test, we caught four trout, weighing in total 9 lb 6 oz, on 5x leaders and No 18 Black Gnats; there was much drifting weed from the cut in progress, and the leader caught strands of drifting *Ranunculus* as fish were played – but nothing broke!

It is not a matter of showing-off to fish fine. I fish as strong a nylon as conditions allow, but trout have the final say. If your casting is accurate and delicate, and the fly is right, but trout reject your offering after taking a look, suspect too thick a leader. Pre-stretched nylons enable one to fish extremely fine, but beware of the moment of strike, and other shocks which are not well withstood.

★

All other items, such as nets, polarized spectacles, fly boxes and so on have been considered in Chapter 2.

Natural insects and artificial flies

Ephemeroptera

Commonly known as 'upwinged flies', these have a segmented body, six legs, two or three long tails and, usually, two pairs of upright wings, of which the forewings are the largest. Some members have only one pair of wings. They may be identified on the water as they float with wings together and erect, like a butterfly with closed upright wings. In flight the tails of the larger members hang prominently below the body, giving a parachute-like appearance.

Flies of the group include: mayfly, large dark olive, iron blue, March brown, blue-winged olive, *Caenis*, the spurwings, pale watery and others. Do not worry too much about correct identification and imitating them exactly; there are too many members of the group and too many life-cycle stages for this to be practical. Instead, appreciate and recognize each progression in the life-cycle of the Order. Then, having identified the stage, present the trout with a floating general-pattern artificial of the same size and stage or, if in the underwater nymphal period, with one of two nymphal patterns.

Life-cycle

The female lays her eggs on the water surface; the eggs sink to the river bed and hatch after an indefinite period, depending on the species, water temperature and month of the year. Hatches may take days or months. The females of some species crawl down weed stems or bridge supports to lay their eggs underwater.

Nymph The egg hatches and a nymph emerges to pass through a series of skin moults over several months. This stage is spent near or on the river bed, clinging to stones or weeds and sometimes burrowing into the river bed or bank.

The dun When the nymph is mature, it propels itself to the water surface, breaks through the surface film and the nymphal case, or shuck, splits. The fly struggles free of the case to sit on the water surface, where the wings unfold and dry. Wing drying may take a few seconds or a full minute, depending on whether the day is warm and dry, or cool and wet. This emergence is readily seen in the mayfly although, to the angler who has not studied the subject, a mayfly dun just appears, apparently from nowhere; the educated observer will have seen the struggling nymph from which the dun emerges, and the flight of the dun, and will remark on the transparent nymphal shuck left behind on the surface. The dun period may last for minutes or one or two days.

Spinner Duns are dull in colour, whilst the final stage, the imago, or spinner, is shiny. The transition is accomplished by the dun moulting and shedding its skin. I once watched a mayfly make this progression on television: the thorax case splits and the spinner emerges – body, wings and tail – it is miraculous. Male and female spinners mate over land, the male dies and the female returns to the water to lay her eggs before dying. Dead spinners are known as *spent*. They float downstream, wings flat and lifeless in the water film, from which they are taken by trout. The spent of the mayfly is known as a *spent gnat* and is imitated by a fly of that name, that of the blue-winged olive is imitated by the Sherry Spinner and that of the iron blue, by the little Claret Spinner, of which a suggested dry fly is the Houghton Ruby.

Presence

This is the most important order of insects to the angler, mainly on the chalk streams, but almost universally elsewhere. Some like slow-moving rivers, others fast rocky streams, and some, such as the pond olive, are found on still waters. They are present in various months of the year and at different times of the day: mayfly in late May and early June; large dark olive in March and April; March brown in March and April; iron blue in April and September; blue-winged olive in July, August and September. That is just a smattering. We could delve further, but this is not necessary in order to catch trout.

I do not wish to discourage detailed study of insects. The more complete one's knowledge, the better one enjoys a river day and, perhaps, catches a greater number of trout, but the Law of Diminishing Returns applies. The insect expert cannot carry a sufficiency of artificials to match the naturals at all life-cycle stages. The angler who knows that a pale watery is about 0.2 in. long and a medium olive is 0.3 in., and can recognize the two, is unlikely to catch many trout if his leader is too thick, his casting cumbersome and he knows little of fish vision. As will be seen, a small selection of artificials in a variety of sizes is sufficient for most needs.

It is important to consider time of day, the weather and the month of the year. For example, the large dark olive rarely hatches before noon in April, seldom when the air is colder than the water, and the hatch is over by tea-time; the iron blue may hatch throughout a rough windy spring or autumn day; the mayfly from 10 o'clock in the morning until pub-opening time at noon, and then again in the late afternoon; the blue-winged olive in the evening in August, late afternoon in September and after luncheon in October. Gather experience on which hours to fish – by fishing! One will soon find that there is little point in expecting a consistent rise on a hot July day, other than in the evening. Equally, late evening is barren in the chill of April.

Trichoptera

A description and the life-cycle has been given in Chapter 3. Although this order is of importance to the river dry-fly angler, one only needs to take account of a small number of naturals. This limits the artificials I carry to four: Grannom, Red Sedge, Brown Sedge and Caperer.

The grannom is the first sedge we see in spring in the West Country. Brown in colour, it is of small size and the female has a green egg sac beneath the abdomen. It hatches in April during the afternoon.

In the nineteenth century the chalk streams were fished for two main periods: the second half of April and the last 2 weeks of May and the first few days of June. Those weeks coincided with the presence first of grannom and then of mayfly. Due to the distances some anglers had to travel to reach the chalk rivers, and the time this took, these weeks were usually the only ones spent on the river. The grannom was really a preparation for the mayfly and was credited with bringing trout into the habit of surface-feeding after the winter. There is limited truth in this proposition. On my home river, the Dart, we see prolific hatches at the same time as the large spring olive, but few rises by trout. So, the grannom encourages fish and angler, but to a sparse extent. There are natural large and small red sedges, caperers, cinnamons, silver, grey, black, brown, marbled and the Welshman's button.

But, as I have written, four artificial patterns suffice, of which the Caperer is the most productive of catches on the chalk rivers and the Red Sedge on upland streams.

The sedge season starts in earnest in the warm weeks of June, July and August. Walk up the river in September and inspect caddis cases – all are empty. Their peak hour is dusk, although many emerge onwards from tea-time in mid-afternoon. Sedge weeks are the warmest and mellowest of the season and the evening rise, with its sounds of plops and sploshes and the sight of widening rings upon the water, the culmination of the day.

Plecoptera

These are the hard-winged flies. They have two antennae, two pairs of wings and two tails, which may be so short that they do not extend beyond the folded wings, as in the yellow sally.

Their life-cycle comprises the egg, which hatches underwater into a nymph, which swims to the surface to emerge as the adult fly. Mating then takes place and the eggs are laid on the water. The nymphs are sometimes referred to as 'creepers'. They are eaten by trout and I have found many in the stomachs of small West-Country sea trout.

The order is of limited interest to the chalk-stream angler, for these insects prefer the faster rocky streams and rivers of the north and west. My own observations in Devon lead me to the conclusion that they hatch intermittently and individually in summer, and not in the numbers associated with hatches of olives.

They may be imitated by: Yellow Sally size 14, Stonefly size 10, Partridge and Orange size 14, Willow Fly size 14 and other patterns. Although the naturals fly regularly whilst I am fishing in summer on Dartmoor I do not carry any of these patterns. My experience being that their flights coincide with those of sedges and olives, I continue to present the patterns for Ephemeroptera and Trichoptera which feature in the table on page 78, and with success.

Diptera

This order has been discussed in Chapter 3. It is sufficient here to note that hawthorn in April and May, crane fly in August and September, and gnats, midges and reed smuts are all present on rivers and eaten by trout.

Suitable dry flies are listed in the table on page 78.

Reed smuts are so small that they are beyond my ability to imitate, but trout feed on them, revealing their presence and opening targets for my No 18 Black Gnat, which brings about their downfall.

Observing the natural fly

Look at the fly on the water. Is it large or small, dun or spinner? Is that trout taking a floating insect or nymphing? Success hangs upon these points and responding correctly to the observed situation.

If asked the most important factor in choosing an artificial to match a natural on which trout are seen to be feeding, I would put forward *size*. On 14 June 1992, I was teaching two boys to fish dry fly on a moorland stream. The sky was bright, the air hot, and the water low and clear. Not promising. A few large brown sedge flies hatched in the morning. We fished a No 12 Brown Sedge with some success until trout ceased to be attracted and the sedges no longer flew. We reduced the size to a No 14 Kite's Imperial with a pale hackle, to which two trout responded. In this there was no logic, but one should change a losing game! The day became hotter. At luncheon in the shade of a tree we saw yellow sallies, black sedges and needle flies. Trout stayed low. Then there was a rise and a pale watery landed on the arm of one of the boys. It would be hard to find anything more perfect than that small two-tailed insect. Wings erect, it sat, with tail whisks moving slightly in the breeze. It was tiny compared to the sallies and sedges, and whether the trout had risen to one of his relatives, I do not know – but it was there and surely others were too. To the 5x leader we knotted a No 18 Iron Blue. There are no iron blues on Dartmoor in June but the size was right. The two best trout of the day made mistakes, played their part and were returned to the river.

Patterns of artificials

Flies

Greenwell's Glory, Gold Ribbed Hare's Ear, Olive Quill, Tup's Indispensible, Blue Dun, Little Marryat, G. & H. Sedge, Poult Bloa, Lunn's Particular, Sherry Spinner and so on, and so on and so on. What a gathering to delight the manufacturers of compartmented fly boxes and the commercial dressers of flies. I do not say that they are *all* unecessary, but would draw your attention to a simplification between dun and spinner patterns. Dave Walford, a keeper of long experience on the river Test, said to me:

'I use very small dressings of a Lunn's Particular, just one-and-a-half turns of hackle on a No 16 or No 18 hook. [This artificial is a winged spent pattern of a medium olive spinner.] When the duns are on I pop the wings up, and when the spent's on I pop them down.'

He squeezes the wings into the required position with his fingers. One fly for dun and spinner; one compartment of the fly box saved; a simplification.

In the table on page 78 are listed the flies commonly seen on rivers during the season. The list is by no means complete, but simplifies dry-fly fishing. The angler who is able to identify these 15 insects, or groups of insects, is on the way to success. It is true that the list, and the suggested artificials, takes little account of duns and spinners requiring separate patterns, except in the case of the Sherry Spinner and Lunn's Particular. Also listed are 13 artificial flies, sometimes in two or three sizes, and three nymphs. In the case of Kite's Imperial it is wise to carry both dark- and pale-hackled flies to cover many olives other than the blue-winged. My patterns are hackled and thus cannot land upside-down with the exceptions of Grannom, Grey Wulff which has two hair tufts for wings, Red and Brown Sedges, Sherry Spinner, Daddy-long-legs and Lunn's Particular. Special credit must be given to that final fly – it is splendid in the evening when olive spinners die and float, wings outstretched on the surface of the river.

Through the high summer *Caenis* (Angler's Curse) species are common. To imitate, one would need a No 20 or No 22 hook. I must admit that, as these minute flies hatch in clouds, I can see no reason why trout should prefer my artificial. Beaten before I start, I usually go home!

Nymphs

A small selection is all that is required to meet most situations:

No 14 Pheasant Tail The dressing material is a few fibres of the tail of a cock pheasant and fine copper wire.

No 14 Pheasant Tail Dressed with silk instead of wire – this will fish in the surface film.

No 18 Black Buzzer As a midge pupa.

I do not carry a mayfly nymph. On some waters nymphs are prohibited throughout the season; on others before 1 July. As mayfly hatch before July there is little reason to carry the nymph and it is much more enjoyable to hook a rising trout to a floating fly. Neither am I addicted to the Grayling Bug, which closely resembles a maggot, although I accept that it has a place in winter fishing for grayling.

Natural flies and their artificial equivalents

Naturals	Dry flies	
April	Large dark olive	A dark Kite's Imperial No 14
	Grannom	Grannom No 14
	Iron blue	Iron Blue No 18
May	Mayfly	Grey Wulff No 10
	Iron Blue	Iron Blue No 18
	Medium olive	A pale Kite's Imperial No 14
	Medium olive spent	Lunn's Particular No 14
	Black gnat	Black Gnat No 18
	Hawthorn	Hawthorn No 12
	Midges	Black Gnat No 18
June	Mayfly	Grey Wulff No 10
	Medium olive	A pale Kite's Imperial No 14
	Medium olive spent	Lunn's Particular No 14
	Pale watery	A pale Kite's Imperial No 14 or 16
	Black gnat	Black Gnat No 18
	Midges	Black Gnat No 18
	Sedges (various)	Red Sedge No 12, Brown Sedge No 14
July	Blue-winged olive	Greenwell's Glory No 14
	Blue-winged olive spent	Sherry Spinner No 14
	Small dark olive	A dark Kite's Imperial No 16
	Small dark olive spent	Lunn's Particular No 16
	Black gnat	Black Gnat No 18
	Midges	Black Gnat No 18
	Sedges (various)	Red Sedge No 12, Brown Sedge No 14
August	Crane fly	Daddy-long legs No 10
	Blue-winged olive	Greenwell's Glory No 14
	Blue-winged olive spent	Sherry Spinner No 14
	Black gnat	Black Gnat No 18
	Midges	Black Gnat No 18
	Sedges (various)	Red Sedge No 12, Brown Sedge No 14
	Small dark olive	A dark Kite's Imperial No 16
	Small dark olive spent	Lunn's Particular No 16
	Caperer	Caperer No 14
September	Crane fly	Daddy-long legs No 10
	Blue-winged olive	Greenwell's Glory No 14
	Blue-winged olive spent	Sherry Spinner No 14
	Iron blue	Iron Blue No 18
	Medium olive	A pale Kite's Imperial No 14
	Medium olive spent	Lunn's Particular No 14
	Midges	Black Gnat No 18
	Caperer	Caperer No 14
	Sedges	Red Sedge No 12, Brown Sedge No 14

Senses of the trout

The cone of vision

Trout have binocular vision covering an area to their front but this is monocular to each side; to the rear there is a narrow arc into which they cannot see. They are thus able to judge the distance to an approaching fly being carried downstream towards them on the surface – and take it accurately. To each side, the single eye alerts them to danger. From behind, the angler may creep upstream without being seen.

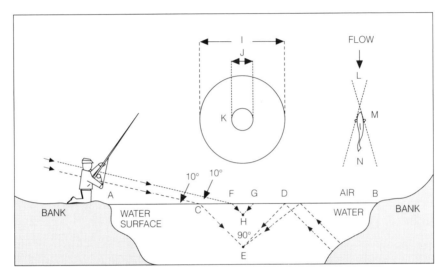

19 The cone of fish vision. A-B River 30 ft wide. B-D River bed is reflected down to salmon, at E, from the surface mirror. C-D 9 ft window of vision of salmon at E, at 4 ft depth. F-G 2¼ ft window of vision of trout at H, at 1 ft depth. I 9 ft window of vision of salmon. J 2¼ ft window of vision of trout. K A fly on the water surface is invisible to trout at H.

An angler kneeling at A would have his head visible to trout at H, if his cap is 3 ft above the ground. His head and shoulders would be visible to salmon at E.

What a fish sees: with binocular vision (L), it can judge distance in order to seize a fly; with monocular vision (M) it can see approaching enemies; in the blind area of approach (N), the angler casting upstream is not visible.

Trout may also be approached from the side if the angler keep sufficiently low. As may be seen from the illustration above, for a trout at a certain depth there is a circular area of the surface in which it can see floating objects. The deeper the trout, the larger this surface circle. At the circumference of this circle, rays of light hitting the water at an angle greater than 10° to the surface are refracted down to the trout; at less than 10° to the water surface the rays do not penetrate and the trout is unable to see above-surface objects beneath such an imaginary line. Within the circle, rays of light are refracted down to the eye of the trout, except those at 90° which travel vertically down to the fish.

If an angler keeps within an angle of 10° from the edge of this circle he is invisible to the trout but, as he approaches the edge of this vision cone, first his head, or the tip of the rod if he is casting but not his body, will be visible. If he stands on the edges of, or within the circle, or so that he is entirely above the 10° line when standing on a bank above the water, he is entirely visible. The practical interpretation of these facts is that the lower the angler keeps, the less likely he is to be seen by the trout; also the deeper the trout, the greater is the surface circle of its cone of vision.

It is a blessing that water runs downhill. The dry-fly fisher, casting upstream whilst wading, stands on the river bed at a point where it is lower than the bed beneath the trout, which is 15 or 20 yd higher up the river. This does not mean that the angler is entirely invisible if in the area of monocular vision but, unless the fall is very steep in which case he may be out of sight, at the least some of him will be below the 10° line. He will also be invisible if almost, or directly, behind the fish, in the blind area resulting from the obstruction of the trout's eyes by its body.

Conversely, the wading wet-fly angler, if casting downstream, stands on the river bed where it is at a higher level than that beneath the trout. He is also ahead of the trout and in the area from which food arrives and where vision is concentrated. It is thus necessary for the angler casting downstream to keep extremely low to avoid detection.

'He's a "hands-and-knees" man' is a complimentary observation on the angler who creeps on all fours along the river bank to approach a rising trout. By contrast, it has been my misfortune, if beginners forget their instructions, to see them standing on a boulder or high upon the bank to obtain a better view of the river and any rising trout. When, after a couple of hours, they have failed to catch anything and every trout has fled under the bank or beneath a bed of weeds, the penny drops and the approach is made with care. If one cannot keep low, at least one may be able to cast from behind a static object or with a tree or bush as a background. The worst situation is for rod and angler to be outlined against the sky.

The depth at which the trout is positioned, as we have seen, governs the diameter of the surface circle in which it can see floating objects – in our

Hiding behind the rushes, the angler holds his rod high to act as a shock-absorbing spring, and keep the line out of weed beds.

particular interest, flies. At a depth of 1 ft the diameter of the 'window' is just over 2¼ ft; at 6 in. it is just over 1 ft and, when a trout is just under the water film, 3 in. below the surface, its circle of vision is no greater than the spread of the fingers of one hand. In terms of fly presentation, this means that accuracy is required when a trout is rising in shallow water and is, therefore, at a shallow depth. That fish's circle of vision, being small, requires us to place our fly in an area which may be no greater than that of a dessert plate. If this is not appreciated, and your fly lands an inch or two outside the dessert-plate circle, you may think that the offering has been rejected because it was not on the menu of the day. It is more probable that it has not, and could not have been, seen.

Hearing, vibration, taste and smell

Trout cannot hear an angler speaking or shouting above the surface of the water, but it is likely that they are able to receive the vibrations of underwater sound. The squeak of the iron hob nails on a boot on river-bed rock is probably perceived, whilst the angler who shouts at a cow licking his tackle bag on the bank remains unheard.

There are sense organs in the lateral line on both flanks of the fish. These pick up changes in water pressure and thus enable a river trout to remain head-on to the current; if positioned sideways on, the pressures on each flank are unequal. The lateral line also receives minute pulses when other fish or predators swim into the area, or an angler runs along the river bank. There is thus no need to whisper the information to a companion that 'a trout has risen over there', but you ought not to trip over his tackle bag in your hurry to approach and tell him the good news. If a bull approaches your friend from behind, a shout will do no harm. Many times I have seen anglers jump down from a bank on the edge of a river in order to approach a rising fish. Such an action, and the resultant vibrations, are fatal to success; so also is the cast which lands heavily on the water, even if it is outside the window of the quarry.

It seems unlikely that taste and smell affect the dry-fly angler, although fish possess both senses. I would not be so categorical in respect of smell and the sub-surface fly or, for that matter, other baits fished in the water. To consider this subject further the reader is advised to study the section dealing with these matters, written by Professor Peter Behan in the book *Salmon & Women* (Witherby, 1990). For myself, I do not worry about taste or smell in dry-fly fishing, but rub my hands in earth before knotting sub-surface salmon flies to my leader or preparing natural baits.

8 Dry-fly fishing on the river

One of the peaks of dry-fly fishing is an engagement with an experienced trout. There you are, seated on one of those wooden benches placed 10 ft back from the river bank. It is 10.30 am in the final week of May or early June on a chalk stream. Dew is still on the grass, swallows and swifts are overhead and a gentle breeze blows, for once, upstream. Ziiiip – the air parts before a swift descending from tree-top height to feed on mayfly which have started to emerge. Attention returns to the water surface where life is being released. Nymphs pierce and struggle through the clinging water film and emerging mayfly duns tread down their nymphal shucks, drying their wings in seconds as they drift downstream and lift into the air. A swallow descends and the 2-year span of egg, nymph and dun ends after 15 seconds of flight.

Widening rings of rises now spread across the water and, wonderful as it always is, trout, formerly tucked out of sight, appear in channels between the beds of weeds. Good trout too – fat and amiable as they feed, accepting the bounty of the mayfly emergence. A dun drifts down, wings erect, tail whisks curved towards the sky and legs pricking the water film as it drifts and dries its wings. Mr Portly, a 2 lb trout, strolls across, lifts, gulps and eternity descends on the dun. The water smooths on Portly's patch. That is the sad part; a perfect insect is no more. That dun will not moult, become an iridescent spinner, mate, lay eggs and die, drowned, wings outstretched upon the water.

Enough of observation. Mr Portly is still feeding and the dun must be avenged. You haven't a gossamer mayfly in your box! No matter, that No 10 Grey Wulff will do the trick, Turle-knotted to the point of a tapered 3x leader. Portly rises again, a yard beyond the intervening fast channel. A straight cast will not do; the line will be pulled by the fast water and the fly will drag. Warned of unnatural actions, the trout will go down and live to feed another day. No. A curly cast is the one; a cast which will not pull and drag before the fly has seduced the trout; a wonderfully crooked cast, such as we all make inadvertently, commonly, and when not needed.

On your knees you lengthen line. Swish, swoosh, swish, swoosh and, parachuting, the Wulff settles a few feet short of Mr Portly's window vision. He is undisturbed and accepts a passing natural. With shaking hands, tranquillizer taken, you place the second cast perfectly. The old trout rises, locks on to the Wulff with a suspicious eye, backs down with head just inches from the fly – and takes. A second of suspense follows Mr Portly down, a timeless pause, the rod is raised, bends over, and you know you have him firm. The scene now changes from southern chalk to the West Country, Wales and Scotland; to moorland brooks and Highland streams and 8 oz trout. Mr Portly is replaced by Mr Skinny, a senior member of a numerous tribe of darting, wary troutlets.

The banks of the brook are high where the water has cut a passage through the peat, the bed is firm and the waterway two rod lengths wide. There are no weeds, boulders abound and caddis cases 1 in. long lie in profusion in little bays and backwaters.

The June sun sinks below the hills, the breeze dies and Mr Skinny ventures out of a rocky hole to take his sedge-fly supper. Weighing 12 oz, Skinny knows his place – the best place at the neck of his little pool where first pick may be made of drifting morsels. Minor 6 oz specimens swing in downstream to take a lesser chance. Caddis larvae, now changed into flies, heads and legs protruding from the ends of sandy cases, creep up the sides of boulders. Reaching the surface, the sedges emerge, dry and take wing. Some fall upon the water to the delight of the feeding Skinny tribe. In the failing light there are plops and slurps and other greedy sounds.

Watching from the shelter of a nearby drystone wall you see the head of a wading angler above the bank. Just a head, as he creeps and stalks upstream, and a waving casting rod. Forwards and backwards, forwards and backwards, forwards . . . Twitch – the rod zips up at lightning speed, a red-spotted 7 oz trout is hooked, drawn in and tweaked free of barbless hook. The troutlet flicks away. Mr Skinny returns at once, shaken, to his hole. The angler blows upon his fly, water drops mist away and he re-oils the No 14 Red Sedge.

There are no benches on the moors; wading is required; the response to a rise is fast; the 5x leader is fine and a 12 oz trout is a monster.

Preparation of tackle

Run the fly line up through the rod line guides. In so doing, place the rod butt on a bank or seat so that the rod is horizontal. In this position the task is easier and, if the line is momentarily released from the fingers, it will not run back through all the line guides.

Now attach the leader. This may be done by the double sheet bend if there is a loop at the end of the leader and a single overhand knot at the end of the line, but such a junction is bulky. Instead use a braided loop connector as illustrated on page 26 or needle-knot 1 ft of 20 lb BS nylon into the end of the fly line, cut off the loop of a knotless tapered leader and join the nylons with a blood knot. The line/leader joint may then be wound into the rod tip when netting a trout and the fly is unlikely to catch on this streamlined junction when casting. The disadvantages in dry-fly fishing of the needle-knot method are: the removal of the coloured loop renders the leader strength undefined for future use; the leader, if wound a few inches within the rod tip, may be pulled inside the line guides by the weight of the fly line, causing the fly to be pulled up to the tip of the rod. Personally, I do not remove leader loops when fishing by day (and one does not have to with a braided loop connector), for I can see and ensure that the junction knot remains outside the rod tip when netting a trout. The needle-knot arrangement has an obvious advantage when fishing for sea trout in the dark.

The leader should now be greased with solid Mucilin from the line junction to within 3 ft of the point. This final yard should remain ungreased in case one wishes to change from fishing a dry fly to fishing a nymph, which may be required to penetrate the surface of the water. The line should not be greased. A floating line floats because it is less dense than water. If greased, the chemical preparation may cause the line coating to crack and let in water and the line will sink. A floating fly line sinks because it is either dirty or worn and cracked. If the line is double tapered, as are my floating lines, it must then be reversed.

At this point of preparation, hang the net on your belt loop and put on polarized spectacles and a wide-brimmed hat, both of which aid fish spotting. For the catch, place a polythene bag in the rear pocket of your fishing waistcoat. In the front pockets store the following: compartment fly box, solid Mucilin, Supafloat, spare leaders, artery forceps and midge cream. A pair of small scissors may be hung about the neck. The priest, also corded around the neck, may hang to thigh level and then be placed in a trouser pocket. If using home-made leaders, a spool of tippet nylon should also be carried. For myself, I use Leeda, knotless tapered leaders until they have been shortened by about 1 ft through fly replacement – they are then discarded at home.

The fishing

Arrival at the river

Before setting up the rod, look at the water to observe clarity, insect life, the presence of weed and, if possible, the size of trout and whether they are rising. These matters bear upon the decisions to be made on leader length, strength and profile, coupled to the likely size and pattern of artificial fly. A large fly requires a heavier nylon point than a small dry fly.

Where is the wind? The essence of dry-fly and nymph fishing on a river is that the artificial move in the manner of the natural, that they are carried downstream by the current without interference, known as drag, by the line

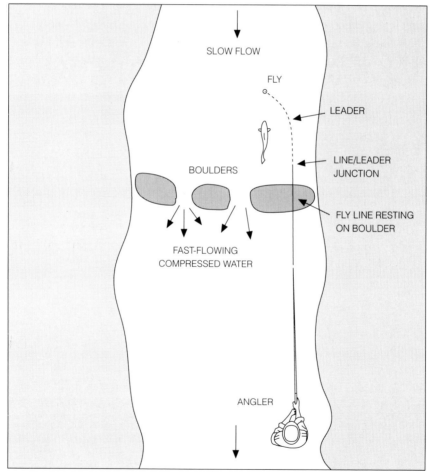

20 Dry fly. Drag elimination in a fast-flowing rocky brook. The fly line must be kept out of the gaps between the boulders or the line will be pulled downstream, causing the fly to drag.

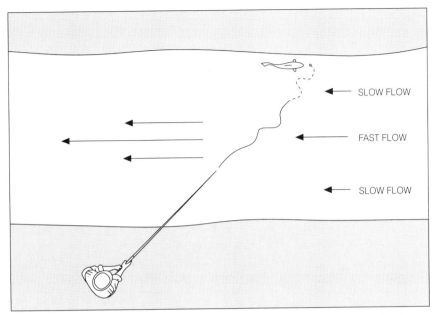

21 Dry fly. Elimination of drag when casting to a trout in slack water on the far side of
    a current. To create a wiggly line, aim high in the air. As the line straightens,
    pull back the rod and then push forward. In the time taken by the current to
    straighten the wiggles downstream the fly will have drifted over the trout.

or leader. To this end the cast must be made upstream, to drift back towards
the angler, or up and across, or across. Even downstream is permissible if a
curly cast is executed and the fly has a short drift over an observed feeding
trout – *provided the fly does not drag.* The wind has a marked effect on dry-fly
fishing, for floating flies are light in weight and, by their stiff hackles, wind-
resistant. It is hard to cast a large dry fly against the wind; a small fly is easier
and a nymph, being streamlined and possibly heavier, cuts through an
adverse breeze.

An upstream wind is helpful in carrying forward a long leader and in ruffling
the water surface as it presses against the flow. A rippled surface breaks up
the outline both of the leader on the water and the angler against the sky.
A downstream wind may be counteracted to some extent by a short leader of
$7\frac{1}{2}$ ft, which should be thick at the butt and steeply tapered. Such a leader
might be 0.025 in. at the butt and reduce in diameter to a point of 0.006 in.
(5x) or 0.007 in. (4x).

Choice of bank from which to cast should exercise the mind. If the day is
calm, being right-handed would lead you to the right bank, from which you

Upstream dry fly. Keep low.

may cast up-river with the right hand close to, or just beyond, the river's edge. If right-handed, and unable to cast with the left hand, fishing from the left bank means reaching across the body to place a fly beneath your own bank. If left-handed, it is efficient to cast upstream from the left bank. These

Upstream dry fly. Either keep low or cast 'cross country'.

suggestions are based upon the fact that, if you look downstream, the left bank is to your left and the right bank to your right. This is the same for all rivers. If there is a cross-wind I would prefer to fish with the wind at my back, unless the sun is low and also to my rear. Body silhouette and one's shadow across the water frighten trout.

If fishing a brook a few feet wide where one may wade, or a river where this is allowed, the right-handed person will creep upstream beneath the right bank, and vice versa for the left-hander. There is much to be said in favour of wading to confer concealment, and much against it, on account of fish and weed disturbance, and the disruption of invertebrate life.

Tempting a trout

Time is not wasted by studying the river for signs of insect life and trout activity, but one ought to watch from the lower end of the beat with plenty of upstream fishing space ahead.

Two courses are now open: to cast to a rising trout or to fish the river. The first is preferable and the second, although sometimes frowned upon, understandable. In the 'good old days' when the hours of pleasure were longer, and one had time to stand and stare, it was unacceptable to fish the river without a rise in sight. The approved system was, and is, as follows: sit down below a likely stretch of water, wait for a rise, identify the insect eaten, ascertain visually that the trout is worthy in size, match the insect, and cast to that fish until it is caught or 'goes down'. That is the classic style, the most satisfactory and true method of dry-fly fishing. It has been followed by many generations.

The second system is to work upstream, casting to all likely places whether or not a trout has risen. This disturbs a considerable length of water, particularly if the angler is wading. I try to follow the individual-trout method, without wading, on a stocked stream, but wade and cast to all the likely places on the Dartmoor brooks where the river bed, being of stone, contains little weed to be broken under foot. On my moorland brooks there are few large trout to be discerned, and each fish hooked is stranded on a rock or beach, unhooked and released without being touched by hand.

Examine the individual-trout method. It has a long pedigree. Watch for a rise, then creep nearer to mark the exact position of the fish, which is almost always above the place where the rings of the rise were first seen. The rings are downstream of the fish because of the delay between the rise and the

Wading in a trout stream is hazardous.

sighting of the rings, which are carried downstream by the current in the interim. How often does one hear a rise and whirl about at the sound, but the delay caused by swivelling the neck allows the rise to drift several feet.

The second rise fixes the position. Is he takable? This cannot always be determined, but sometimes a dorsal fin sliding through the surface, or a tail which waves 'good-bye', gives a clue. Siege may now be laid to that fish. Which artificial fly is to be placed before its eyes? On most days one can anticipate which flies are likely to hatch or be blown upon the water. Therefore use mayfly in May and early June, blue-winged olive in July and sedges during summer evenings. Even so, identify the fly or, at least, the size. Now, knot an imitation or a dry fly of the same size to the leader point. This should then be suspended in the Supafloat bottle, withdrawn and blown upon to free the hackles of excessive floatant. False cast the fly until dry. I usually touch the hackles with my upper lip: if cold the fly is still wet with floatant; if warm, the Supafloat has evaporated and the waterproofed fly may be cast. If the fly is used before it is dry the floatant will be washed off and the fly will sink.

All is ready. The moment has arrived to plot the trout's downfall in the final phase – correct placing of the fly. This must drift over the trout without being dragged by line or leader. Drag is circumvented by the study of the relative speeds of water currents close to the fish. If the trout is directly upstream of the angler, he may cast directly up the river and the fly will drift down naturally. If the trout is in slow-moving water on the far side of a faster current, the fly will be dragged by the faster movement of the fly line as it is washed downstream. What to do? Cast a wiggly line that lands in crooked form upon the water, as S-shaped as a swimming grass snake. By the time the current has straightened the line, and drag commences, the fly will have drifted over and out of the trout's window of vision – or been taken! To cast crookedly, pull the rod tip back and then push forward just before the line alights on the water.

Another method of avoiding drag is to alight the line on an intervening weed bed, bank or upstream boulder, just allowing the leader and fly to alight on the far, or upstream, side.

At all costs the fish must not be 'lined'. In other words, the line must never penetrate the area of its surface window. That the leader has to enter the window must be accepted, but the less it does so the better. There seem to be spots for a fly to fall which tempt a trout: just behind its head is one; slightly to one side, the angler's, is another.

If casting directly upstream to a trout close to one's bank, it is likely that the fly will overshoot the trout by 12 or 15 in. It will then drift back to the angler who must recover line over the forefinger of the hand on the rod at the same speed as the drift. If line is not drawn in, a loop will form downstream of the rod tip. This will delay contact with the fly when the trout rises and the strike may be too late.

That the trout may not take the fly is everyone's experience. If in shallow water, its window is small and may not have been entered by the fly, which thus has not been seen. There may be two naturals coming down, one is being eaten, the other refused – the one your fly represents. Despite a hatch of duns, which you thought to be the prey, it may be taking almost invisible reed smuts. Continue the siege. It is easy enough to look for another fish, but admission of early defeat will not improve knowledge or technique. As long as the trout continues to rise, keep at it. Change flies, try smaller and larger patterns. Don't give up, or little will be learned.

In these days, when almost all of us are short of time, it would be unreasonable to expect someone not to 'fish the water' on days when rises do not develop. If one only has a single day a fortnight on a river, and on that day the river is dead, what is one to do? Sit in the hut for 8 hours waiting for activity? Go home? No. Fish the water. Cast to likely places. Try a nymph if this is allowed.

Nymph fishing

As in dry-fly fishing, the choice is open to fish the water or attempt to take a trout which is seen to be taking nymphs. The latter course demands observation of the quarry, and the former of leader and line.

Fishing the water by casting a nymph upstream into possible lies is just as likely to be frowned upon as fishing the water with a dry fly – only more so. To begin with, a weighted nymph is required, for the intention is to fish at a depth equal to that of unseen feeding or non-feeding trout. We are not at this stage considering the trout which is taking nymphs in the surface film. It is visible; for it, an unweighted, Skues-type nymph should be presented and will be acceptable to the most demanding purist as well, we hope, as the trout.

To fish the water, knot a Pheasant Tail nymph to the leader point, of that pattern in which fine copper wire has been used as the tying material. Grease the leader to within 1 yd of the point. The nymph will thus sink and the leader butt will float to act as a 'float' and thus to indicate a take. Cast upstream to that certain place, allow the nymph 3 or 4 seconds to sink, then tweak back slightly faster than the current whilst watching the greased nylon. If the floating leader twitches or moves forward, feel for the fish by raising the rod.

Have you heard of the 'black hole'? I become dreamy and my eyes unfocus when the 'black hole' comes to mind. These takes happen on smooth rivers – mine was on the Dun at Hungerford. The trout was not invisible. It was a substantial 'cruiser' who kept its territory patrolled on a leisurely circular course. Lesser trout were displaced. No doubt this one fed from time to time to sustain its bulk, but on that afternoon, between its luncheon and its tea, it strolled and kept its mouth shut. When close enough to be seen, it was too near to risk a cast. When far enough away to be attacked, its shadowy form, plump as it was, faded, but always in the same direction.

Upon my knees I lengthened line and cast across the dark water to pitch the nymph ahead of the likely track. All now stilled. I held my breath. The nymph sank. Delicately I drew in one foot of line, and then the leader slid forward and down into the 'black hole'. Remember, when the leader tweaks or slides forward, raise the rod. I did, and the trout was there. You do not have to see a trout to fish the weighted nymph, but the leader must be watched with concentration.

Trout feeding on nymphs demand accurate presentation of a weighted or unweighted Pheasant Tail nymph. Polarized spectacles are essential for nymph fishing in rivers. To my mind there are two situations to be addressed. These are: the trout taking nymphs at some depth and the trout picking-off those hanging below, or stuck in, the water-surface film. The former requires the weighted pattern and the latter the unweighted pattern.

The trout which is seen 2 ft below the surface, swinging from side to side, sometimes dashing downstream for a couple of yards, but always returning to the same position, is taking drifting nymphs. Some of these may be rising to the surface to hatch; some are just being carried along on the current for unexplained reasons, but it is eating them. You can see its mouth open and, sometimes, a look of satisfaction as it shuts. Certainly, an alert trout. Pitch the coppered-wired nymph 2 yd above its lie, allow it to drift, sinking as it is washed downstream, then lift the rod when it is just ahead or to one side of the trout's nose. This movement is known as *induction* and its response as the *induced take*. It may turn itself up or out to take. The moment you see those white lips open – strike. There is no need to wait. In the time lag between your brain's intention, and the rod tip's execution, its mouth has shut and you will hook it solid.

Fishing the unweighted nymph is different, neither more difficult, nor pure, nor demanding. Just different, to cope with another circumstance – the bulge which stretches the water film raised by a trout feeding on nymphs. These have risen to the surface for a purpose, to emerge. The leader should be greased to within a foot of the nymph. The almost weightless Pheasant Tail, silk-tied instead of wired, may be moistened with spit to fish in, rather than on, the water film. Cast upstream and, as with the dry fly, allow the nymph to drift without drag. Strike as the water bulges.

Much has been written about the study of 'rise forms'. This term envelopes the different waves, rings, splashes and other disturbances of the water surface by feeding trout. There are supposed to be the sip, the slash, the double-whorl, the suck, the bulge, the hump, the porpoise roll and many other forms of feeding gymnastics. Some you are supposed to hear! The interpretation of these movements by angling wizards, the Merlins of the Piscatorial Court, verges on academic fantasy. They are supposed to indicate the exact insect on which a trout is feeding.

Look, instead, for the insect, and see it being eaten – then you will know. The movements which interest me are those which indicate whether a trout is a surface or sub-surface feeder. A fish which does not break the surface with its mouth is not taking a floating fly – go for it with a nymph. There is a movement which I find helpful. The trout which waves its tail in the air in shallow water, as it grubs on the river bed for caddis, shrimps and snails, is best left alone. It is a time-waster, blind to activities in the upper world and to almost every offering.

Hooking, playing and netting

Trout which appear to rise to a dry fly do not necessarily take it into their mouths. They may just bulge the water surface upwards whilst making a close inspection. Others take the fly, give a stimulating tweak in a flurry of water – and come off! Some are firmly hooked through correct response to the rise by the angler. A decision has to be made: a quick strike or a slightly delayed raising of the rod.

There will always be fish which bend the rod for a moment, and then the hook comes away. How to increase hooking success is a matter for debate. For myself, I tend to react slowly to large trout and quickly if they are small. A large trout has a wide bony mouth. A No 18 hook is small and partially protected by the stiff hackles of a dry fly. It is not surprising that the small hooks fails to take hold in the centre of the mouth, for it may skid over the hard, gristly, inside surface, unless pulled into the 'scissors' at the corner of the jaws.

The scissors hold is more likely to be achieved if the strike is made from behind or above the fish, when it has turned away from the angler. This is likely to be obtained if there is a short pause betwen the visual rise and the response. The larger the trout, the longer one should hold one's breath before raising the rod, but the difference is only between 1 and 3 seconds.
The distance between trout and angler should also be taken into account. React more rapidly to a rise at 18 yd than to one at 8 yd. The strike to a far-off fish is subject to some delay in the straightening and lift-off of the line. The time loss is short for a nearby trout.

The reaction should be different on West Country and Highland streams where food is short, trout are swift and, by comparison, tiny. Watch them – they are quick to grab a morsel before the chance is lost on a rapid, tumbling rivulet. They flick to the surface to take a passing insect or spit out a dry fly before you have thought 'Jack Robinson', let alone said the words. React swiftly and, as the rod bends, leap upstream to stop the fish taking permanent refuge under the boulders which litter the river bed.

Inconspicuous in the rushes, the author plays a river Test brown trout.

Methods of playing hooked trout depend on their size and the type of river. In all cases the tip of the rod should be kept high to absorb shocks and keep the trout close to the surface. A hooked trout which succeeds in descending to the river bed may take the leader around a tree root, under a stone or into a bed of weeds. The fish held near the surface may often be steered around, over or through obstructions.

A distinction must be made between dealing with large and small trout. The little wild brown, 8 in. in length, only presents an initial risk upon being hooked. It may dart beneath a rock, between two rocks, or through a tunnel. The angler's immediate reaction on hooking these fish must be to forget concealment, jump forward with rod held high and keep the tiny out of trouble. An 8 oz trout is not going to break a 6x leader of 2 lb BS. It may be beached, the hook tweaked free and then released. If it has to be touched, make sure your hands are wet and cold.

Reaching out with
a telescopic net.

There is no need to hold most of these little fellows if a barbless hook is used – just run your fingers down the leader and shake the fish free. If you do not possess barbless hooks, file off the barb whilst holding the bend of the hook in your artery forceps.

The large trout, by which is meant a fish above 1 lb in weight, and particularly those of 2 lb and above, need firm and alert handling. Upon hooking the fish, close the gap between you and the trout whilst keeping out of sight. This usually means moving upstream along the bank and kneeling in the verges. It is always a help if river-keepers leave the edge of the river untrimmed – one may then crouch behind this fringe of vegetation. If the trout rushes downriver, follow until you are again adjacent to it. If the fish enters a bed of weed it may usually be drawn out from downstream, sometimes by pulling on the line by hand.

The leaping trout must trigger an immediate response – drop the point of the rod; the fly will not come unhooked, although there is a slight risk of release if the hook is barbless. Some anglers do not lower the rod tip to slacken-on an airborne trout, but it is my practice and few fish escape. The trout which thrashes on the water surface is counteracted by reducing rod pressure, conferring on it a moment to sink beneath the water.

The hook should be removed with artery forceps.

The hook should be underwater if the fish is to be returned.

The time will arrive when the trout tires. Now slide down the bank into the water or crouch out of sight in riverside vegetation. Extend the net, sinking the meshes with a small stone in the bag, draw it over the rim and lift it on to the bank. If the trout is to be released, hold it with a wet hand through the meshes of the net. This is a firm hold. Remove the fly with your fingers, or

A trout should be dispatched at once.

Cleaning a trout at the river to inspect the stomach contents and establish diet.

artery forceps if the hook is in the back of the mouth. Return the trout to the water by immersing the net and twisting it over, thus turning it inside out. If the trout is exhausted, it is as well to hold it, immersed and head-on to the current, in your hands until it recovers and swims away.

It may be anticipated that some trout are going to present problems in the playing as soon as they are hooked. These are heavy fish, in channels between beds of weeds and on the far side of weed strands flowing and swaying in the current. It is necessary to take firm action as soon as the fish is hooked. Hold the rod low over the water to pull it straight downstream. Sometimes a trout of 2 lb or more can be skidded across the surface of intervening weed beds, but only if there is rapid downstream movement by the angler at the same time. These downriver rushes are often 40 or 50 yd movements.

Trout which one intends to keep should be knocked on the head at once by the priest. The fish is then kept fresh by being placed in a wet bass hung in a tree; evaporation of water in the bass will keep the catch cool. If a bass is not available, place the trout in a polythene bag in the shade, marking the place with a cut rush, piece of ragwort or a stick across the path. Do not leave trout in the open – magpies will peck out the eyes. Clean the catch before leaving the river for home, but don't throw the intestines in the water; bury them. On a hot day the flesh of a trout will separate from the rib bones if left uncleaned in the sun.

9 Wet-fly fishing on the river

This method of river fishing has been viewed by some as less skilled than imitating insects with a floating artificial fly. This is unwarranted when applied to anglers who cast upstream, note the feeding actions of trout and pay attention to the construction of soft-hackled flies and the depth at which these should be fished. There is substance to the thought that the method lacks finesse if winged lures are cast downriver. Where such substantial creations are swept across the water by the current, reliance is placed on trout taking without discrimination. Such fish are not common!

In the 1940s I caught my first Dartmoor brown on a Peter Ross cast down and across. How pleased I was, and how ignorant to be satisfied with a thoughtless system which lacked a rational explanation for its limited success. How can a fly without swimming ability and almost powerless, hold its position or move upstream against the speeding water flow? The system lacked scope for thoughtful development. It could be argued that to fish a wet fly upstream is more skilled than fishing a dry fly. The wet is invisible to the angler whereas the dry may be seen and response made to the rise of a trout. Just because dry-fly fishing is obligatory on chalk streams there has arisen the thought that it is the finer skill. Neither view may be argued to a conclusion due to the variables of ability, knowledge and conditions and, the more one seeks wet-fly knowledge, the wider becomes the field for research.

For me, the gathering of some competence has been achieved with the assistance of those skilled in the method on Dartmoor streams. From the north came thought-provoking letters from Dr Ronald Broughton, Chairman of The Grayling Society. Some fish have fallen due to persistent upstream casting, others by whittling down hook sizes, the thinning of dressings and fishing when the time was right and fly was on the water. We shall never know all the answers. Success must be pursued with tenacity.

Recently, struggling for trout in March, I sought the wise guidance of a man, Dartmoor by birth, and my senior in every way. He has caught them all:

salmon, peal and wild brown trout. Greenheart rods, jungle-cock cheeks,
Perfect reels with ivory handles, line driers too, are all to be found in his four-
roomed cottage. My letter sought his assistance on March trouting 1000 ft
above the sea; a bleak fortnight of the year after opening day on the 15th of
the month. His reply was as follows:

> The Cottage
> Dartmoor

Dear Charles,

I am flattered that you should ask me about trout fishing on the river in March but, for
what it is worth, here it is:

I have always preferred to fish upstream wet with only two flies. On the point Blue
Pheasant Tail, on the dropper Partridge & Red with gold binding, or March Brown.
In all cases the flies are hackled and not winged.

Best conditions are mild weather, even temperature and wet, with the river at a good
height. If the water is dead low and the weather cold the going is very hard indeed.
But when there is a good head of water I have taken fish with snow on the ground, or
in a cold east wind.

The fish are hungry and will take quite freely for an hour or two. The best time to fish
in March is between noon and 3 pm. Later than that the rise is generally over for the
day unless the temperature is exceptionally mild. There is little to be gained by
starting early. Watch out for those dark olives drifting down the river like ships in full
sail. They seldom appear before noon and are gone by tea-time. The big cannibal trout
will take a fly in March. My biggest on March 31 many years ago was 3 lb, taken at 4
pm. He had a trout of ½ lb inside him! On another occasion a large trout of more than
1 lb had a mouse in its stomach. Those were the days; we shall never see the like again.

> Yours ever
> David

Then again, on a wet July day, the trout of a Dartmoor stream failed to
appreciate my Kite and other dry concoctions. After struggling for some
hours, with scant reward in drizzling rain, I came across a tweed-clad friend.
This hands-and-knees man, whose skin is waterproof, showed me an
outstanding catch of trout and, on request, the fly which he had fished
upstream. This Blue Upright, normally a dry fly in the West Country, had
been dressed by himself on a fine-wired No 16 Partridge Captain Hamilton
wet-fly hook. The body was of peacock quill, the hackle of blue hen wound
only at the head and the tail whisks, just three or four, were from the same
feather. The result was an illusion, the phantom presence of a fly.

Dr Ronald Broughton says that there are large hatches of various olives, pale
wateries, iron blue, gnats, stoneflies and yellow sallies on the rivers Ure,

Nidd, Wharfe, Hodder and Derbyshire Wye and other clear waters flowing over limestone. He remarks:

If trout are being lazy and taking from just below, or within the surface film, my fly ('wet', soft-hackled and wingless) must be there too, and if further under the surface, then there. Anywhere else and there is no hope. And if it doesn't look like the natural and behave as such, then again – fishless!

One gathers from these contributors of supreme experience that upstream casting, observation of natural insects emerging and egg laying, thinly hackled flies and fishing at the required depth are some of the keys to obtaining a tug on the leader.

Wet flies

These flies fish beneath or in the water surface. They should be sparsely dressed with the soft absorbent feathers of a hen and are better hackled than winged. It is true that a winged Invicta, cast upriver, will kill when sedges hatch in summer evenings and a winged Greenwell may take a toll when olive duns hatch, but the *cognoscente* fishes hackled. Exceptions abound in angling; T.E. Pritt's Fog Black, a favourite of that doyen angler and author of the nineteenth century, has tiny grey wings to imitate the black gnat.

Recently, I received a presentation of wet flies suitable for wild trout and grayling from Dr Ronald Broughton, with notes relevant to each:

I am sending you some Northern spiders to try on the chalk streams and Dartmoor. They are often used in the top 6 in. to 12 in. or even right within the surface film – the soft mobile hackle giving movement akin to a fly struggling with the disasters of eclosion. They are used, as well, as ascendant nymphs in the deeper waters. Generally these days, some flies are without doubt 'look-a-likes' and caricatures of specific naturals, and some are more general. So here they are:

Snipe & Purple – mainly represents iron blue. Can be taken for a gnat, and was so on the Houghton water in November by grayling.

Jackson's Blue Midge – *the* most perfect copy of a smut rising to the surface in its bubble of air.

Pritt's Fog Black – a black gnat.

Broughton's Pupa – my dressing of the pupa of the little black midge of limestone rivers caught under the surface film in quiet corners. It works on the chalk streams as well.

Dotterel Dun – early summer olive, and pale watery nymph.

Waterhen Bloa – this, without doubt, is the nymph corresponding to the Blue Dun, i.e the olive of late spring and early autumn.

These flies are dressed shorter on the hook (much of the shank being bare) to get the fly down through the surface film as fast as possible and, with no great weight, they fish just below the surface. Try them, and let me know how you fare with them. Hopefully they will work for you and tempt the trout to the hook.

Yours

Ron

So, there they are, the select group to deceive the most discerning trout and grayling.

To this one ought to add the Pheasant Tail Spinner, a wet dressing, to deceive trout when iron blues, pale wateries, or blue-winged olive are on the water. There is no reason to imitate the male spinner, or Jenny, of the iron blue, for the female spent are more commonly on the water. At such times a wet Pheasant Tail Spinner is taken readily.

In 1931 H. F. & G. Witherby published *The Art of Fly Fishing* by Lt Col. W. Keith Rollo, an angler of northern streams. His wet-fly selection is as follows, the dressings being hackled, with the exception of Greenwell's Glory, Wickham and Invicta. I have converted his Pennell hook sizes to the current Redditch Scale:

1 My particular fly, which we will call the 'Blue Dun Hackle'. It much resembles the Blue Upright. Hook size: No 14 and No 13.

Hackle Grizzly blue-dun hackle with a nice sheen on it.
Body Peacock quill.
Tail Two or three wisps of a blue-dun cock's hackles.

2 Dark Partridge & Orange, ribbed gold wire or yellow silk. Hook size: No 14 and No 13.

3 Light Snipe & Yellow. Hook size: No 14 and No 13.

4 Dark Snipe & Purple. Hook size: No 14.

5 Waterhen Bloa. Hook size: No 14 and No 13.

6 Greenwell's Glory. Hook size: No 14 and No 13.

7 Wickham. Hook size: No 11 and No 10.

8 Invicta. Hook size: No 10.

Rollo's flies were dressed on hooks tied direct to gut, with the exception of the Wickham and Invicta where, being in larger sizes, eyed hooks were used.

I must confess to carrying few wet patterns, preferring to fish dry if this presents a chance. To cast a dry fly against an adverse wind is hard going, for the fly has little weight and much wind resistance. Under such circumstances, and in early spring, I may change to wet, taking advantage of the slim shape and slight additional weight to cut through an adverse breeze. Invicta No 14, Greenwell No 14, Waterhen Bloa No 16 and a Black & Peacock Spider No 14 find places in my box. In a corner will be found a wet Blue Upright. In addition I employ a No 16 winged March Brown to act as a nymph in the surface film, the wings having been trimmed off to short stubs. This skimpy offering has its attractions and is my smallest, wet trout-tempter.

The fishing

Casting upstream

The choice has to be made: whether to cast up or down the river. If one accepts the fact that natural food drifts downstream, then, if the wet fly is to act in a natural manner, it must be cast upstream to drift down. A decision between up or down does not have to be made if imitation is the aim, for one cannot argue against this phenomenon. Disregarding this assessment, anglers sometimes cast downstream. Why? Two situations would persuade me to follow that course: a strong wind blowing down the river and a full-coloured water flow after rain, when I might cast down and across with a slow-sinking fly line or an ancient cracked floater of which the tip sinks.

In addition to presenting the wet fly in a natural manner when casting upriver, the angler is approaching from behind the trout. As has already been observed in Chapter 7 trout cannot see in a narrow arc to their rear. Furthermore, the angler is at a lower level than the trout, whilst the opposite applies if he is casting downstream. The lower the angler, the smaller the proportion of him is visible to the fish, if any is in sight at all. These two advantages allow the stalking of trout. The strike from behind a trout is more likely to succeed in placing the hook firmly in the scissors of the jaws. When casting downstream, the fly may be pulled out of the mouth of the trout, which is facing the angler.

Having looked at the advantages of upstream casting, consider the practice. Many anglers fish a team of flies: point, first dropper and top dropper, or bob. A team of three flies presents trout with a choice. If one of the team is favoured, the other two could be changed until the members of the team are identical. Recently, fishing an Invicta on a single dropper and a Pheasant Tail nymph on the point, the Invicta took trout whilst the nymph failed. I then fished the Invicta in both positions and both took fish.

There are risks to using more than one fly on a leader: the free-trailing hook may catch on weed whilst a trout is being played and the free fly often catches in the meshes of the landing net. Particularly when learning, stick to one fly on the leader, but change if it fails to tempt. It may take a little longer to find an acceptable fly in this way, but simplicity and lack of tangles are advantages. Because the fly drifts back to the angler, casting has to be frequent. Three or four times the number of throws will be made than with the downstream method. The length of line outside the rod tip is likely to be short, perhaps 20 or 30 ft due to the low profile of the wading angler, who is able to approach fish to within two or three rod lengths. As the line drifts back it has to be gathered over the forefinger of the rod hand at the same speed as the water flow. If slack line is allowed to curl on the surface downstream of the rod tip, the strike to a taking trout will be too slow.

Now, the strike. Observation and keen eyesight are requisites for discerning the sub-surface movement of a taking trout. This may be revealed by a flash, a moving patch of light colour, which is the flank of the fish, or a humping of the water surface. The trout may not be seen if the fly is a few inches below a rough surface, but the floating line will check, as is the case when nymph fishing. Any check or twitch should trigger a strike by the angler, that quick lift of the rod tip to set the hook. 'Strike' is a term with which we are familiar, but it is misleading in intensity. Whilst the upward flick of the rod tip must be as fast as light, the rod finger on the line must have a featherweight touch. Let the line slide out from beneath the finger as the rod tip bends or the leader, if it is of the 5x or 6x classification, may break at the point.

Where to cast

Some brooks are so narrow that one just casts ahead to the right and left of the main rippling current. If 12 o'clock is straight upstream, one would normally search an area between 10 and 2 o'clock. If the river is wide and one is wading beside the true right bank, it is sensible to cast to the nearside first and then across the fast run to the slack water at the 2 o'clock position. If this is not done, trout on the nearside will be 'lined' before being presented with the fly.

Keep the rod up when casting across a fast current to slacker water on the far side in order to keep line out of the rapid flow. This helps to prevent the fly being dragged downstream. It is also helpful in this situation to move the tip of the rod downriver whilst pointing at the drifting fly, the rod being almost at right angles to the bank. This manoeuvre also slows the advent of drag. As already pointed out, a 9 ft rod is better than a 7 ft model in such situations and in almost all aspects of river trouting other than casting in restricted circumstances.

Trout lie in many places: in front of and behind submerged boulders; before a waterfall or weir; to either side of a main rough current; at the tail of a pool before it breaks into the stickle leading to the next pool; in a back eddy where the fish will face into the current, but will be pointing down the river; in the open spaces of a weed bed; under bushes; beneath the overhang of a washed-out bank on the outside bend of the river; a yard or two below the point of entry of a minor feeder stream.

Casting downstream

As previously described (page 102), the downstream cast has certain disadvantages. These do not rule it out when certain circumstances prevail, one of which is that it suits the beginner. The cast made down and across is easy to accomplish for the current straightens out both line and leader.

A downstream wind assisting the cast is also helpful and may persuade the practised fishermen to cast with the current rather than battle against a gale.

Takes are transmitted to the angler by a pull on the line. Visual indications of a taking trout do not have to be seen or recognized – a help to those of tender years making a start and to ancients with failing sight.

Downstream wet fly. The angler should be below the bank, not outlined against the sky.

It is better to kneel than stand up, particularly when casting downstream.

The system may also be employed in the conditions of a minor spate, when fast-flowing coloured water makes upstream casting and line recovery difficult, and the fly cannot be made to fish deep. Then, a slow-sinking or sink-tip line and a winged wet-fly pattern of the Peter Ross, Mallard & Claret or Black Pennell type will often produce a trout (and sometimes a salmon!). I have no shame in using sunk flies which are no more than lures for downstream fishing, because the fly, held against the current, cannot be imitative of insect life.

The downstream caster should fish a longer line than that which is comfortable for the upstream method. This is largely because of the difficulty in keeping out of sight. Don't forget that the river bed beneath the angler is higher than the bed beneath the trout. In addition, the fish is looking upstream with binocular vision, and there is no blind area, as is the case when approaching from behind. So, cast a long line and keep low.

If, looking downstream, we now consider 6 o'clock to be the centre of the stream, our cast, if we are centrally placed and wading mid-river, should be from 4 to 6 o'clock and from 8 to 6 o'clock. Such placings of the fly will sweep the stream at a slow speed. If the cast is made to 3 or 9 o'clock, drag on the line will whip the fly past trout at the outside extremities of this wide arc. If the narrow arc system is used, the same width of river may be covered but a longer line must be thrown.

Part 3

Salmon fishing

10 Salmon, rivers and fishing conditions

My home is 750 ft above sea level on Dartmoor. Most of the winter mornings are spent writing at my desk, which faces over open country to the west and Bodmin moor. To the east of the garden gate, ponies and sheep graze on sparse moorland grass which slopes up and away to the heather-covered hills, which are topped by tors of granite. By lunch-time my labrador is impatient for the moors and off we go by car to Princetown, 1500 ft high, and the salmon-spawning streams of the upland moors. The final week of November is the time to go, and the first 2 weeks of December. I park the car and, thumbstick in hand, explore a mile or two each day. Some streams chosen by salmon are only a few feet wide; others are the width of a minor road with passing places. They all have this in common: where salmon spawn the bed will be of gravel and small stones of walnut size. There will be no silt or mud to clog the river bed. Such an area is usually towards the tail of a pool where the depth decreases and water speed increases to sweep the river bed clean.

Life history of the salmon

The hen fish cuts a trough in the stony bed by turning on her flank and flapping her tail. The lifting tail sucks up stones which are washed into a bank below the redd by the water flow. The redd is just a depression 4–5 in. deep, 2–3 ft in length and about 18 in. wide for a 10 lb hen. In this she lays her eggs, about 700 per 1 lb of the hen's body weight. When extruding her ova the hen turns on her side, then muscular spasms and flapping force the eggs from the urino-genital pore, from which they sink to the bottom of the redd.

A cock fish is usually in attendance, either in the redd or just downstream. He will move close to the hen, force sperm-containing milt from his vent, and so fertilize the eggs. The hen then covers the redd with small stones and gravel and moves on to cut another redd elsewhere. Sometimes a hen is unable to extrude her eggs, or does not do so for some reason. Such a fish, known as a *baggot* or *rawner*, may be caught in the early weeks of the new season.

A grilse, in December, leaping on the spawning beds.

A cock grilse lifted out by hand. The upward hook of gristle on the lower jaw develops late in the season and is called a *kype*. Hen salmon do not have a kype.

When landed the fish maybe bright in colour but, if killed, the colour fades and the fish becomes dark. If held up by the head, eggs may dribble from the vent. These fish, like kelts (spawned male and female fish), are termed *unclean* and must, by law, be returned to the river.

Finding redds is not difficult for the salmon-watcher; look for patches on the river bed which are lighter in colour than surrounding areas, due to disturbed algae and detritus. To watch salmon spawning, stand back some yards from a likely stretch of river and observe. Sooner or later there will be a disturbance of the flowing water as a cock fish chases away a rival, or dorsal fins may be seen cutting through the water surface. Creep forward on hands and knees, then wriggle to the edge of the bank to look over – spawning fish may be observed a few yards, or even feet, from the watcher.

To fish intelligently for salmon the angler must follow the subsequent development of the fish, know when it will appear in the river after its time at sea, and when it must be returned to the water by law. He must understand the terms kelt, grilse, smolt and parr, amongst others, and be able to recognize these stages in the life history.

Alevin

Provided that they do not become covered with silt, and therefore rot, the eggs will hatch in about 90 days if the water temperature is in the region of

39-41°F. If warmer or colder, a shorter or longer period will be required. An *alevin* emerges from the split ova case and is sustained for a month by a sac of yolk suspended beneath the chin. The yolk absorbed, it starts to feed and is known as a *fry* until about 2 in. in length, when it becomes known as a *parr*.

Parr

Parr are sometimes caught when trout fishing. Being small they would, of course, be returned, but the angler ought to know the difference between salmon parr and small brown trout.

Salmon parr have the following characteristics:

1 The body is slightly built and torpedo-shaped.

2 The tail is distinctly forked.

3 An imaginary perpendicular line from the back of the eye will not touch the maxillary bone.

4 There are 8-12 finger marks, even in width, well defined and regularly spaced along the sides.

5 There is no white line on leading edge of fins.

6 There is no red, black or orange colour on adipose fin.

Brown trout can be distinguished from salmon parr by the following:

1 The body is thicker than that of the salmon parr.

2 The tail has a shallow fork.

3 An imaginary perpendicular line from the back of the eye will pass through or touch the maxillary bone.

4 The finger marks are less numerous, wider but uneven in width, less defined and irregularly placed along the sides.

5 There is a white line on the leading edge of the fins, particularly the anal.

6 The adipose fin is coloured with red, orange or black.

So far the developing fishlet has spent the first months in the headwaters of the river where it will also spend the first 2 years of its life if feeding is sparse, as on the moor. In some chalk streams only 1 year is spent in the river before the migration to sea because a more generous food supply has resulted in faster growth. During the more usual 2 years, the fishlet gradually moves downstream feeding and growing as it goes.

Smolt

After the 2 years, when the parr is 8–10 in. in length, and weighing about 8 oz, the finger marks on the flank disappear. It then becomes silvery in colour, is termed a *smolt*, and migrates to sea in March, April or May. Both parr and smolts must be returned to the river if caught by accident.

Grilse

We now lose sight of the fish for a minimum of 14 months, during which time it feeds voraciously in the sea. After this period, and known as a *one-sea-winter* fish or *grilse*, it may return between the end of June and autumn at weights between 3 lb and 6 or 7 lb, the later entrants being the heavier. Grilse then run up the river to spawn in the headwaters as described.

Multi-sea-winter salmon

Other salmon may swim as far as Greenland and return after two, three or four winters at sea. Three- and four-sea-winter salmon are now rare, and two sea-winter salmon are reducing, whilst the percentage of grilse in the annual entry increases. These population changes are probably due to the multi-sea-winter salmon being at greater risk of high-seas' netting. The weight of two-sea-winter salmon may vary between about 7 and 25 lb but is likely to average 9 or 10 lb.

A salmon's life history may be ascertained by taking scales from the flank and examining the growth rings under a microscope. Three times I have requested this information on large Devon salmon from the South West Water (now National Rivers Authority) laboratories. The results, which are most untypical, are shown in the table below:

Ages of salmon taken in Devon

Weight	Source	Stage
19 lb	Dart	two-sea-winter
20 lb	Dart	three-sea-winter
24 lb	Lyd	two-sea-winter

It will now be easier to refer to two- and three-sea-winter fish as salmon and one sea-winter fish as grilse. In Scotland, all salmon are called *fish*, and sea trout are *sea trout* unless small, in which case they are called *finnock*.

Grilse are slimmer than salmon, as may be seen in the photographs on page 109. This slimness limits the available methods of landing them and this problem will receive attention in due course.

Salmon enter our rivers from January until December, although very early and very late entries take place in a few rivers. For example, the Helmsdale opens in January and the Camel closes in mid-December, to take rivers at opposite ends of the British Isles. A more general national picture is for salmon to start entering in March and grilse in late June, and both to continue, when water levels permit, until late autumn. Certain rivers have unusual runs: the Deveron produces three-quarters of the salmon catch in September and October; the Camel and Fowey do so in the last 2 weeks of November and the first 2 weeks of December.

The upstream journey

During the first 2 or 3 days after leaving the estuary, fish carry sea lice. These small suckered lice attach themselves along the back of a salmon and close to the vent, but drop off after a short time in fresh water.

If a salmon enters a river in February, when the water temperature may be in the region of 40°F, it will not travel far upstream in the first few weeks. The fish will also be reluctant to jump over white-water weirs or waterfalls. As the weeks pass, the water warms, and so does the body of the salmon, which becomes more active. Obstructions will now be jumped and 4–5 miles may be covered in 1 day or, in spates, 10–15 miles. By May, at water temperatures in the region of 60°F, the small upland rivers will have reduced in flow to the extent that fish decline to run until there is sufficient rain to raise the level of the water. The rise and fall of water level in a river, following rain in the catchment area, is called a *spate*. Between spates, salmon and grilse lie in deep pools but become restive when rain falls. Even before the water level rises, fish may be seen to move to the head of a pool to investigate the chances of moving upstream. As soon as the water lifts most of them continue their upstream journey and may cover many miles in 24 hours, spreading the population throughout the whole river and to the spawning areas by July. Those fish which reach their ultimate destination by mid-summer are in no ripe condition to spawn, but remain, waiting, under rocks or the bank, hidden, until the mating months arrive.

Recognition of a kelt

A hen salmon which enters the river in March weighing 10 lb might be found to weigh only 6 lb after spawning, when it becomes known as a *kelt*.
They may be distinguished from fresh fish as described below.

In a kelt:

1 The line of the back and belly are parallel.
2 Gill maggots are almost invariably present.

3 There is a distinct ledge at the back of the skull where the body thins.
4 The fins are frayed.
5 The vent is suffused and prominent.
6 The belly is normally black.

In fresh fish:

1 The back and belly are convex to each other.
2 Gill maggots are only present if the fish has been in the river for some time.
3 There is no downward ledge behind the skull.
4 The fins are not frayed, but are often pink at the leading edge, due to friction on rocks during the upstream passage.
5 The vent is firm and compact.
6 The belly is pale and the back is dark.

These identification signs have been noted in an NRA publication, and I amplify them as follows. Gill maggots are sometimes said to be present only on kelt, thus serving as a means of identification. This is not reliable, for I have found gill maggots in salmon in late spring, May and summer when on their upriver journey. Neither is colour to be relied upon, for a 'well-mended' kelt may have silver-coloured flanks and appear bright and fresh, although thin, but, if killed, the colour will fade to a dark shade and the flesh found to be white, soft and tasteless.

Kelts are often caught in the opening weeks of the salmon season if these fall in February and March. Few kelts remain in the river by April, having either succeeded in reaching the sea or died. In addition to the physical signs of recognition, kelts behave differently from fresh salmon. They usually find resting places in quiet waters, sometimes known as *kelt alleys*, leap regularly for no apparent reason and fight with little energy when hooked because of

Salmon kelt, taken in March and returned alive when spinning for springers.

their depleted state. A kelt, or unclean fish, must, by law, be returned to the river. This should be done at once, with wet hands, and the kelt held head-on to the current until it has recovered sufficiently to glide away.

Types of salmon rivers

These may be divided into rain-fed rivers and those which are sustained by springs rising from chalk aquifers. Of course, all rivers are sustained by rain, but these two classifications separate those where rain falls on the catchment area and runs *down* into the river from the spring-fed rivers in which rain falls, soaks into the underground sponge of chalk and then rises *up* into the river. Spring-fed rivers are more stable in their flows than those which are rain-fed; they experience rises and falls in levels, and increases and reductions in flows, but at a steadier rate of alteration.

Rain-fed rivers

These are subjct to rapid rises in water levels and, sometimes, to almost as rapid falls. In February and March it is likely that both large and small rivers will continue to enjoy the benefit of winter rainfall by the steady drainage from water-laden land, and they will be running full. By the second half of April the smaller river will probably have fallen to a level at which salmon cease to run, if there has been no rain within the last week. Successful fishing will come to a halt. Subsequent runs of salmon and, in the main, the catching of fish, will depend on spates, and this situation will continue until the end of the season on 30 September. The river may rise again and run steadily, and fish be caught, if rains arrive in October, November and December and if the river remains in season.

Spates

A spate in a small river is likely to take place in the following sequence of events: rain falls in the catchment hills and fills the brooks and feeder streams, which run down into the main waterway. The river in which they collect rises by 2 or 3 in, a small spate, or by 1 or 2 ft, a heavy spate, and a bulge of water runs down the valley. The rise may be rapid. A lift of 6 in. sometimes occurs within 30 minutes, and 2 hours may see the level increase by as much as 1 or 2 ft. This rise may continue, if rain falls steadily in the hills, until the river is in flood. If a flood state is reached, the fall from the peak level can be rapid when rain ceases to fall in the hills. Commonly, a reduction of 6 in. is experienced in half an hour, 1 ft in the next 2 hours, and a further 6 in. in the following 6 hours, followed by a steady dropping back over 24 hours to a level an inch or two above that prevailing before the spate commenced. The rise and fall on a small river can thus be over within 2 days, or even less on the smallest steep-falling salmon streams.

This study of small spate rivers reveals their unpredictable nature. After the middle or the end of April, fishing for resident salmon, and the entry of fresh fish from the sea, depends on spates. The most numerous salmon entrants into our rivers in the last 10 years have been grilse. They arrive onwards from the end of June – well into the months of low water and intermittent spates. If there is only one river rise in August there will be 2 fishing days and 29 days in which catches are almost non-existent. Not only that, but the first spate after a drought is usually one of dirty acid water, washing away the debris of the drought weeks. Few salmon will be caught unless there is more rain and a second cleaner rise. These observations on lack of catches in drought conditions apply where fishing methods are restricted to fly. If bait is permitted – worm, shrimp and prawn – the picture is not so bleak.

It is now apparent that the spate river has its main run of fish, grilse, during the weeks most subject to low water. It is also clear that catches are restricted to just a few days, unless there is a wet summer. Because the main salmon rod take during the last decade has occurred, to the extent of about 60 per cent, in July, August and September, it is obvious that there have been a few days of heavy catches and many blank days between spates. The fact is that summer fishing in small spate rivers is unreliable and, the higher up the river into the hills one fishes, the quicker will the water run away. If such a river is 20 or 30 miles in length, it is possible to enjoy 2 days of good fishing: the first on the upper reaches as the water level starts to fall; the second on a lower section closer to the sea.

Great rivers

Large rivers running for long distances may commence in the hills and then continue through lowland agricultural fields for 20, 30 or 50 miles and even greater lengths. In these, the rise in the water level by 2 or 3 ft following rain may be rapid and even dangerous, because the catchment area is large, particularly if the lower reaches are restricted in width and run through a gorge. They are also fed by tributary rivers which are subject to their own rises at the same time. Although the rise may be great and the water too dirty to fish, due to silt washings from ploughed land, the fall will be at a slower rate than in the little river. Alterations in water conditions thus take place over a longer time span. The water may remain fishable, being sufficiently clear, for an hour after the river starts to rise. There may follow 2 or 3 days of brown, mud-laden, unfishable flow and then many days of excellent water, with the river dropping just an inch or two a day after the initial substantial fall. Even this drop will cease if there is snow-melt from the hills.

Such a river may not have to rely on immediate rainfall until much later in the season than the small spate stream. Further, even when at a low level, there is sufficient flow and depth for salmon to enter and run. There will be more good fishing days in a season on such a river, the runs are more predictable and, as always, you pay for this in fishing rents, which are higher than those on smaller streams.

Spring-fed rivers

The spring-fed river is different from the two categories just described. To begin with, it is only honest to comment, those running into the sea along the south coast of England have almost ceased to experience salmon runs. In the 1970s I had a salmon rod at Broadlands, on the river Test, and experienced excellent fishing until 1975. In 1976 there was a bad drought and salmon catches dropped dramatically and then continued to fall. Mile for mile, salmon catches on the river matched any in the British Isles in the 1950s. In the early 1970s the estate grossed in the region of 300 or more salmon and, in 1975, I and the rod with whom I shared took 30 fish. In 1991 the catch was 6 fish for the whole 4 miles of estate water, despite the addition of double banking to the top beat. The same reduction has taken place on the lower Itchen and, at the time of writing in 1992, there are worries concerning the Hampshire Avon.

It is against this background that chalk-stream salmon-fishing methods will be described, for hope is not dead. The National Rivers Authority, other organizations and private individuals are taking a multitude of steps to recover these rivers: clearing the spawning beds of clogging silt; installing fish passes and counters; radio-tracking salmon and introducing hundreds of thousands of smolts. Postscript: (October 1993). Due to these steps towards recovery, there has been a marked improvement in the 1993 season salmon rod catch on the rivers Test and Itchen.

Chalk streams

As I have written, the chalk river is fed by rising springs and has a more stable flow than the rain-fed river. If one is allowed to use fly, artificial spinning bait and the natural baits of prawn and shrimp, there will be few days in the season when one fishes without a chance, because of high or dirty water.

I used to go to the river once a week or once a fortnight, always anticipating that the water would be in order, and this was usually found to be the case. Of course, even if fish were present, all was not entirely rosy. Chalk rivers are alkaline, weed growth is often prolific, and weeds have to be cut. Weed cutting took place on agreed dates about four times a season for periods of a week or 10 days. Drifting cut weed in those days rendered fishing difficult. Whether one was casting a fly, spinning or ledgering a prawn, the cut weed caught on line, prawn and fly at almost every cast. When playing a salmon, the line often became entangled in drifting weed or the fish took refuge in a growing bed of *Ranunculus*.

In the sport of fish spotting, however, the chalk stream stands supreme. When the water clears in late spring or early summer, after the fuller winter flows, salmon may be seen. To locate the quarry through polarized spectacles and then go to work to catch that fish is a fascination and a challenge now too rare. The fish lie on the grey/white bed of the river, at the tails of pools, off groynes, between weed beds, below tree roots at the river's edge and in many other places. Rain may temporarily spoil the water clarity but it will also enliven fish, and one may continue casting to their known lies with every chance of success. But, as pointed out, I speak of the past, whilst trusting that runs will again be established.

In years gone by, the chalk streams, particularly the rivers Frome, Hampshire Avon and the diminutive Piddle, which runs out at Wareham, experienced runs of heavy salmon, of which some were over 30 lb or even 40 lb in weight. Such multi-sea-winter salmon are now extremely rare and the runs are primarily grilse.

Finding salmon lies

A salmon lie is a place where a fish pauses on its upstream journey, sometimes for only an hour and sometimes for days, depending on the water conditions. From the time a salmon enters fresh water from the sea it ceases to feed. In almost all cases it will never feed again and will die in the river, for very few spawned fish succeed in completing a return journey to the sea after spawning. If a hen fish leaves the sea in spring it is plump and the two roes in the body cavity are small. If that fish were caught and cleaned at the end of September in the upper reaches of the river, the roes would be so large that the body cavity would be filled, but the quality of the flesh would have been reduced. The fish has converted its body flesh and fat into roe and into energy, which has been used to survive and accomplish the upriver migration. The fish needs to conserve energy, and thus body weight, by choosing lies where it may pause without working hard to hold its favoured position.

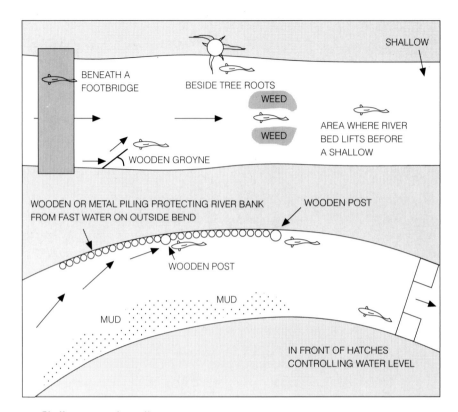

22 Chalk-stream salmon lies.

A lie will provide:

1 A place where the fish may rest in almost complete equilibrium with the water current.

2 Good water flow supplying oxygen through the mouth and out of the gills.

3 Security in 4-6 ft of water.

Such places alter as the water level rises and falls in a pool and are unlikely to be found in rapids, where the fish would have to work hard to maintain position.

At the height of a spate, fish are mainly running, but they sometimes pause at the tail of a pool after surmounting rapids. In effect, they stop for a breather. You should fish constantly in the tail of the pool under these conditions, because salmon are unlikely to be caught elsewhere.

As the spate subsides, salmon and grilse move further into a pool and, as the water falls back to a low level, go to the neck or head, where they may remain, sometimes with their heads and bodies hidden by the bubbles of the run-in.

The confluence of two streams sometimes creates a salmon lie.

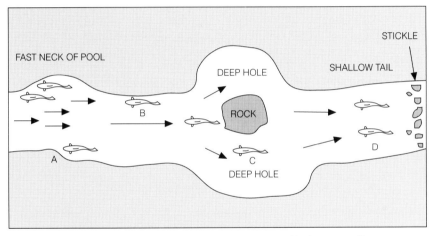

23 Spate-river salmon lies. Points A, B and C are occupied in low to medium water and C and D in high water. D is the only place, in a full spate, to catch a fish. The water is too fast-flowing and dirty at A, B and C.

It follows that, to know the lies in a river, it must be fished at all heights – a lengthy process, the gathering of this knowledge. My advice on 'learning' a beat on a river is to go there season after season after season, or to employ a gillie who knows the water. It is no good constantly trying different rivers, unless you are accompanied on each by a local who knows the water. Weirs are a source of salmon in high water, not below the weir but above the sill, just before the water pours over the lip. There they rest, tails to the ridge, recovering after their leap.

In high water, salmon may be caught above a weir by day, casting from a position upstream and out of sight.

In low water, sea trout are also caught above weirs at night, by casting flies upstream whilst standing in the fish pass.

Boulders are favoured, not behind the boulder, where the water is turbulent, but in front or to the side. I once asked a North Country river-keeper where he considered salmon and trout lay in relation to a large boulder. He replied that salmon did not feed and that, water comfort and stability being their priority, they rested in front or to one side. Trout, on the other hand, when in a feeding mood, would patrol around a boulder, picking up food swept into the whirlpool to the rear. From my own observation, this is also the case with a man-made groyne jutting out from the bank; salmon will lie off the end and slightly downstream, but not in the slack water to the rear where a trout is sometimes found. There is no doubt that salmon also lie on top of flat rocks, but not round boulders. There is a riverside tree I climb to spot fish through my polarized spectacles. They may be seen, 3-4 ft below the surface, grey shapes with waving tails, on top of a flat shelf of rock several feet long and wide. I imagine that the water hits the shelf and is deflected upwards, and the salmon, chin to stone, rest just beneath the current thrown over their heads.

The places where salmon lie vary with the height of the water: the higher the water, the lower down the pool they will be, towards or at the tail. The sides of pools and runs are more likely than the centres to hold salmon in high water. In low water the opposite is the case for the edges will be too shallow and fail to provide security.

In high water in a wide river, there is little point in casting to the far bank unless a lie is actually known to be on that side. Even if this is the case, success will not come if the bait or fly is swept away from the lie at high speed. It is far better to fish your side of the river carefully at a controlled speed. Running salmon rarely take when swimming upriver in a spate, but sometimes they pause momentarily and can be caught at the river's edge. I recall a day on the Deveron when the water covered the bank. I fished on, standing on the grass in 2 ft of water whilst salmon and sea trout, avoiding the pressure of the main current, swam past my feet.

There is no short way to learning a river other than via a local or gillie. I have fished my home water for 35 years; last season an 11½ lb salmon and a 4 lb grilse came to my fly and were landed from previously barren places. Learning never ceases: water levels rise and fall, gravel banks shift and boulders roll but, in time, by looking at a strip of water, you will know by experience the likely places to find fish.

Fishing conditions

Time of day

Air temperature and time of day are linked, the passing of the hours bringing changes in water temperature. In March, if the air is warmer than the water by 6 or 8°F, the water will warm by 1 or 2° by lunch-time. This slight increase may trigger a salmon to respond between noon and 3 pm, after which hour the air cools and the air/water temperature gap closes. In hot summer weather the hours from dawn to the middle of the morning are likely to provide the best chance. This is because the water has cooled overnight, and so has the air, but, with the coming of day, the air warms faster than the water, establishing the right conditions of air temperature being higher than that of the water.

Summer evenings enhance one's chances, particularly with fly, after a fishless day. Continue to fish until dusk. The air/water temperature gap may not be good, but the sun is off the water and salmon sometimes move from deep cool lies to faster-running areas at the rippling heads of pools.

The three instances above, of early spring afternoons and then dawn and dusk in summer, should be disregarded if the river is in splendid order. When there is a full flow, the air is warm, midges are about, there is ten-tenths cloud cover and it is raining, fish through the day until exhaustion calls a halt.

Weather and water conditions

These are inextricably linked, for the state of the water ultimately depends on past and present weather. Whilst weather determines fishing conditions, in that it controls water levels and flows, the actual conditions of cloud, wind and rain are not as important on fishing days as the state of the water they have produced. Thus, if the water is in good fishing order, I will sally forth, even in a heatwave or a snowstorm. If the water is desperately low, or in flood, I might await a better day, even if the sky is cloudy and a warm damp wind is blowing from the south-west providing ideal weather.

Weather

What is an ideal day? I like rain. Whether on a chalk stream or a rain-fed river, whether the water be high or low, in spring, summer or autumn, rain raises my expectations. In March or April, my hands wet and white with cold, fish take as a full river rises and falls daily by 5 or 6 in. When the Aga in the house is surrounded and overhung with wet clothes, and I am in a hot bath at the end of the day, there may be a salmon on the kitchen table. In May, and onwards through the season, when in spate country, I rarely fish for salmon unless it is raining or has been raining in the previous 1 or 2 days.

In a chalk river the water usually remains stable in flow, but rain excites stale fish, stimulating them to take the fly or bait.

A thunderstorm raises the chances. Fish when the storm has passed and not when lightning flashes. A carbon-fibre rod is a personal lightning conductor and one does not seek to be electrocuted. Put the rod down until the storm has passed.

Wind is a help, particularly one which blows upstream and pushes against the current to create waves. If a gale blows upstream, it is possible to take salmon in a wide flat pool which, in calm conditions, would have a glassy surface. This is even possible in low water. Cast across the pool, take two or three steps upstream and strip the fly fast across the river. I will tell you what will happen and describe the system in detail in Chapter 13.

A dull, damp, warm day is good for fish catching in summer. The cloud should be low, grey and cover the sky. White cotton-wool clouds, bright with intermittent sunshine and drifting across a clear blue sky, reduce chances to a minimum. Rather a clear blue sky than the cotton-wool condition. Bright sunshine does not preclude the catching of fish but it does reduce the chances when shining straight down the river, particularly in the mid-day hours. Not only is the fish facing into the sun but the fly line casts a wide shadow on the river bed. This shadow precedes the line and fly to warn fish, if the sun shines from upstream and projects the shadow downstream. Thus a river which runs from south to north is at a disadvantage, for fish face into the noon sun. I do not like to fish with the sun at my back, particularly if the sun is low. In such a state one's shadow stretches across the water, the silhouette of the body is stark and the fish will possibly be dazzled when rising to a fly close to the surface and moving towards the sun. All in all, let the sun take a holiday on another river.

Air temperature can be decisive. It controls the temperature of the water, raising it, in a heatwave, to 65°F or more, at which level fish become reluctant or, in early spring, keeping it below 40°F, which results in lethargic salmon, dull with cold.

The best conditions are met when the air is warmer than the water and the water is between 45 and 60°F. At this upper figure, if the air continues to be hot through long hours of summer daylight, the advantage begins to be lost. When cooler air arrives, there will be a period of poor fishing, possibly lasting for some days until the water also drops in temperature. In such a period recently, in June, I was fishing for trout. At the end of the day an experienced friend approached me with three brownies, which was also my tally. We had both hoped for a heavier bag. He questioned, 'Was the air too cold, or the water too warm?' I thought for a moment, remembered testing the milky-warm water with a cold hand, and replied that trout had been reluctant to rise into the warm surface water. It can be so, and this applies also to salmon.

Water

So we come to the second truth, that, whilst weather controls water over the long term, desirable water does, in the short term over-rule the need to worry overmuch about the weather. In other words, in a spate river with falling whisky-stained water after rain, fish all day even if the sun is bright, the air is hot and there is not a breath of wind.

Spates should be studied and water levels watched. Anticipation is the key to taking full advantage of a spate. Work out from experience the crucial hours to fish.

Outside my kitchen window is an inverted dustbin lid. If the lid fills with rain, not over 2 days, but in 8 hours, a spate is likely to arrive on my home river. Off I go. On the way I cross a feeder stream in the car. I peer over the bridge and, if the brook is running full, a spate is in the making. Do not wait for the water to fill the river further downstream where you fish: be there ready in advance to cast as the water rises. The first half an hour, or maybe only 15 minutes, are precious moments when fish take. After that, as the water rises, continue to fish, but the chances of a take are reducing.

Salmon run on rising water; lies are vacated and fish are hard to find, other than in the wide tails of pools where they rest after negotiating rapids on their way upriver. The water continues to rise but the rain has stopped. Now, watch a grassy sloping bank where the water is lapping at the edge. As soon as leaves, twigs and broken grass start to be stranded in a tide mark in England, or empty floating whisky bottles in Scotland, commence your main effort. There may be no response for 2 or 3 hours as the river drops back from the peak level, but the magic moment will arrive unless the water is dirty and acid.

The first spate after a period of drought is not the most productive, but it washes the waterway clean and brings up a few fish. These are hard to catch in the acid dirty flow, but a second period of rain, and a second rise, will bring clean water and catches.

Water colour in a spate can render fishing impossible if the colour is brown, due to mud. One has to await a change in colour from brown to green as clarity is re-established. In a chalk-based river, heavy rain, and the resultant washings from road and ploughed field, may render the water too thick for success but a clearance will arrive. A moorland river may run a whisky-stained shade with no detriment to the fishing but, if the colour becomes brown or peat black, due to a deluge, fishing will be poor until it clears.

11 Landing and playing salmon

Successful fly fishing, spinning, prawning and the use of the shrimp terminate in landing fish. As the methods for securing salmon are the same for each system, they will be considered in a chapter of their own. There are six ways of securing salmon: hand-tailing and gill-flap gripping, beaching and the use of a wire tailer, the gaff and the net.

Landing salmon

Beaching and hand tailing

There are those who go to the river without any landing equipment, relying on beaching the fish or lifting it out by hand. This is satisfactory in certain rivers and on some beats where banks slope gently into the water. The angler who does not possess a net, tailer or gaff, having become used to the hand and beaching on the home river, will lose fish on beats where equipment is a necessity. Such waters may have steep banks, fast, deep flows and large fish, any one of which may render the hand landing method inadequate or impossible to bring into use.

Some rivers are suitable but, in any case, one should know how to use the hand which may, in emergency, be all that is available. At any rate, it is always there! I habitually carry a Gye net but, one day, whilst playing a grilse, the release tab on the sling holding the net to my back caught in a bramble. Being freed, the net fell in the river. I lifted out the grilse by hand and later recovered the net.

There are two ways of tailing a salmon and one of gripping a grilse. The physical differences between one- and two-sea-winter fish determine the method. Their tails are different. The two-sea-winter salmon has two knobs or swellings of gristle at the base of the tail: one on top and one underneath. These knuckles form a *wrist* in front of the broad sweep of the tail. This wrist may be gripped by the ring formed by the thumb and forefinger of the hand, providing a hold firm enough to lift out a 20 lb salmon.

Beaching.   Hand tailing.   Hand tailing.

There is controversy over whether the thumb and forefinger should be closest to the head or the tail of the fish; in other words should the palm of the hand be over the tail or towards the adipose fin. The position of the angler, in or out of the water, determines the choice. When beaching a fish and pushing it up the bank, the palm of the hand should be over the tail. If lifting a salmon onto a steep bank whilst wading, because there is no beach, the palm of the hand must be towards the adipose fin and the thumb/forefinger ring immediately in front of the tail. In either case, the grip is enhanced if the hand is first wiped over grit, sand or mud, or wrapped about with a handkerchief.

A grilse has a slim tail without gristle swellings. It cannot safely be hand-tailed, but it can be lifted out. Place the hand across the top of the head of the fish with the forearm lying back towards the tail. Press in the gill flaps with the thumb on one side and the first two fingers on the other. A good grip will be secured under the top bone of the skull. Almost invariably this will cause bleeding from the gill filaments and no time should be lost in thumping the fish upon the head with the priest.

The author leaps to the bank with a hand-tailed fish.

Beaching is safe. Play out the salmon, lead it towards a gentle slope and keep it swimming forwards by rod pressure until it is stranded. Then move behind the fish, push it up the bank and lift it clear, the grip, on this occasion, being with the palm of the hand over the tail. When playing out the fish prior to beaching, do so, if possible, standing in the water. If perched on the bank, erect, obvious and silhouetted against the sky, the position does not lead to relaxed acquiescence on the part of the fish.

Wire tailer

This is a superb instrument for losing fish. Imagine this situation. You are in the river playing a salmon; the tailer is around your back in the carrying position. With one hand, the other being on the rod, you must release the wire-and-brass ring from beneath the clip half-way along the shaft, then slide it to just beyond the shaft end to form the noose. The hand must be passed through the leather loop on the handle or a heavy salmon may pull the grip out of your hand. During these manoeuvres you will have spoken to the fish, directing it to keep still whilst the noose is moved over its tail and up towards the adipose fin. You then pull and, if you are lucky, the noose settles around the salmon's tail-wrist and it may be lifted out of the river. If the loop slides off the tail, the wire has to re-set with your third hand. Conservationists have arranged that the tailer is allowed on all rivers at all times of the season. It does not work on slim-tailed grilse.

Tailer. The brass ring is moved forward to the end of the shaft when about to tail a salmon.

Tailer in use on a two-sea-winter salmon.

Tailer. Safe carrying position.

Gaff

This is a metal hook which pierces the side of the fish to lift it out of the river. Gaffed salmon, being wounded, cannot be returned to the water. In some areas, the use of the gaff may be prohibited before the middle of April in order to preserve kelts and after the end of August to ensure that heavily gravid hen fish may be returned. On many rivers it is totally prohibited.

There is a case for the gaff. If a river is deep, with steep banks, it may be difficult to net a fish, particularly if the current is strong and sweeps the net aside. A really large fish may present a problem for a 24 in. net. Whilst I do not like the gaff, and have declined to use one for many years, it does not do to be dogmatic.

To gaff a fish, first play out the salmon. It is a mistake to take a quick slash at a passing active fish; it may be lost due to the gaff touching the leader. Place the gaff across the back of the salmon at the dorsal fin, draw in firmly and continue to pull and lift until the salmon is on the bank. Do not hestitate once the fish is on the hook. The salmon must be killed at once.

Net

A small net will only hold a small fish. A large net will accommodate both large and small. Choose a capacious net with a diameter of at least 24 in. and a ring of metal. Avoid those dreadful collapsible nets, the arms of which lock open into a Y-shape. The arms of the Y are joined by a cord. The first risk with such a contraption, usually described as a grilse net, is that it may be too small. The second is that it may fail to open and lock. The third is that the cord will sag, drawing the arms together if a heavy fish, or even a grilse of 5 lb, becomes balanced across the mouth. The fish may then slide backwards out of the net and be lost.

There are Gye nets by Sharpes of Aberdeen of 18 in. frame diameter for sea trout and 24 in. and 30 in. for salmon. Leeda Tackle market a similar Gye with a 25 in. diameter frame, the handle of which extends to 73 in.; this is my preference.

The net is carried on the back, held in position by a Peel Sling with a quick-release Velcro tab (as illustrated on page 129). The shaft slides cross the mouth of the net for carrying. There will always be small problems when carrying large nets and this is so, to a limited extent, with a Gye, in that the handle protrudes below one's waist and the end of the shaft above the shoulder. I cut off the top end of the shaft, shortening it by about 6 in. and

Carrying a Gye net. The shaft has been shortened to below shoulder level.

To release the Gye net, pull the Velcro tab.

then re-fit the stop plug, which prevents the shaft sliding out of the net-frame bracket whilst leaving sufficient length at the end of the shaft for the Peel Sling ring. If the shaft is not shortened it will extend above the shoulder and may catch in tree branches when fishing in enclosed rivers.

The 30 in. net is not to my liking; it limits mobility. Too large to be easily carried by the single fisherman, it has a place when transported by a gillie or placed at a static fishing stand. It is, of course, the safest of the nets. All Gye nets have shiny aluminium frames, eye-catching in both shop and river. Paint the frame green or scared salmon may be stimulated to extra effort at the final moment. Do not paint the shaft or it will not slide in and out of the frame bracket.

It is easier to net your own salmon from river level, than have this done by a companion with whom you must co-ordinate your actions. There is a case for assistance when fishing from a high bank, from which the fish cannot be reached by the angler, and from which he cannot descend. If this is the position, the angler must have a clear view of the netsman and release rod pressure as the fish enters the net. Twice, when netting for inexperienced rods, I have had the fish pulled away as it was about to slide down into the net. The first occasion was with a 5 lb grilse – it was re-netted without much trouble. The second was a 19 lb salmon which had to be gripped by hand at head and tail and sat upon.

To net a salmon

Leave the net on your back whilst the salmon is being played. If released too early from the Peel Sling, you may find yourself running down the river after the fish, rod in one hand, the other on the reel, and the net – well, sort that out for yourself.

When the fish is almost, but not quite cooked, lower yourself into the river or kneel close to water level on the bank. Let the place be a quiet backwater away from strong currents. Place the net beside you on the bank. Now, persuade the fish upstream, turn it, reach out with the net and run the fish downstream, head-first through the mouth of the partially submerged net frame. The current will wash the salmon down into the bag and it will be facing the wrong way to swim out. Always try to net a salmon head-first into the net. If netting from behind, the fish can swim forward and escape.

Do not attempt to draw a fish from below you, upstream into the net. In this case the first item to reach the net rim will be the leader; if the fish runs downstream into the net, with the rod point upstream, the leader will be behind the head of the fish and lying along its body in safety. I have suggested that netting take place before complete exhaustion has rendered the salmon incapable of swimming against the current. The upstream movement of a salmon prior to netting cannot be achieved in heavy water if the salmon has insufficient energy left to move against the flow. A salmon, wallowing exhausted downstream of the angler, is sometimes too heavy to be pulled back by a fly rod and, in this case, a dangerous strain is placed upon the hooks.

This salmon has been netted correctly – head first.

Stag-horn handle with two wires for carrying fish.

Remember that tube flies and Waddingtons have treble hooks (page 144). One or two of the hooks of the treble may still be free outside the lip of the salmon's mouth. If one of these catches in the meshes of the net, it will pull the other(s) free and the fish will escape. It is thus unwise to scrape a fish over the rim of the net. To avoid this, do not net in shallow water but select a position where the net frame may be sufficiently submerged.

Sometimes a fish has to be drawn across the river into the net because there is insufficient space upstream. In this case the head of the fish must be kept at surface level and the net frame be half sunk to avoid free hooks touching the meshes. Whilst this position sometimes has to be accepted, it may result in the hooks being pulled out of the mouth of the fish, which is facing the rod.

Having the salmon safely in the bag, draw it ashore, then lift the net and fish by gripping the rim. Do not lift by the aluminium shaft; it will bend.

All this may sound complicated. It is not. The net or beaching are the safest ways.

Playing salmon

The methods of hooking salmon will be described in Chapters 13, 15 and 16.

The cone of trout vision has been described previously (page 79). The same physical rules apply to the transference of light from above-surface objects to salmon in the water. If the angler can keep at less than a 10° angle upwards from the water surface at the circumference of the window of vision, he will be out of sight. Remaining hidden whilst playing a salmon is desirable.

When a salmon is hooked it is probably unaware of the presence of the angler. It cannot know what has happened and why it is being pulled out of alignment with the current. It must be a confusing situation to the fish and, the longer the salmon remains ignorant of the whereabouts of danger. and the identity of the threat, the better. If the fish sees the angler standing on the bank, body and rod bent over the water in a threatening position, it reacts. The reaction may take the form of a fast run downstream; it will, certainly, be to fight with vigour. Therefore, the longer the angler remains out of sight, whilst wearing-out the fish, the better. The rod point, even though visible, ought to be held high to act as a spring to absorb the shocks of the fight and minimize stresses on the hook-hold.

If wading waist deep in a wide river the angler is likely to be outside the angle of vision of the hooked fish. It may be wise for him to remain still for some time, taking steam out of the salmon before wading to the bank.

Kneel when fishing a small river. The author with two grilse.

Furthermore, because the angler is closer to the fish than if on land, less line will be off the reel and beneath the water surface; one ought to keep the length of drowned line to the minimum, another reason for keeping the rod tip high. A long length of line under water, pulled along by the fish, puts considerable strain on the hook-hold which may tear free. So, in a great river, don't move at once to the bank unless the fish is small and easily controlled.

On a small river, keep out of sight by either kneeling a few feet back from the edge of the river or operating from behind a screen of vegetation. If wading, keep tucked in close to the bank.

Almost all salmon are hooked when downstream of the angler and they should not be allowed to remain in that position. Throughout the fight it should be the aim of the angler to keep opposite or downstream of the fish. If the fish remains downstream of the angler, not only is the salmon able to offset the pull of the line by the pressure of the current, but he remains in a dangerous position for a fast run back to sea. Thus, in a small river, as soon as the fish is hooked, the angler should move down opposite to the quarry whilst using every endeavour to keep out of sight.

The salmon should be played from opposite or below the fish. Too much strain will cause the salmon to become violent, thrash on the surface or leap. Extremes of movement, particularly jumping, are dangerous but may be kept to the minimum by steady, rather than excessive, rod pressure. Some people maintain the pressure of the rod, keeping a tight line, when a salmon jumps. That is not my practice. I do my best to react sufficiently quickly and drop the point of the rod when the salmon becomes airborne; it then falls back on a slack line which cannot strain the hold of the hook.

Pressure should at once be resumed after the leap. Forewarning of the intention of a two-sea-winter salmon to jump is given by a sudden burst of speed which terminates in the leap. Grilse give little notice, popping up at any time.

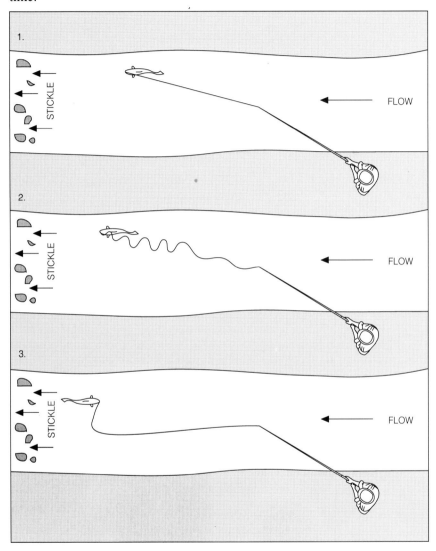

24 Stopping a salmon swimming out of
the tail of a pool.
(1) The fish heads quickly for the pool tail.
(2) The angler drops the rod point and opens the bail-arm of the spinning reel for
2–3 seconds or strips 3–4 yd line off the fly reel. *Line goes slack*.
(3) The fish feels no resistance, needs to breathe and turns to face the current.
The angler tightens gently and walks the fish upstream.

My views of the tight-line/slack-line alternatives are based on the speed of movement under water and in the air. Movement is sharper in the air than when damped down by water. Sharp, twisting, head-shaking jumps loosen hooks if the line is tight.

A salmon should be encouraged to run upstream, for it then fights both current and rod pressure. Additionally, there is rarely danger in an upstream run which finishes when the fish, overcome by rod and water pressure, comes back close to its starting position.

When a salmon is static opposite the angler, it can be persuaded to move upstream by a gentle sideways strain with rod held low. To counteract this unbalancing pull, the fish heads slightly forward and towards the far bank, thus presenting its nearside flank to the current and having to swim ahead or lose control.

Danger arrives when a fish swims downstream. Such movements can be rapid, cover many yards, and need a finely calculated response. If in a long pool with clear banks, the angler can also walk downriver, keeping adjacent to the fish. If there is a grilse on the end it can usually be stopped by rod pressure. Not so a 10 or 15 lb fish with the water under its tail, particularly in a small pool 25 or 30 yd in length. To keep a fish in such a small area of water is usually possible if one is quick and cunning. When the salmon heads for the run-off, but still has 8 or 10 yd to go, release all pressure. This is done either by dropping the point of the fly rod and stripping a couple of yards of

A staff for safe wading.

On reaching the bank, when playing a fish, the staff should be discarded.

line off the reel or by opening the bail arm of a fixed-spool spinning reel for 2 seconds. In four cases out of five, the salmon will swing around and face upstream without leaving the pool. The fish has to face the current in order to breathe, by water passing in through the mouth and out of the gills. The fish, having faced about, is now static in the tail of the pool and may be *walked-up*.

The aim of walking-up is to move the salmon from a downstream position to a point higher up the river. Gently tighten on the salmon with the rod out over the river, at right angles to the bank and horizontal. One is therefore pulling from a position as near to directly upstream as possible. Slowly increase pressure, moving forward a step at a time without winding the reel; the salmon will start to slide forward through the water. The clicking vibration of winding a reel may be transmitted down the line and upset the almost-unconscious progress of the fish. When the top of the pool has been reached, the angler should again move level with the salmon. It must be emphasized that a salmon will not stop at the tail of a pool on the release of pressure if the slackening is made too late and it is already within the water suction at the head of the next set of rapids.

If a salmon does run out of the tail of the pool it may be lost if the angler cannot follow. Usually one can pursue the fish if given time to negotiate obstacles. Time may be gained by releasing all pressure on the salmon, which will usually wait, facing into the current, some distance below the angler. A loop of free line, part of that released by the angler, sometimes forms downstream of the resting place. The slight pull of this loop from below has a steadying effect. If permanent access is available to a particular piece of water, it is advisable to cut back branches and remove obstacles which would prevent one following a runaway.

It is unwise to take to a full river after a fleeing salmon if you cannot follow on the bank, unless the river is intimately known. I have accepted the risk from time to time, if fishless after a long drought or having been given my orders by my wife to stock the larder. Before launching yourself, be sure to remove wallet, cheque book and flask from your pockets. If you drown, the paperwork will not be needed; if you don't, you will need the flask.

12 Fly-fishing tackle and artificial flies

Rods

Fly fishing in large and small rivers requires rods of differing lengths. Fishing in warm and cold waters, with floating and sinking lines, suggests a requirement for rods differing in power, in that a rod of authority is needed to raise a sunk line to the surface. Less power is needed to fish a floating line. Small restricted rivers, overgrown with trees, may require single-handed rods. Needs differ; the choice is wide. If I had to select one salmon rod to cover all situations the choice would be a 13 ft carbon, taking No 9 lines of different specific gravities, and a 10 ft stiff trout rod. Having gathered some experience of differing situations, I hope that I shall not be called upon to make this impossible choice and can continue to employ the weapons on my rod racks. All of these, with one exception, are in carbon fibre. Split cane in particular, and also fibreglass, are too heavy by the standards of today. My rods will now be described.

14 ft, AFTM No 8/10, tubular-carbon
Cordon Blue by Bruce & Walker

In the south of England there are no really large, first-class salmon rivers other than the Wye. A 14 ft rod copes with the need to cast, and lift out of the water, a sinking fly line in the cold waters of spring when one has to get down to fish. It is suitable for rivers of medium width: the Hampshire Avon, Frome, Tamar, Teifi, Coquet, Helmsdale, Deveron and similar others.

The Cordon Blue will roll, Spey and overhead cast. It has the sensitivity to fish a No 9 floating line, 12 lb BS nylon and small flies on large rivers in summer. If restricted to the fly on a large river, and thus unable to spin deep in early spring, a 15 ft AFTM No 10 should be added to execute long casts with a fast-sinking line, strong nylon and heavy tube flies or Waddingtons.

13 ft, AFTM No 9/10, tubular-carbon
Gold Medallion by Normark

This has a crisp action with plenty of power. Having taught people to cast for many years, I have noticed that they learn and perform better with a stiff rod in the overhead cast than with a soft one. The wider line loop thrown overhead by a soft rod tends to fall lower towards the ground on the back cast. This rod copes satisfactorily with sinking and sink-tip lines on medium/small rivers and with a floating line on a large river, shrunk to summer width and level. This is a sensible, attractively priced rod of good quality with Fuji line guides. It is well balanced by a No 9 fly line.

12 ft, AFTM No 9, graphite
Salmon by House of Hardy

This rod belongs to my daughter, Lara. We have both killed fish with it over the past dozen seasons. Amongst the collection, it is my favourite. Light in weight, narrow in the tube and on the stiff side, it controls salmon with authority but is overweighted by the suggested No 9 line. Our preference for this rod is a No 8 floater; it would not be used with a sinking fly line, for which a longer rod is to be preferred. It is no longer manufactured, having been replaced by the two shortest rods in the Hardy double-handed range: DeLuxe 12½ ft No 8/9, and Favourite 12½ ft No 9.

12 ft, AFTM No 8/9, spliced split cane
Scottie by Sharpes of Aberdeen

The three pieces are bound together over the splices by black insulating tape. There is no need for anyone today to possess this rod, which is steeped in tradition and waterproofed by resin impregnation. It has a slow rolling action, is sweet to handle, completely reliable and will withstand knocks that would shatter a carbon tube. To see the rod bent into a fish in an uninterrupted arc is a delight.

Why do I take it to the river, mounted on the roof of my car, which cannot then be parked in town in case a vandal snaps off the rod tip with his fingers? Nostalgia: memories of days which have passed; those years when superb Kingfisher silk lines were greased to float, sank of their own accord, and cut into the wind like knives; for plus fours, rubber overtrousers and brogues, malt whisky in the evening and footmarks on the dew at dawn.

10½ ft, AFTM No 7/9, tubular-carbon
Salmon & Sea Trout by Bruce & Walker

This is single-handed, but has a 4 in. screw-in butt extension to support the wrist when tucked into the tummy whilst playing a salmon. My particular rod is finished with matt varnish which does not reflect the sun when I am casting. It handles a No 8 floater and is sufficiently powerful to bring a salmon to the net.

There is little to be said in favour of short, single-handed salmon rods on medium rivers. They lack the length to mend the fly line as efficiently as a longer rod; the line cannot be lifted over tall bushes when playing fish, neither can it be cleared when a hooked fish takes the line around an underwater obstruction, unless the snag is close to the bank. Longer rods are better at controlling lines and fish. The short, single-handed rod has a place when one is wading within a canopy of trees in a river narrow enough to spit across. It is also to be preferred over a double-hander when casting from a boat.

Fly lines

The choice of lengths, profiles and densities is wide; prices range from cheap to unnecessarily expensive; shades vary through the spectrum, as in Joseph's technicoloured dream-coat, and manufacturers' and trade names abound. You cannot try them all, and I doubt whether there is much to choose between the top manufacturers' lines. I will describe the lines which find places on my salmon fly reels. They are all made by 3M Scientific Anglers of the USA and are all 27 yd long and double tapered.

Floating lines　Air Cel, colour light green.
Sinking lines　Wet Cel 11, colour dark green.
Sink-tip lines　Air Cel Supreme; this has 10 ft dark-green sinking tips at both ends, whilst the main floating body is light green.

All these lines may be reversed when one end is worn. All execute roll, Spey and overhead casts. In AFTM No 10 and above, Scientific Anglers also produce double-tapered lines which are 35 yd long.

My lines are three-quarters of the way up the price ladder. An excellent line, just half-way up the price scale is the Leeda 'Hi-Tec' Gallion. It may not last as long as the Scientific Anglers' line just described, but it has a smooth finish, shoots easily through the line guides and comes in a free, foam-lined, red, floating fly box. The floater is light green but I am not keen on the noticeable brown shade of the sinking line.

Not less than 100 yd of backing is needed behind these lines to fill the reel spool and cope with a runaway fish. This should be of 20 lb BS. The type may be braided – Milwards produce a good, white braided polyester – or monofilament. The former may be spliced to the fly line or joined by the Albright knot; the needle knot or nail knot are used to join monofilament to the fly line. It is not easy to judge the length of backing needed to fill the reel spool if the backing is wound on first. Instead, wind on the fly line, attach the backing and fill to just short of capacity. Then pull off both line and backing, and reverse. The end of the backing should be taken around the reel spool and secured with the Arbor knot.

My fly lines are backed by 20 lb BS Maxima Chameleon taken from a 600 yd spool. This extra-large capacity mono spool allows me to wind any length of nylon on to the fly reel without having to join sections of 50 or 100 yd; sometimes one needs 120 yd, or more, to fill the reel spool and this can all be in one uninterrupted length.

Reels

In my view the best fly reels are made by House of Hardy; their prices match the quality of the product. I would suggest the following:

St John reel For DT8F fly lines and 100 yd of backing.
Marquis Salmon No 1 For DT9F fly lines and 100 yd of backing.
Marquis Salmon No 2 For DT10F and 100 yd of backing.

These three reels have adjustable drag and a spare check-spring and pawl inside the back of the reel casing. The spare spring is rarely needed; I have used one once only in the 35 years I have owned St John reels. They are readily changed from right to left-hand wind but, if this is done, the line and backing have to be stripped off and re-wound. Spare spools are available to hold lines of different densities and these may be fitted in a few seconds. These reels are not the most modern in the current Hardy range but they are simple, reliable and cost half as much as some recent models. The reels in the Marquis range have exposed rims for finger-control braking. The St John spool is enclosed but this does not worry me for I always apply pressure to a salmon by passing the line under the forefinger of the hand on the butt of the rod. Adjustable drag is essential in a reel, not to control the salmon, but to be set light in order that delicate finger pressure may alter resistance. Do not purchase any reel without this facility; the non-adjustable drag may be set hard by the manufacturer, resulting in too much pressure on the hook-hold or the necessity to give line by pulling it off the reel by hand when playing a fish.

It is sensible to purchase a large simple reel to recover line rapidly, rather than a smaller multiplier which has a greater number of working parts. If the single-action reel has a larger diameter drum than is required to accommodate the line and backing, line recovery will be greater for each turn of the handle. Large simple reels are the sensible choice.

My own reels are St Johns, a Hardy Viscount 150 and a Hardy 3¾ in. Perfect; the St Johns are for DT8F lines and the other two are for DT9F. Both the Viscount and the 3¾ in. Perfect are no longer made (smaller

Perfects are still manufactured for lines up to DT7F). Spare spools are available for the Viscount and St Johns, which can also be changed from right- to left-hand wind. The Perfect is either right- or left-handed – it cannot be changed. Of all the reels in my house (there are about 40), my favourite is the Perfect. Go to tackle auctions, seek out one which is large enough for salmon lines – they are perfection and an investment which increases in value. I have never found the Hardy factory decline to repair out-of-date reels.

An excellent reel, priced at about 80 per cent of the Marquis range, is the System Two, manufactured in Cornwall by British Fly Reels and marketed by Leeda Tackle. Sizes cover all lines from AFTM 2–13. All models have a fully adjustable, stainless, caliper disc-drag and are ambidextrous, i.e. for right- or left-hand use. Spools are easily changed. Much lower down the price scale is the Leeda Dragonfly Imperial 120. This is of carbon construction and light in weight. Attributes include adjustable disc-drag, ambidexterity, easily changed spools and proven reliability.

Leaders

A tapered leader is unnecessary for salmon because casting is down and across the river or across. The current then straightens out any crookedness in line and leader. If 50 yd spools of 20, 15 and 10 lb BS Maxima Chameleon are carried, many requirements will be met for salmon, trout and sea-trout fishing:

20 lb BS Used for: large, heavy, salmon tube flies; the butt sections of home-made tapered leaders for still-water wet fly and lure trout fishing; the butt of sea-trout leaders.

15 lb BS Used for: for my own Black Dart, Copper Dart and other medium tube flies for salmon; the second section of trout and centre of sea-trout leaders; the trace in salmon spinning.

10 lb BS Used for: single-hooked low-water salmon flies, small tubes and small doubles; the third section of trout wet-fly leaders; the point of sea-trout leaders.

These varying strengths of nylon allow flies of different sizes to work freely in the water. The movement of a low-water single of size No 6 or No 8 would be severely restricted if knotted to 20 lb BS nylon. All, even the 10 lb BS, provide the strength to land large salmon. I do not think the thickness of Chameleon nylon particularly matters if deterrence of salmon is considered. Some seasons ago I put this to a trial, fishing my tube flies off 20 lb BS Platil in the summer, and took nine grilse. I admit that the tubes were 1 in. or more in length and I was fishing in spate water.

Look along the leader
to see wind knots.

For floating-line salmon fishing, the leader ought to be about 10 ft in length.
Draw this straight off the spool, tie a blood-bight loop on one end and join
this loop to the fly line with a double sheet bend. This produces a bulky joint
which may be watched when a salmon rises to the fly; if the knot moves off,
raise the rod, because the fish has taken the fly. When using rods of 12 ft or
longer, there is no risk of winding this knot into the top rod ring when
landing a salmon, for the knot can be seen and the leader is shorter than the
rod. When fishing with the 10½ ft rod, the junction may be made by blood
knot to 1 ft of 20 lb BS monofilament needle-knotted into the fly line. This
joint can be wound through the rod tip. As an alternative, the leader length
can be reduced to 9 ft and the blood-bight loop and double sheet method
used. A braided loop connector is an additional method. When fishing with a
sinking fly line, the leader may be reduced to about 7 ft in length, an
advantage when fishing heavy flies.

The treble hook of a tube fly, and the straight wire loop of a Waddington,
should be knotted to the leader with a tucked half blood. Eyed salmon flies
should be attached with a two-turn Turle or, if the eye is large, the two-circle
Turle.

Droppers, to fish two flies on a leader, may be provided by cutting the nylon
at the chosen position along the leader, re-joining the ends with a blood knot
and leaving one end 6 in. long to form the dropper. Attach the dropper fly to
the end coming from the top section of the leader and cut off the end coming
from the lower section of the leader close to the knot. In this way, a salmon on
the dropper is attached directly to the upper portion of the leader, which is
tied to the fly line.

Flies

Trout, sea trout and salmon are able to appreciate colour. Before studying
this section on salmon flies, the reader is asked to refer to the discussion of
non-imitative flies for still-water trout (page 41). The principles of trout-lure
colouration are also applied to salmon flies but hooks and body designs are
different. Salmon do not feed in fresh water. If a fish enters a river 25 miles
long in April, it has roughly 7 months in which to swim that distance to the
spawning beds. This could be covered in a couple of days instead of over 200.
How are those almost endless weeks to be spent? In boredom! It must be so.
What is there to do? Perhaps, after a month, there is rain in the hills, followed
a few hours later by increased water flow down the valley, with the strange
tastes of peat and other soil washings. Excitement indeed. The salmon stirs.
Suddenly, a strange, orange, shrimp-like thing appears, swinging at a most
unlikely pace across the river, holding its own against a current which would
sweep away a natural creature of that size. This stimulates closer inspection
(up it comes), a tasting (the take) and a return to the lie to chew and savour
(the hook slides home as it turns). The angler, hopping in excitement on the
bank, is consumed with fear that the hook will come away and the fish be lost.

There are two intentions in the design of a salmon fly: to attract the fish and to
ensure that, once hooked, it remains so until landed. If it is accepted that the
colours needed are red, orange and yellow, one or more of these and a striped
red or black body, these may be dressed on all types of hooking devices. It is
only between the different designs of hook, and the body on to which the
dressing is mounted, that we need to make a choice. A salmon fly must have a
correct balance between weight and bulk. A fat lightweight fly will skid on
the surface of the water when held against the current by a floating fly line.
There are many different hook patterns. For quality, and the fulfilment of
specific needs, I always purchase hooks by Partridge of Redditch. The
Managing Director fishes; he knows about hooks.

Hooks

Single hook

Reference should be made to the drawing of a hook on page 56. Large hooks
of sizes 1, 1/o, 2/o and above are of thick metal, which requires considerable
force by the rod to be driven into the jaw of a salmon. They usually have long
shanks (a 2/o may be 1 1/2 in. in the shank and longer still if eye and shape are
added) which put considerable leverage on the hook-hold when pulled from
many directions during the playing of the fish. Having a single point, they are

less likely to obtain a purchase in the mouth than a double or treble. These three disadvantages dissuade me from their use.

I am not utterly opposed to small flies dressed on single low-water hooks. These are of fine wire which readily penetrates the mouth of the fish. The shank of a No 6 or No 8 may be only ¾ in. in length, exerting less leverage on the hook-hold. They swim well, being slim with little water resistance, and thus do not skate.

Attractive flies may be dressed on these hooks. Salmon take them, but there are defects: the fine wire may break if the salmon takes the line around a rock or leaps on a tight line, and the hook has only one point.

Double hook

The increased hooking power of two points is an advantage; a little extra weight over the single is another. In large sizes, leverage by a long shank is a weakness. If using a double, choose a short shank. Shrimp flies are often dressed on small, short-shanked double hooks and are fished in the dropper position or on the point. I am quite happy to use a dropper when salmon and sea-trout fishing from a boat but eschew them in a river where the free fly may catch on an obstruction or in weed and pull the other fly out of the mouth of the fish.

Up-eyed treble

Types are: the Esmond Drury, Partridge x2b and Partridge grsx2b Grey Shadow. The Grey Shadow finish is very hard, protecting the points for a long time and the hook from corrosion.

Fly patterns are dressed directly on the shanks of these hooks. I am not fond of the large No 2, for these are overheavy and their shanks are long, but must admit to taking a fish of 14 lb on one without any trouble. Attractive small flies may be dressed on Nos 10 and 12; such little offerings are engulfed by the fish and one, two or three of the points take a firm hold.

Partridge-Waddington shank

Originally the Waddington consisted of a wire with a loop at each end. To one loop the leader was knotted with a tucked half blood, whilst the other loop was closed after being passed through the eye of a treble hook. Thereafter, the treble could not be replaced. The hook was kept in line with the wire by a piece of cycle-valve rubber and the dressing was applied to the wire between the two loops. The disadvantage of this arrangement is that a damaged hook resulted in the whole fly having to be discarded.

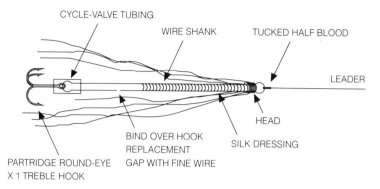

25 Partridge-Waddington shank. The shank is dressed from the head
    to just above the gap.

Partridge improved this system with their vib double Waddington shanks in
eight lengths between 0.4 and 2.2 in. These consist of two parallel wires as
illustrated in the drawing above. Close to the end of one wire is a 0.08 in. gap
for the fitting and replacement of treble hooks, the gap then being closed by a
fine wire binding. The best hooks for these shanks are Partridge xi, round-
eye, outbend trebles. Needle-eyed trebles are unsuitable.

Waddingtons are slim, swim well and are efficient at hooking fish on their
treble hooks. But the complications of hook attachment do not attract me
when compared with the simplicity of hook replacement in tube flies.

Tube flies

The tube may be of polythene-lined brass or aluminium, or just polythene. In
the metal types, the tube should be wide enough to accept the needle eye of a
Partridge x3 outbend treble. If the eye is pressed into the tail of the tube and
gripped tightly by the plastic lining, the hook will be held in line with the

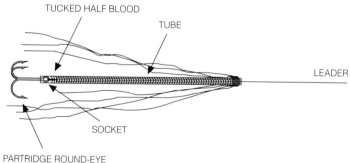

26 Veniard Type B Slipstream socketed tube. The tube is dressed
    from the head to just above the socket.

tube. It is unsatisfactory if the eye of the treble cannot be inserted into the tube, for the hook will turn sideways and hang down.

Instead of metal I prefer Veniard Type B Slipstream, socketed polythene tubes. These are formed of one tube inside another, the inside tube being shorter at the tail, thus forming a socket. At one time I used these with the black, needle-eyed Partridge x3 treble, but I now prefer the round-eyed x1, which is gripped more firmly in the socket. The advantage of the tube fly is the ease with which the treble may be replaced. When netting salmon, treble hooks are often bent when one of the points catches in the meshes of the net. If this happens the hook must be replaced; do not bend it straight because this weakens the hook. In fact I almost always replace my trebles after each salmon in case one of the hooks has been slightly strained. At the time of writing (1992), the cost of an x1 treble is £0.55 – a mere trifle compared with the value of a salmon to the angler and the other costs of putting the fish on the bank.

I use Type B Slipstream tubes in lengths of 1, 1¼, 1½ and 2 in. The tube is quite fat in order to accept the treble eye into the socket. Fat tubes create water resistance when cast downstream and skate on the surface if light in weight and fished off a floating fly line. I therefore wind fine lead wire beneath the floss silk of the body dressings or make the body of 0.40 mm copper wire. A Type B Slipstream tube shorter than 1 in. is not attractive, being too fat for the length; for smaller flies use the up-eyed trebles already described (page 143).

Fly patterns and their uses

It has not been my practice to describe fly dressings if these are known patterns regularly featured elsewhere. The Black Dart and Copper Dart tube flies are not in fly-dressing guides because they are my own preparations. They are therefore described in detail, together with three known patterns. These three may differ slightly from standard dressings in simplicity and the hook. They should suffice for all situations, the two smallest being on No 10 or No 12 up-eye trebles and the largest a 2 in. Type B Slipstream.

Black Dart

A dozen or more years ago I designed this tube fly to incorporate desirable colours, stripes, correct weight and a short-shanked treble hook. The stripes are in the form of tinsel, ribbing the body, and jungle-cock cheeks, which are themselves striped in yellow and black. The fly may be dressed on tubes of 1, 1¼, 1½ and 2 in. in length. My favourite is the 1¼ in. All four Black Dart tubes have the same frontal area. The 1 in. length necessarily has less lead wire and is thus lighter and liable to skate in fast water when fished off a floating line. A sink-tip line solves the problem but one cannot always be bothered to change. As a substitute, to avoid skating on some waters, I dressed the body of plain 0.40 mm copper wire (see Copper Dart, below).

Tube Type B Slipstream, socketed.
Hook Black Partridge x 1, outbend treble, No 8.
Tag No 16 oval gold tinsel.
Body Black floss over close turns of fine lead wire. The lead is stopped short of the head where the bucktail wing is to be tied in.
Rib No 16 oval gold tinsel.
Wing Orange bucktail
Cheeks Jungle cock. A long feather, three-quarters the length of the tube; one each side.
Head Black varnish.
Silk Black Naples.

Copper Dart

As stated above, this is dressed on a 1 in. tube to act as a substitute for the 1 in. Black Dart if it skids on the water. It may also be used if the fly is required to fish a few extra inches below the water surface off a floating line.

Tube 1 in. Type B Slipstream, socketed.
Hook Black Partridge x 1, outbend treble, No 8.
Body Side-by-side turns of 0.40 mm copper wire over a single winding of black Naples silk.
Wing Orange bucktail.
Cheeks Jungle cock. A feather three-quarters the length of the tube; one each side.
Head Black varnish.
Silk Black Naples.

Hairy Mary

This is well known as a single-hooked low-water fly in size Nos 6 and 8. It is very effective, but the broken-hook worry dissuades me from its use. Instead, I carry it tied on a 1¼ in. Type B Slipstream tube. The word *carry* is deliberate; it is not fished unless a salmon rises to the Black Dart or Copper Dart but refuses. The Hairy Mary is then substituted to offer alternative colours. It should be noted that the body is still black, striped with silver tinsel, and has a few turns of yellow floss above the socket.

All these tube flies are fished off 15 lb leaders.

Tube 1¼ in. Type B Slipstream, socketed.
Hook Black Partridge x 1, outbend treble, No 8.

Tag No 16 oval silver tinsel closest to the socket, about six turns, and three turns of yellow floss above.
Body Black floss over side-by-side turns of fine lead wire.
Rib No 16 oval silver tinsel.
Wing Natural brown bucktail.
Head Black varnish.
Silk Black Naples.

Stoat's tail

This, the smallest of the five flies, is used in warm clear water in summer. The leader should be of 10 lb BS nylon and the hook the up-eyed, treble, Partridge GRSX2B already described (page 143).

Two tufts of black hair may be tied in just behind the eye, one on each side or as a single tuft on top. The body of black floss may be ribbed with silver tinsel if desired. The tail of a stoat is not readily acquired in these days when there are fewer gamekeepers to set traps for vermin. My supply comes from stoats squashed upon the road; the tail is always undamaged.

If an up-eyed treble is not available, and neither is a stoat, proceed as follows: cut ½ in. from a Biro tube, press the needle eye of a black No 12 Partridge x3 into the end, catch a black dog and bind a few of its hairs to the head of the tube. Black cotton may be obtained from the emergency sewing kit on bedroom dressing-tables.

Hook Up-eyed, Partridge GRSX2B black treble, No 12.
Body Black floss silk.
Wing Stoat or black dog.
Head Black varnish.
Silk Black Naples.

Shrimp fly

If you wish to fish a dropper, this is the fly. Note the predominance of the colours red and black.

Hook Up-eyed, Partridge GRSX2B black treble, No 10 or No 12.
Body Tail half in red floss, front half in black floss.
Rib No 16 oval silver tinsel.
Throat hackle Hot orange.
Cheeks Two small jungle-cock feathers.
Wing Orange bucktail.
Head Red varnish.
Silk Red Naples.

13 Fly-fishing techniques

Preparation of tackle

Fly lines

Water conditions govern fly-line density. Whether to use a fast-sinking, sink-tip or floating fly line depends on the state of the water. It is necessary to consider the temperature of the water and its volume and clarity.

Fast-sinking fly lines

The Wet Cel 2 is used almost exclusively in water at a temperature of 45°F, or below, and thus before mid-April and after mid-October. The intention is to swim the fly close to the level of a cold lethargic fish resting on the bed of the river. The fact that this can rarely be achieved, due to the lifting effect of fast-flowing water, does not alter the fact that it must be attempted on a 'fly-only' river. As I doubt that a Wet Cel 2 sinks a fly much deeper than 18 in. in the full flows of early spring, a still faster-sinking line may be employed. Try the Wet Cel 4, Hi-Speed-Hi-D, which has a very fast rate of sinking. High-density fly lines are difficult to raise in the water, after their swim across the river, before executing the next throw and the line cannot be mended once it has sunk below the surface. Despite these limitations, it is no good fishing a water at a temperature of 40°F with a floating fly line.

There are two additional situations in which a Wet Cel 2 might be used. Salmon usually rest close to or on the river bed, regardless of the temperature of the water, although they may move into streamy runs in hot evenings. If the water is cold they are reluctant to rise up to take a fly fished just beneath the water surface; they may also refuse if the water is hot, above 65°F, although a fish, rarely but possibly, may be taken by sinking the fly towards the deepest lies.

Finally, if water clarity is poor in a spate, when the water temperature at 55°F suggests a floating fly line, a sinking line may carry a large gaudy lure to a depth close to fish where it can be seen.

For myself, I rarely use a fast-sinking line if the rules of the river allow me to spin in cold, very high or exceptionally coloured water.

Floating and sink-tip fly lines

From the middle of April, often until the end of October, the temperature of the water will be above 50°F. Their bodies warmed, salmon leap and, being no longer lethargic, will rise to take a fly fished just beneath the surface of the water. Late spring, summer and early autumn are the periods when floating and sink-tip lines are fished. Even at 45°F, as I have proved, fish may be taken on the floater if the water is clear and not too high.

Until recent seasons I fished through the warm months with a floating fly line. Fish were caught. There was all the excitement of seeing them come to the fly, take and go away, and of timing the vital rod-raising moment. But, in certain circumstances, more fish might have been hooked on a sink-tip line. Which to use? Study the water. If it is low and clear, use the floater; if coloured (but not thick) and in full flow, try the sink-tip. Deep holes are better fished with the fly 6 in. or 1 ft below the surface; again the fast-sinking line has a use. On 2 days in September 1992, when I was fishing in heavily stained, warm low water, the sink-tip brought me two grilse. If the water had been clear the floater would have been the choice.

It is wise to carry both lines. I mount on the rod a St John reel, on which is the Air Cel floater, and thrust a spare spool with sink-tip into my pocket. A method of converting a floater to a sink-tip is marketed by the Orvis Co. as their Sink-Tip System. This pack, at moderate cost, is comprised of two, different density, brown and green 6 ft sink-tips. These may be looped to the end of the floating fly line if this already terminates in an Orvis Braided Loop Connector. The sinking tips are not suitable for fly lines lighter than AFTM No 8.

Selecting the fly

In cold water, i.e. 45°F and below, full flows and poor clarity, fish a large fly. In warm water, of low level and with just a stain of whisky shade, select a smaller fly.

A full range of fly sizes is described in Chapter 12. Of course, the three variables of water temperature, clarity and rate of flow are rarely present in just these two combinations. One may arrive at the river to find low, clear, cold water; high, clear, cold water; dirty, warm, low water or other permutations. These variables must be considered in selecting a size of fly in

which one will have confidence. It is unwise to be dogmatic. In salmon
fishing never say *never* and never say *always*. Experiment. Vary unproductive
offerings. Fish down a mile of water with one fly and, if fishless, work back
up with a different pattern or, at least, vary the size.

In Chapter 12 I wrote that I use the 1¼ in. Hairy Mary tube solely as an
alternative fly. That was the case until recently! Then, fishing without success
in heavily stained water with a 1¼ in. Black Dart, I recalled fishing in a
similar circumstance on the same river of late August and early September
1974. The water then had been high and rather dark, but yielded six salmon,
from 5–15 lb, to a size 1/0 Hairy Mary single in 2 days and 4 afternoons.
Perhaps the Hairy Mary tube should again have been given a swim in
September 1992 – it brought the two grilse on the sink-tip line, as already
described. Even so, my favourites remain the Black and Copper Darts.

The size of fly which brings the best response varies from river to river. It is
sensible to take account of local knowledge when tackling a strange water.
Thus, on the river Tamar, flies tend to be much larger than on the clearer
moorland rivers. Tamar waters are cloudy; peat and granite waters are
clearer. The river Test is inexplicable; large flies of single No 4 or a 1¼ in.
tube are needed, even in that gin-clear water at a temperature of 65°F. One
morning on the Test, in August 1975, I took three grilse on a No 4 single-
hook Silver Doctor, at a water temperature of 68°F, using a floating fly line.
Those fish refused a smaller No 6. Yet, on the northern Scottish rivers, a low-
water No 6, No 8, or a wee No 12 Stoat's Tail on a Partridge GRSX2B black
treble hook might be selected by the gillie. You must experiment, but only
after local advice has been taken and tried. If you want to upset your gillie
when on a fishing holiday, insist on disregarding his fly selection and use a
pattern which works on your home river. Do this when tackling-up on the
first and an uncomfortable week will follow. If his choice fails to take fish you
might then, deferentially, suggest your favourite pattern.

Water conditions are not the only factors governing fly choice. Fishing styles
vary, calling for different sizes and patterns. The most successful salmon fly
fisherman I know, based upon fish taken per day fished, uses just one fly
throughout the season and, wonder of wonders, in one size – 2 in. The fact is
staggering at first glance. Are all our wiles and variations unnecessary? I think
not. He only fishes one river and only when it is in spate. In other words, he
waits until conditions suit his fly. The lesson to be drawn from this strange
example has little to do with flies. It is that success largely results from
knowing the river – every little eddy, pot, wrinkle and the lies in a long glide.

★

On 24 September 1992, the day after writing about fly selection, the following experiences were enjoyed. I decided, soon after dawn, that I would write in the morning and fish in the afternoon, there having been two-thirds of a dustbin lidful of rain overnight. At 8.30 am the telephone rang. 'Would you like to photograph a 10½ lb sea trout taken on fly during the night,' asked the caller. We agreed to meet at the river at noon, he bringing his peal. Between the telephone call and the photographic session, my informant, a supremely skilled fly man, fished down a mile of river and then worked back again, covering the water a second time without raising a fish. After our meeting he drove off to find a taxidermist, for a 10½ lb sea trout is the fish of a lifetime.

I decided to cover the water for a third time and started off at 1.00 pm with a 1¼ in. Hairy Mary tube. This is not my normal practice and I usually only carry this fly to persuade difficult fish, yet the afternoon was being started with a Hairy Mary. I have also noted that the fly had recently taken two salmon without them having first risen to another fly. However, some conclusions may be drawn from my experiences of this day.

On leaving the car the water level was recorded by a stick thrust into the tide mark in a sandy bay. The flow was at a medium rate and the water the shade of light-brown, Cherry Blossom boot polish, but not turbid. The Hairy Mary was knotted to the leader.

After ¾ mile, and trying all the usual lies and likely places, a 6½ lb cock grilse snatched up the fly as soon as it hit the water. He was a determined, courageous fish. Hemmed in by bushes, up to my thighs in water, I could go neither up nor down. He rushed to the tail of the pool but turned when I slackened line. After returning to the middle, and executing a pirouette upon his tail and some underwater research into the snagging possibilities under the far bank, to my astonishment, off he went upstream. I pulled him back to the lip at the tail of the pool above. Sight of the net stimulated him to a second run upstream then, out of steam, he was drawn into the net.

One might imagine, the Hairy Mary having recently taken three grilse, one of which was now with me on a carrying string, that I would have continued with the pattern on my way back to the car, fishing as I went. I decided otherwise. The Hairy Mary had already been shown to any resident salmon on the way down. It had not interested those individuals, for one has to believe that fish are always present. Fish down with one fly and go back with another. On went a 1¼ in. Black Dart which must, at least, be the correct size.

In a glide, where 5 years ago a salmon straightened my hook, leaving me in despair, a 6 lb hen grilse swirled after the fly and hooked herself. If I had known then that the treble was firm inside the lower jaw, much anxiety would have been saved! Again I could not move. There were rapids above, rapids below and deep unwadable water. I was stuck. In such circumstances, one can usually kill a fish in a small pool by keeping low and, unseen, with rod held high, gradually tire out the fish. Excessive pressure encourages leaping – don't apply the full strength of the tackle. When a fish goes to the tail of the pool, slack off momentarily and in good time. When it goes up, increase the resistance. In the end a salmon exhausts itself without leaving the pool, through swimming head-down to counteract the near-vertical lift of a rod held high. I netted this grilse and walked back to the car.

Why had success come to me and not to the sea-trout champion, for his was the greater skill? Maybe, for four reasons:

1 The water started to fall after he left, dropping, according to my stick, by 3 in.

2 A cold north wind, present in the morning, ceased to blow.

3 The water must have warmed a trifle, for olives started to hatch and trout to rise.

4 Fishing down with one fly and back with another gave the second grilse a choice.

The first three reasons had nothing to do with skill. They illustrate the need to fish in a spate river during those few hours when atmospheric and other physical changes stimulate fish.

The fishing

Droppers

When fishing a river, as opposed to a salmon loch, there are risks in adding a dropper to the leader. These arise when a fish has been hooked and is being played. The salmon in a chalk stream may run through a weed bed; a rocky river may see the fish dash between or under obstructions, such as boulders, or tree roots reaching out from the bank and trailing beneath the surface. The tail fly, if the fish is on the dropper, will hang behind and may catch in these snags, pulling out the dropper in the mouth of the fish. The risk is not so great if the salmon takes the point fly; even so, there is the chance that the dropper may hook on to something, even the meshes of the net at the final moment. Troubles with a second fly are less likely to arise when fishing from a boat in open water. Even there, fish sometimes take refuge beneath the boat, where the free fly may catch on the metal rubbing strip along the bottom, or even on an oar.

The commonest fault in double-handed casting. The rod butt moves away from the body, the rod tip drifts back beyond the vertical, and the back cast drops.

The correct way of double-handed casting, with the butt close to chest.

Casting

Be taught to use a double-handed rod by a professional. Assuming that you know how to execute overhead, side, roll and Spey casts, which should you use? Circumstances order the style.

The Spey casts are used when obstructions on the bank, deep ravines in which you have to cast and other physical obstructions would prevent the extension of the line in the air to the rear if one attempted to cast overhead. They are also employed when fishing a heavy fly which might hit the angler if cast overhead, particularly when using a sinking line and large fly in early spring or late autumn. The overhead cast may be dangerous in the vagaries of a strong wind. The Spey casts are more likely to be used on a wide river, particularly when wading. They are not often necessary on a small open river where the short overhead cast is less obtrusive. Over many miles of water on my home river there are only two or three lies which necessitate a single Spey and none at all requiring the double Spey, which may only be made when wading.

The roll cast is seldom used unless it be to roll a sinking fly line to the surface at the end of its traverse across the river, or before going into a Spey or overhead movement, because the roll does not enable the angler to switch his fly across the water to the far side.

Mending the line

This is a tactic by which the speed of travel of the fly across the river may be reduced or increased, by an upstream or downstream mend.

After the initial cast is made across the main current, towards the far bank, the line is lifted and switched upstream. This removes the belly created in the centre of the line by the current and slows down the passage of the fly if the rod is then held out at right angles to the bank. Such an upstream mend slows the passage of the fly across the river. The mend should lift over the line without moving the fly; in other words the final yard of line, and the leader, are not lifted from the water surface. This manoeuvre may be used to hold the fly in the centre of a run, or on the far side, for a considerable time, or almost

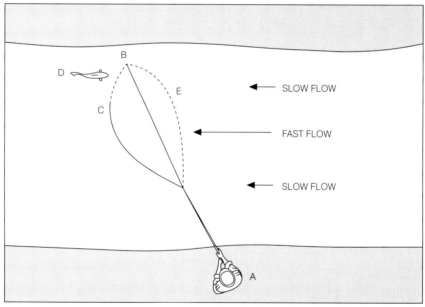

27 An upstream mend (to produce the opposite result of backing-up). If an angler at point A casts a fly to point B in order to cover lie D, then the fly will be swept past the fish at speed to point C by the fast water pushing a downstream curve into the line. If he casts to point B, and at once lifts the line over to upstream curve E, without moving the fly and leader, the fly will swim more slowly past D during the time taken for the current to straighten the line.

indefinitiely if second or third mends are made. Second and subsequent mends are only possible with a floating or sink-tip line. A sinking line, once beneath the surface, cannot be mended, but 1 or 2 yd of slack line may be thrown upstream as soon as the cast is made; the rod should then be held out over the water at right angles to the bank, in order that the line pivots from a point (the rod tip) as far out as possible. As I have written, casting and mending should be learned from a professional. All the diagrams and photographs in the world fail to teach the Spey casts. I know, from those who have tried and then come to me to learn.

Backing-up

This produces the opposite result to upstream mending. It increases the speed of passage of the fly across the river instead of slowing it down.

I was taught to back-up the fly on the river Helmsdale in June over 30 years ago. Having fished down a long pool, the gillie tied on a different fly and instructed me to back it up. Starting at the tail of the pool, the fly was cast out at right angles to my bank and straight across the river. At once, I took two or three steps upstream and stripped-in the fly. The combination of my upstream paces, stripping-in line and the belly created therein by the fast-moving current mid-river caused the fly to sweep at speed in a curve across

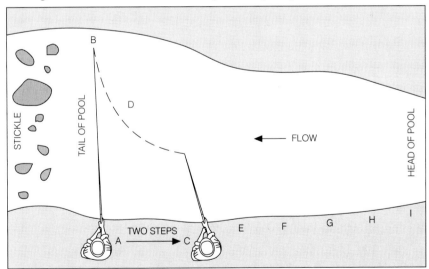

28 Backing-up the fly in a fast curve in a stream (to produce the opposite result of an upstream mend). The angler at point A casts a fly straight across the pool to point B, takes two steps to point C, and strips the fly along track D. He repeats the process at points C, E, F, G, H, I etc., until he reaches the head of the pool.

the river. Half way up the pool a salmon took the small No 6 low-water, single Hairy Mary. It seems that flies retrieved in a curve are more tempting than those moved on a straight course. This is confirmed by: the illicit use of the curving passage of a dragging mayfly on a chalk stream; the high percentage of takes to the fly by trout as the line curves before straightening behind a moving boat; the success of the still-water bank angler who casts straight out, takes three or four steps to right or left and strips-in the line in a curve. I put the system to use from time to time and, memorably, some years ago, when I rose nine salmon in a morning without hooking one. Failure was not due to the wrong size or patterm of fly, for alternatives were tried. Failure was inexplicable. Something different had to be set in motion. I backed-up the 2 miles which had been covered by conventional downstream casting. Two fish chased the fly and both finished on the bank.

On some rivers a large fly is used in this tactic, on others a small size. Experiment. Don't become hidebound. Always change a losing game, and sometimes change when winning if the physical conditions of air or water alter.

Concealment

It is most unlikely that a salmon will take a fly if the fish has first seen the angler or a waving, highly varnished rod. Read again the section on cone of vision on page 79. There, it is pointed out that anglers casting wet flies downstream are more easily seen by trout than those casting flies upstream. Almost all salmon fly fishing is accomplished by downstream casts.

Study also the diameter of the trout's window of vision in relation to the depth at which it swims. The closer a fish is to the water surface, the smaller is its window. In general, salmon rest at greater depths than trout, close to the river bed, and their windows are thus wider. An angler on the bank is more likely to have a portion of his body, and the rod, above the 10° angle from the circumference of the window than would be the case with a trout.

Fishers creep up on feeding trout, taking every care to remain unseen. Few take this trouble when salmon fishing and yet the chances of frightening fish are greater, particularly as the angler may not know the exact position of the fish. One often sees an angler who has not considered these matters standing tall on the bank, or on a boulder mid-stream, casting with an almost vertical rod. One rarely sees such a person carrying a salmon.

The risks of being seen are less when wading and casting in chest waders in a wide river. In such a situation the angler is almost certainly below the 10°

A 15 ft fly rod enables the angler to keep back out of sight.

angle, and so is much of the length of his rod. This is even more the case if casting a long line.

Stalking salmon is thus of greatest importance in small rivers; and only marginally less on those of medium size, particularly if casting from the bank. One's chance of remaining unseen may be increased in many ways, particularly if the exact lies of salmon are known and one may make a calculated approach. A long rod enables the angler to keep back from the edge of the bank; the cast may be made with the rod horizontal, the line extending 2 or 3 ft above the water surface, rather than casting with the rod in the usual vertical position; a long throw keeps the angler away from the fish.

Personal concealment is vital to success: cast from a kneeling position; wading, tucked below the bank; from behind a bush; cut your silhouette by positioning yourself in front of a tree. I often move forward almost doubled up, with creaking spine, to cast to a known lie.

I doubt that the colour of the clothes you wear makes much difference to concealment from a salmon. It is true that fish see in colour but consider for yourself the difficulty of distinguishing the colour of the feathers of a bird high in a tree. Recognition of the bird by colour is almost impossible, for it appears black when outlined against the sky. Salmon view us (if we are careless) in silhouette against the sky and thus are doubtlessly unable to distinguish the colours of our garments.

Having argued that colour camouflage makes no difference to the fish, I put forward that it is of considerable importance as an indication of attitude. The angler who wears a red coat and casts with a shining, superbly varnished, flat-surfaced hexagonal rod does not merge with a country background. The rod should be round in section and matt-varnished and the angler's clothes should be the colour of moss on the trunk of a tree.

Hooking

The techniques of hooking salmon differ between large and small rivers and also between the responses to the fly fished off floating or sinking lines. The suggested courses of action largely depend on whether the angler sees the interested fish come to the fly, an event he is unlikely to discern when using a sinking line. This is particularly so when long casts are being made in a wide river and the angler is wading deep. In almost all cases of hooking salmon, the response by the angler should be much slower and more deliberate than when fishing for trout.

Look first at the options available when an unseen salmon gives a pull to the fly fished off a sinking line. There are only three. The first is simple – pull back! This is likely to be an automatic action by both novice and sleepy fisherman. Both will be startled and respond in this way when there is a pull to the 3457th cast made that week. The chances of hooking, or failing to hook the fish are about even.

The second is to hold a loop of line, about 4 ft in length, dangling below the forefinger of the hand in front of the reel on the butt of the rod. This loop is released if a draw is felt on the sunk line. The intention is to allow the salmon time to take and turn away with the fly. The angler, then pulling from behind or to the side, will set the hook in the scissors of the salmon's jaws. This is all very well if one remains constantly alert and in a state of keen anticipation but this is not an easy state to maintain on a cold spring day when fish are known to be scarce.

The third method is the best: fish directly off the reel. Set the adjustable drag to the lightest resistance. If the reel is not adjustable, alter the drag-cams, bringing into use the cam for left-hand wind if one is winding on the right, and vice versa. In this way the angler will wind against a greater resistance than that applied to the fish. Now, cast out and let the line sweep across the river whilst the rod, held low, points directly to the fly and follows it around.

The line is not touched but leads directly to the reel. If a salmon takes, the reel will release line, allowing the fish to turn away. At the same time that line is being drawn from the reel, the angler should sweep up the rod, still without touching the line. The extra friction of this movement, and the delay, will almost certainly set the hooks.

I shall couple together the responses made when flies are fished off floating and sink-tip lines. In both cases the depth at which the fly is fishing usually brings the salmon sufficiently close to the surface for it to be seen. The method of fishing off the reel is still as good as any other style in a wide river where long casts are being made. The short cast, and the rise a rod's length off, call for a different reaction and considerable self-control. The worst reflex is to strike as the salmon rises into view. Almost certainly it will not have reached the fly, which will be pulled away. The flurry of the lifting line may also frighten the fish, which will fail to come again.

If it has just taken the fly, but has not turned away or down, the fly may be pulled out of its mouth. Watch the salmon, wait for it to disappear from sight, then raise the rod and feel for your fish. If it is on, give a firm lifting pull. Not only wait, but also drop the point of the rod as the fish goes down, to allow it an extra 1 or 2 ft of line. None of this applies to the unseen fish which aggressively snatches up the fly, almost pulling the rod from your hand. Your response should be to pull back. The best advice one can give a beginner who sees a salmon lift to his fly is to do nothing at all. Let the salmon hook itself. If it fails to touch the fly at least it has not been disturbed and may be tried again.

A variation on doing nothing is to watch the line/leader junction knot as a salmon rises. If this knot slides away beneath the surface, raise the rod. This, of course, is only possible with a bulky visible sheet bend. I don't mind a fat knot in this position if using a 9 ft leader and a rod of not less than 12 ft in length. One is fishing by day and will take care not to wind the visible knot up to the rod tip when playing and netting a salmon. An easily seen junction 9 ft from the fighting fish, is also a useful indication of the depth of the salmon when it is being played. Such a line/leader joint would not be used at night when fishing for sea trout or if salmon fishing by day with a short rod.

Dealing with the reluctant salmon

There are salmon which rise but do not take the first time; there are nibblers and pluckers; there are also suspicious fellows who rise many times but cannot be persuaded to take. I know a deep, small and secret hole into which the water swirls. It is overhung at the top by the branches of a tree and a bush on my bank stands guard at the tail. It is much loved by salmon and by me. There is no room to cast, the line being washed down by the current. If a fish is hooked it has to be played to a standstill in an area the size of two double-beds – or lost.

The place was found by chance. I was sitting on a rock beside this hole, eating a sandwich and emptying a tin of beer. A salmon's head rose above the surface. The head went down, a tail came up, then all was once more smooth. Crouching, and shuffling sideways like a crab, I took the Black Dart in my hand and threw it on the water. The salmon came up as the fly was hand-lined down, and took but did not turn. After a while the hook pulled out. Some months later a second fish was hooked – it jumped on to the bank and slid back, and that fly also came away. A season later the third fish shot up between some rocks, did a U-turn and came back on the other side of a boulder and was seen no more. I called the place 'Lost Fish Pool'.

Two seasons passed. This year I tried a choice and tempting way to right this dismal record. With a sink-tip line and the rod tip on the surface, on my knees, I let the 1 ¼ in. Hairy Mary tube wash down and left it, swaying out of sight. It was, no doubt, 1 ft below the surface. Nothing happened. I drew in 6 in. of line, then let it go, repeating this sink-and-draw for at least 2 minutes. Then there was a nibble, an unseen tasting, a circumspect investigation. I tried to strike but the rod was hard against the tree, the hooks could not be pulled home and the fish retired unseen.

Ten days later the Hairy Mary again sank from sight, was drawn up 1 ft and then allowed to wash back. The process was repeated several times. A salmon took. Forethought had allowed me 3 ft of room for a strike and the treble hook went home. It was very well behaved, this 6 lb fish, never once leaping from those double-beds.

Then there is the fish which rises into view, rolls beside the fly with open baleful eye and, suspicious, slides down out of sight. Try two more casts. If nothing happens, mark the casting place with a turn of your heel on the ground, sit down for 5 minutes, go upstream for 10 yd and fish down on it again with the same fly. Then give a smaller fly a swim. I will continue at a fish if it encourages me. If there is no response to second and third approaches, at intervals of several minutes, I continue down the river, but may return later in the day to back-up the fly at speed over the lie.

I remember one 7½ lb salmon which inspected a No 6 low-water Hairy Mary single in April. It was a sunny day, with drifting clouds and a fitful breeze. I cast solely when the cloud covered the sun and wind ruffled the water. The waiting, and those few casts, filled an hour. It came up three or four times before the fateful take. Persevere, but only if the fish continues to play a part.

One must always be alert for the faintest hesitation in the passage of the fly, just as though a drifting leaf had touched the hook. It is a rare event, but I can remember a number of instances where the touch has been a salmon. Sometimes the fish leaps after touching the fly which, after a cast or two, it usually takes.

14 Spinning tackle and artificial baits

Rods

These may be of fibreglass or carbon fibre. As spinning rods are shorter than double-handed salmon fly rods, there is little disadvantage in fibreglass imposed by the extra weight and the additional wind resistance of the larger diameter tube. The weight of an 8½ ft Hardy Fibalite (fibreglass) spinning rod is 8½ oz; an 8½ ft Hardy Favourite (carbon fibre) spinning rod is 7½ oz. The featherweight burden of carrying one extra ounce is well worth bearing, for the Fibalite is two-thirds the cost of the Favourite. Both rods cast 1¼ oz, and the Fibalite handle is 1 in. shorter, at 22 in., than the Favourite – an advantage. It is often a fault that the handles of spinning rods are too long behind the reel seat. This makes it difficult to switch the rod across the tummy from right to left and vice versa. Such a switch is necessary if casting with the right hand up the butt of the rod and a right-hand-wind reel, because the left hand has then to be moved to hold the rod so that the right hand can wind. Manufacturers seem to imagine that an angler's arms increase in length as soon as he picks up a 10 ft spinning rod. In both of the 10 ft models of the two types named above, the handle has increased to 28 in., a length that tends to get in the way of easy handling.

I use both 8½ and 10ft Hardy Fibalite spinning rods. The shorter of the two is my choice for spinning and the 10 ft rod my choice for prawn and shrimp fishing and when using a Paternoster system (page 167).

Reels

Fixed-spool reels

These may be used to cast both light and heavy baits in open and restricted circumstances. A bait may be flicked out when the angler's situation between trees prevents a full swing of the rod. This is because the bait, drawing line from a static spool, does not have to build up momentum to make a reel drum revolve.

Hardy 8½ ft Fibalite spinning rod with Elarex multiplier reel.

Mitchell 300 fixed-spool reel. Bail-arm open, ready to cast.

A further advantage is apparent if a bait hits a tree branch or other obstruction in mid-flight. A tangle does not form because the line ceases to be pulled off the static spool. This would not be the case with a revolving reel drum which would, for a moment, continue to spin, producing a bird's nest of tangled line.

Without doubt, Mitchell reels, amongst innumerable makes, are the most widely known and used. One cannot describe them all. Mitchell themselves produce 20 fixed-spool models. I am traditional in my approach and therefore rely on the Mitchell 300 reels which have served me well for many years. I still have in use the original five which I purchased in 1977 for instruction purposes; they have survived a battering! The model 300 is left-hand wind and the 301 has the handle on the right; otherwise they are identical. Both are supplied with two spools of different capacity, one for heavy monofilaments and the other for fine. The drag, against which the salmon has to pull-off line, may be adjusted by turning the knob on the front of the spool. At the rear of the reel body is an anti-reverse lever; this must be engaged when playing a fish for it prevents line being pulled freely off the spool, which will then only release line against the drag.

Other suitable models in the Mitchell series are the 2165 and the inexpensive 1160. These have a knob at the rear of the reel body for drag adjustment, a convenient thumb-operated anti-reverse slide, and are ambidextrous. It is a simple matter to change the folding handle from right- to left-hand wind and vice versa. The 2165 is supplied with two spools of different capacity for monofilaments of varied strengths.

For salmon spinning, the large-capacity spool of the 300 and 2165, and the single 1160 spool, should be loaded with about 125 yd of soft 17 or 18 lb BS monofilament. Avoid springy nylon. When filling the spool do not proceed as one would when reeling on a new fly line, allowing the spool to revolve on a

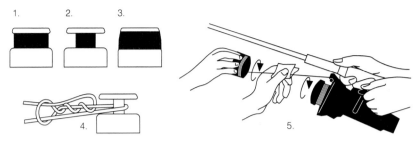

29 Fixed-spool-reel line filling.

(1) Spool correctly filled to within $\frac{1}{10}$ in. of lip.

(2) Underfilled: it will not cast far.

(3) Overfilled: it will shed coils of line.

(4) Attachment of line to spool.

(5) Winding on new line: spools face each other and the line comes *off* in the same direction as it was wound *on* to the spool.

pencil placed through the central hole; this will result in many twists because the reel spool is not winding on the nylon in the same plane as the new line spool is releasing it. Instead, place the spool of nylon on the floor, or ask someone to hold the spool with one of the flat sides facing the reel. Mount the reel on the rod and commence winding. The intention is for the line to come *off* the line spool in the same direction as it is wound *on* the reel spool. If the line spool on the floor is the wrong way up, or faced incorrectly by the assistant, this will be quickly apparent by the twisted line which appears between the two spools, and it may then be turned over.

The reel spool should be filled to within $\frac{1}{10}$ in. of the front lip. If overfilled, coils will come off when casting and tangles will result. If underfilled one cannot cast far. Before starting to fish the drag must be adjusted to that which one wishes to apply to a fish and which will release line before breakage or loss of hook hold occurs. When one is experienced this may be done by hand just by pulling line off the reel. The novice should feed line under the reel bail-arm and through the line guides and then attach the end to a fixed object. Back-off a few yards and apply pressure with the rod; the drag control may then be adjusted to release line at the desired pull.

When playing a salmon, the drag may be adjusted as required by turning the knob on the front of the spool of the 300 models or by altering the rear adjustment of the other models. If increased pressure is required only for a moment, this may be applied by the forefinger to the rim of the reel spool to slow it down as it unwinds.

Multiplying reels

It is unwise for a novice to commence salmon spinning with a multiplier, due to the over-run risks described. Personally, I do not often use them, for their use is limited to heavy spinning baits or to the Paternoster system for spinning and prawn and shrimp fishing with a heavy weight of about 1 oz. Such weights are necessary to build up momentum, start the drum revolving and draw off line. It is barely possible to use a multiplier with lightweight baits and impossible if there is insufficient room to swing the rod.

The sole advantage of the multiplier over the fixed spool lies in the playing of salmon. The thumb, placed on the revolving drum of line, which is on top of the rod handle, applies an infinitely variable brake. Having written of the disadvantages, one must concede that they are a delight to use for early spring fishing in full water, but only in open country.

There are many expensive and beautifully engineered models, particularly those by Penn and the Abu Ambassador series. For myself, I stick to a collector's reel, the Hardy Elarex, which I purchased new in the 1950s.

One may use monofilament or braided line. Milward's green 20 lb BS Sea-ranger terylene-polyester yarn is rotproof, readily visible against the water when fishing and may be purchased in 150 yd spools.

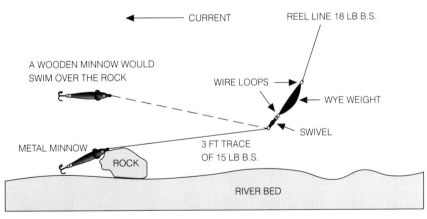

30 A spinning outfit. A wooden minnow would swim above the level of the Wye weight and thus would not catch on the rocks. Note: all knots are tucked half bloods.

Both fixed-spool and multiplier reels require daily lubrication with oil in those places indicated by the manufacturer. Most multipliers have a brake system designed to slow down the drum revolutions as the bait drops towards the end of its flight. It is necessary to set this resistance to match the weight of the bait to be cast. To do so, attach the bait, and any additional weight, to the end of the line and allow this to hang from the rod tip. Adjustment should then be made to the finger knob on the reel to allow the drum to start revolving very slowly.

Weights, traces and swivels

If the reel line is of 18 lb BS, there should be joined to the end a 3 ft trace of 15 lb BS monofilament. If the reel line is of 14 lb BS, the trace ought to be of 12 lb BS, and so on. With these combinations it is likely that the trace will break if a bait becomes snagged in the river bed or elsewhere. One must avoid breakage of the line if at all possible or long lengths of nylon will be left in the river and a new line will have to be fitted to the reel, which will now be underfilled.

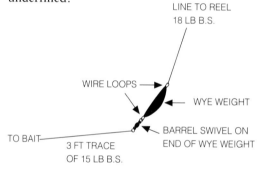

LINE TO REEL
18 LB B.S.

WIRE LOOPS

WYE WEIGHT

TO BAIT

3 FT TRACE
OF 15 LB B.S.

BARREL SWIVEL ON
END OF WYE WEIGHT

31 Making up a Wye-weight, swivel and trace, which must be tied
     to the swivel on the Wye.

If the bait is suspended by a trace longer than 3 ft, the rod point will have to be held too high in the air before commencing the cast. A throw from this position will send the bait through the air in a rising, then falling, arc, and it may drop through the branches of a tree on the far bank. Casts should be made with the bait flying out parallel to the water surface and thus underneath overhanging tree branches. Such a cast may be made if the throw is commenced from a low position with the tip of the rod 3 ft above the ground, the bait just clear of the grass and the line/leader swivel or Wye weight just outside the rod point. Trace and line should be joined by a swivel, either the barrel type or the 'BB' ball-bearing swivel. If additional weight is required, as is the case in most cold-water situations, this may be provided by a lead-free Wye weight and swivel. The Wye is banana-shaped, has a wire loop at one end and a swivel at the other. The reel line is attached to the wire loop and the trace to the swivel, both by tucked half blood knots. It is illegal to use lead weights of between 0.06 and 28.35 g.

This excludes all Wye weights of 1 oz or less (1 oz = 28 g). Lead-free Wye weights are available and should be carried at 8, 11 and 17 g.

Paternoster (ledger) system

If one wishes to fish a wooden Devon Minnow or other bait with built-in buoyancy, or a natural bait, very slowly, just clear of the river bed, the Paternoster system should be employed.

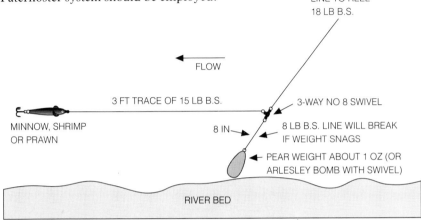

LINE TO REEL
18 LB B.S.

FLOW

3 FT TRACE OF 15 LB B.S.

3-WAY NO 8 SWIVEL

MINNOW, SHRIMP
OR PRAWN

8 IN

8 LB B.S. LINE WILL BREAK
IF WEIGHT SNAGS

PEAR WEIGHT ABOUT 1 OZ (OR
ARLESLEY BOMB WITH SWIVEL)

RIVER BED

32   Paternoster, or ledger. Used to fish bait slowly close to the river bed.

A 3-way barrel swivel, about a No 8 in size, should join the line and trace. From the eye, at right angles to the barrel, suspend about 8 in. of 8 lb BS nylon and a pear-shaped weight of between ½ and 1 oz. The heavier weight will be required to keep the outfit on the river bed in fast water. When cast out, the weight sinks to the river bed, whilst the bait sways in the current 3 ft downstream and about 1 ft above the bottom of the river. A better weight than the pear is the Arlesley Bomb, which has a swivel for attachment to the dropper nylon.

Artficial baits

As will be seen in Chapter 15, some baits are suited to downstream casting, others to upstream; yet others suit fast-flowing water, but not where sluggish currents prevent the full action of the bait unless it is retrieved at an undesirably fast speed.

Devon Minnow

This streamlined bait is suited to downstream fishing in fast-flowing water. It is readily retrieved against the current at the end of its passage across

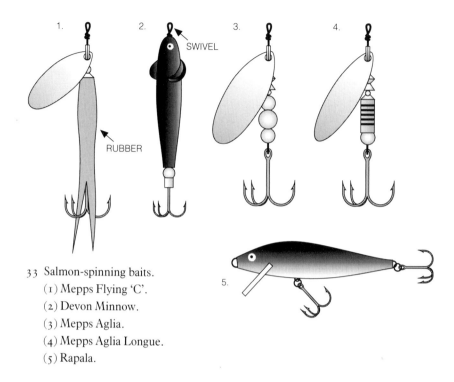

33 Salmon-spinning baits.
   (1) Mepps Flying 'C'.
   (2) Devon Minnow.
   (3) Mepps Aglia.
   (4) Mepps Aglia Longue.
   (5) Rapala.

the river. When the minnow hits the water, it swings a yard or two before
commencing to revolve and is thus not suited to a narrow stream where every
foot of width must be exploited.

I tend to fish this lure in full flows, particularly in March and April, and in
the autumn if there is plenty of water. It is rarely given a swim in summer.

The body may be of metal, plastic or wood. Wooden minnows tend to lose
their coloured paint, but are unlikely to snag on the river bed because they
swim above the weight at the line/trace junction. There is little to choose
between the actions of plastic and metal; both are durable but metal minnows
are expensive. Devons are usually produced in combinations of two colours.
I use Yellow Bellies (green and yellow) in coloured water; Blue & Silver in
clear conditions and, sometimes, Red & Black if the water is peat-stained.

When purchasing Devons, inspect the hook mount, or, as it is sometimes
called, the 'flight'. This should be of plastic-covered steel wire to prevent
rust, with a barrel swivel at the head and an eyed treble at the tail. The body
of the Devon should rest on a red, plastic tulip bead which fits over the eye of
the hook, keeping the treble in line. The ends of the wire should be crimped
within a metal sleeve. Do not purchase flights which have a spade end (no
eye) treble or wire silk-whipped to the treble; the silk may rot, or be cut by

the teeth at the edge of the jaw of a salmon. Ensure that the treble is of a large size, usually No 6 or No 4. The points of the hook should extend beyond the diameter of the minnow body.

Devons are generally available in lengths of 1–3 in. Because I tend to use them in cold full flows requiring a large bait, I carry 2 and 2½ in. sizes. If fished in summer, a 1¼ in. size is useful and, in this length, a metal Blue & Silver brought me my first spring salmon from the river Taw on 15 March 1966. The water was not high – at 1 ft 10 in. on the gauge of *The Rising Sun* at Umberleigh. The river was clear, and warm for the time of year at 47°F, with the air at 56°F – an ideal combination. The sea-liced fish weighed 9¾ lb and came from Sandpits Run.

Mepps spoon

Probably the most popular spoon bait, it is available in many shapes and sizes and colours. The No 1 is the smallest I carry and the No 4 the largest.

Only two patterns need to be carried: the Aglia and the slower-spinning, stream-lined Aglia Longue. I tend to rely on the Aglia: a No 2 for casting downstream into the wide, slow-moving tails of pools and the No 4 for casting upstream or up and across, and retrieved fast in summer. The No 4 would not be cast down in fast-moving water, being hard to wind back against the current.

Colours available are silver, gold and copper. All of these take fish, with gold probably the champion. A friend who used to fish the little river Piddle in Dorset, where there were many salmon in the 1970s, painted his Aglias matt black. He rarely lacked a fish for either the table or his friends.

Plugs

There are many sizes, types and colours. Some float, others sink; some have two trebles, others just one at the tail; some are jointed in the middle. When at school in the 1940s, I followed my flat-footed housemaster along the banks of the slow-moving river Nene in Northamptonshire. With a jointed wooden plug, he killed many pike.

The best jointed plug for salmon is probably the Rapala in 2¾ and 3½ in. lengths. The unjointed, single-body style is also suitable in the 2 in. size. Of the colours on sale, one would not go far wrong fishing the black back and silver belly in clear water and the fluorescent red back and gold belly in coloured conditions.

The plug starts to wiggle, waggle and plunge as soon as it hits the water. This is an advantage in a narrow river.

Floating and sinking bodies are on offer; use the sinking type in spring and the floating pattern if fishing the Paternoster system.

Toby

This is a great attractor as it flashes in the water. Being slim it fishes deep when cast downstream in a cold fast flow. It is also suitable for throwing upstream, followed by a rapid retrieve in summer.

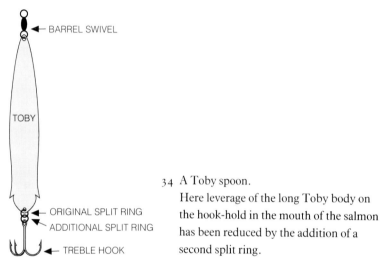

34 A Toby spoon.
Here leverage of the long Toby body on the hook-hold in the mouth of the salmon has been reduced by the addition of a second split ring.

Various lengths, weights and colours are made. If fishing without additional weight, the 1 oz is suitable for both upstream casts in summer and downstream throws in cold water. The trouble with the Toby is that the long body may lever out the hook-hold, if a purchase is obtained in the first place. To increase the chances of landing a hooked salmon, add a second split ring to the single ring joining the eye of the treble to the body.

Flying 'C'

This lure is approximately 3 ½ in. in length. It varies in weight, being marketed at 10, 15 and 25 g (28 g = 1 oz). The 15 g weight is suitable for most conditions. At the head is a small, revolving, Mepps-type spoon in silver or gold. The body is encased in a long sheath of red or brown rubber, with two tails extending just beyond the large treble hook in the tail.

It is a very successful bait in almost all conditions. The red body seems to me to be the most attractive.

15 Spinning techniques

Because there is so much more pleasure to be obtained from fly fishing, one should only spin when conditions are against success with the fly. It is a delight to fish a 'fly-only' river, for one does not have to worry that a chance is being missed by not spinning in high water.

If a river is in spate and heavily coloured, a salmon is more likely to see an obtrusive $2\frac{1}{2}$ in. Yellow Belly Devon minnow than a 2 in. tube fly. The former is a whirr of revolving metal fins and the latter a sedate lure which slides quietly through the water. When the river is cold, below $45°F$, it is easier to fish an artificial bait at the level of a salmon on the river bed than it is to reach that depth with a fly on a sinking line.

If low water has prevailed for some weeks in summer, making fly unlikely to succeed, a large artificial bait cast upstream will cause the downfall of an occasional salmon. To take advantage of these situations, the angler should cultivate two spinning techniques. The first, and most common, is casting downstream. The second is the upstream, or 'up and across', throw.

Downstream spinning

Water conditions

The method is practised at all water temperatures, but finds its main use in the cold days of early spring and late autumn. At any time in between, when there is a full-coloured spate, a downstream cast with Toby, Flying 'C' or Devon minnow may bring a fish to the net.

On some river beats there is a water-level gauge. When the river rises to a prominent mark on the gauge, spinning is permitted. Below the mark, one may only fish the fly. On the river Dovey in Wales, the head keeper of the New Dovey Fishery Association puts out yellow flags permitting spinning, and use of the worm, when the water is high and coloured. At other times the water is 'fly only'.

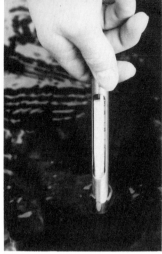

Take the water temperature in early spring.

Mark the level of the river to ascertain rise or fall.

Assume that you have arrived at the river on a March morning at 10 am. Your first action should be to note the water level and whether it is rising or falling – if there is no gauge, stick a twig into the sand of a bay at the edge of the water. When the gauge is inspected at lunch-time, a rise or fall may be apparent. A rise reduces the prospects; falls are encouraging. Salmon run on a rising water and are seldom interested in a bait of any description unless they pause for a rest above a waterfall or weir. If your stick is partially submerged by lunch-time, and you have other work to do, go home early and conserve energy for the following day when the level may have dropped. If the stick is above the tide mark, fish with energy and hope. The next action is to take the temperature of the water and study the clarity. These two conditions, considered together, will lead you to a correct choice of size and colour of Devon minnow or other artificial bait.

Note the temperature of the air. For good fishing this should be warmer than the water. If the air is at 56°F at 10 am, and the water 46°F, the water may warm to 47 or 48°F by mid-afternoon. This rise may trigger a salmon to take a lure. If the air is colder than the water, there is only a slim chance.

Preparation

Choice of bait

The colder the water, and the dirtier the flow, the larger should be the bait. Some would also suggest that the colour be brighter, myself amongst them. The examples given in the following table are a guide for a full river.

In the four examples given, the Devon or Toby are both suitable baits. If the flow is slower, due to a low level, the Mepps Aglia might take the fancy of a fish. The No 3 Aglia in gold would be fished in coloured conditions and the No 2 Aglia in silver is a likely choice in clear water.

Recommended baits for various river conditions

Water temperature °F	Water clarity	Type of Devon Minnow
42	Turbid	2½ in. Yellow Belly
42	Clear	2 in. Blue & Silver
48	Turbid	2 in. Yellow Belly
48	Clear	1½ in. Blue & Silver

These water conditions overlap and the range of variables is immense. Certain of them can be established with a reasonable degree of accuracy. Temperature is a precise measurement and may be obtained with a thermometer; speed of water flow is related to the height of the visible-level gauge; turbidity may also be ascertained without sensitive equipment. Stand in the river up to your mid-thighs. If you can see your boots that, I reckon, puts the water in the 'clear' category.

Choice of weight

In addition to a decision on size and type of bait, the correct weight must be chosen, if extra weight is required. Water temperature guides your intention: if this is below 45°F your bait should fish close to the river bed; if above that temperature, depth decisions are less important, for salmon will take at almost any level. If your intention is to fish deep, you will require much extra weight to hold down a wooden Devon but less, or none, if the body is of metal or weighted plastic. Which weight of Wye to select will depend upon the depth of the river and the rate of flow. Intimate knowledge of the river bed is almost essential to success in early spring for many reasons. To begin with, the avoidance of underwater snags will save you many spinning baits.
The correct weight for particular pools will be chosen with reference to earlier visits to those places. The Wye which suits one pool may not suit another. You have to make alterations as you fish down a beat and proceed from deep to shallow lies at the heads and tails of pools. If the weight is not changed, and is too heavy for a particular stretch, the bait will have to be fished too fast for success, or it will catch upon the river bed.

The fishing

The 'down and across' cast

In cold water the intention is to fish the bait slowly across the river close to the bed. Cast down and across, turning the reel handle as soon as the bait hits the water in order to establish contact. Now, fish; don't wind aimlessly. By that I mean that there are amongst us both 'fishers' and 'winders' – and the winders rarely catch salmon. The rate at which you recover line on to the reel spool should be as slow as possible, whilst keeping the bait off the bottom.
The winder rarely fishes his bait sufficiently deep, constant handle-turning keeping the bait high and travelling fast across the river – fatal to success in early spring.

The rod point should be kept high whilst the bait is fishing the far side in order to keep line out of the water. The point may then be dropped slightly as the bait reaches mid-river and swings to the nearside. If line is not kept out of the river when fishing the far side, the current will form a belly in the line and the bait will be swept across at considerable speed.

If extra depth is required to fish a certain lie, but you do not wish to change the weight, this may be achieved by 'back-winding'. The anti-reverse must be 'off', the cast made and the handle turned to bring over the bail arm and establish contact with the bait. If the handle is then 'back-wound' one or two turns, no more, the bait will sink about 1 ft to a lower level.

The 'down and across' cast is also made in warm water when there is a full flow after rain in summer. The speed of movement of the bait in crossing the river may be increased and it may fish at a higher level. Salmon are active when warm and will rise and chase the bait, just as happens when fishing the fly on a floating line in summer.

Casting upstream

The upstream throw and fast retrieve is more exciting than downstream cold-water spinning. The method is only practised in warm water when fish will chase the bait – often almost to one's feet. It is a heart-arresting moment when a salmon swirls as the bait covers the final few yards; sometimes it takes, but more often turns away with a sweep of the tail and the flash of a curving flank. Upstream casting is not normally used before the middle of May, by which time the water has warmed into the mid-50s. Early June was when one used to start the upstream chuck on the chalk streams, the end of the month coinciding with the arrival of the first grilse.

10 lb salmon taken on No 4 Mepp Aglia cast upstream in June.

Imagine my surprise at an event recorded in my fishing diary:

1991, April 24. 9 lb salmon. Sea lice with tails. No 4 gold U/S (upstream)
Mepps Aglia. Water ¼ up the gauge. Air 51°, water 47°.

Never say never . . .

Tackle requirements vary little from the items used in downstream spinning,
with one major exception – the bait should be large, even in low clear water.

The method works by shocking surprise. Imagine a salmon close to the river
bed, sleepily passing away the days until the next spate. Suddenly a flashing
or whirring mouthful, bent on escape, shoots by above its head. With no time
for thought, its body curves, its tail grips the water and chase is given. Sea
memories and the delightful taste of a crushed herring flicker like lightning
through its mind. One gulp will be enough – sometimes it is, more often
interest fades at the final moment.

So, knot a silver or gold No 4 Mepps Aglia, or a long, light, silver Toby to the
trace. Replace the 17 or 18 lb BS line on the fixed spool reel with one of
14 lb BS, and let the trace be 12 lb BS. No additional weight is required,
for the bait will be retrieved at speed just 1 or 2 ft below the surface.
The lightweight bait is the reason for the reduced breaking strain of the line, for
the smaller momentum will not pull out a heavy line the necessary distance.

The upstream throw should be made beyond a known lie. When the bait hits
the water, pause for 2 seconds to allow it to sink 1 or 2 ft, then reel back at a
moderately fast speed. If a salmon takes at some distance, say 15 or 20 yd, the
line will just stop. Jiggling and a short downstream movement usually follow,
leading one to assume that the fish is small, by no means always the case. As
soon as I feel a fish I make a firm strike to drive in the hooks – if a fish is to be
lost, it is better lost through this strike than after a protracted battle. More
often than not the salmon chases the bait, then turns away at the final moment

without taking. As this final swirl is usually at one's feet, it is as well to hold back from the bank, or crouch on one's knees. Unlike downstream casting, where the take is usually at sufficient distance for the angler to be out of sight of the fish, the upstream take often occurs with only a few yards between fish and fisherman. There is no doubt that anglers are sometimes seen at close range, causing the salmon to veer away. An effective throw may also be made 'up and across'. The last yards of retrieval of such a cast are in a curve, as the bait swings into the nearside. If the point of the rod is turned upstream when the bait reaches mid-river, this curve will be pronounced. We have already seen, in backing-up the fly, that curved movements are more attractive to fish than straight lines of travel.

Releasing snagged baits

If a bait catches on the river bed when cast downstream do not pull the line. Instead, open the bail-arm of the fixed-spool reel or release the check on a multiplier, let 20 yd of line run off, then close the arm or stop the drum by a

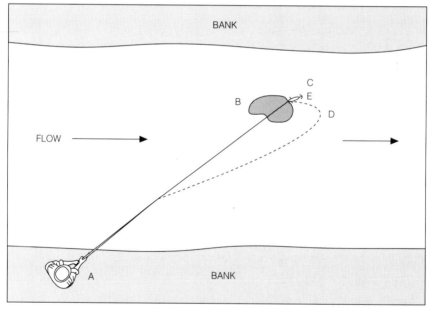

35 Releasing a snagged spinning bait. Whilst spinning across the river, the bait (C) becomes stuck to the sub-surface rock (B). The angler at point A releases the line to form a downstream belly (D). A sharp lift to the rod, whilst the line is trapped beneath the finger, may pull the bait free from behind. An 'otter' may also be allowed to slide down the line to position E. There, swaying on the surface, it may lift the bait free.

turn of the reel handle. A loop of line will have formed 10 yd below the stuck bait. A sharp lift of the rod will transmit a downstream pluck to the bait, which may be released. If the bait does not come away, move below the snag, take the line in your hand and pull from various directions. A handkerchief wound about the fingers prevents the line cutting the skin. If release seems impossible you may have to pull until the trace breaks. Provided the bait and weight are below the surface of the river, they will not fly back into your face.

If the bait is caught on the far bank, above the water surface, a dangerous situation exists. Even more worrying is for it to be caught in the branches of a tree on the river bank. Tree branches bend like bows and nylon is elastic. You have set up a giant catapult. The Wye weight is the bullet and you are the target! Proceed with care: protect your hand with a glove or handkerchief, raise the collar of your coat and pull up your thigh boots to protect the legs. Now, turn your back and walk away with head down until the nylon snaps. The weight will usually hit the ground at your feet; if it hits a rock, one end of the weight will be flattened. I have a hole in the back of my waxed jacket where a Wye went through.

An 'otter' is a device which may release baits stuck on the river bed. Find a piece of dead wood about 1 ft long and 1 in. thick. A length of string with a split ring close to one end is tied to each end of the stick. The manner of construction is illustrated below.

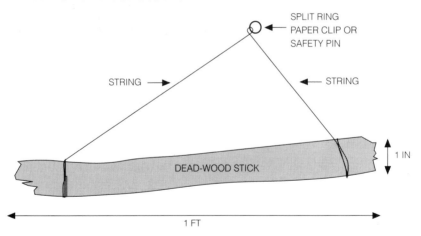

36 The 'otter'. Used to release baits stuck on the river bed.

The line outside the rod tip is passed through the split ring. From a position upstream of the stuck bait raise the rod tip and the 'otter' will slide down on to the water and swim across to the bait. There, from above, it will plunge about and may release the hooks.

16 Prawn and shrimp fishing

If you ask the age-old question, 'If salmon don't feed in fresh water, why do they take prawns and shrimps?', I have to reply that I do not know, any more than I know why they take flies and baits of metal and plastic. I suspect that the rise to take a fly or other lure is triggered by the relief of boredom, aggression, or because of a feeding memory from the months of salt-water migration. If the recollection of sustaining crunchy mouthfuls is the reason, what is more crunchy, tasty and generally true to the eye as natural than an undamaged prawn or shrimp? They are both exceptionally good baits, perhaps too good. Prawn fishing can be overdone. It is an exciting sport if the quarry can be stalked, seen from a hands-and-knees position and persuaded to take a prawn swaying in front of its nose. It may also be practised in a slovenly manner.

Two years ago, on a chalk stream, I saw a fat man, hardly to be described as an angler, in a deck-chair below a fish pass. His rod was in his lap and the line led to a wine-cork float, hanging below which was a prawn which circled the pool on the currents. Prawns scare salmon if persistently presented and, if fish are pricked, they become uncatchable. Whether the fat man was capable of fishing the fly I do not know; he was capable of making that pool unfishable by other methods and by anglers on that day and, perhaps, for days thereafter.

If prawn is allowed on a water, you can bet your boots it will be overdone. Management sometimes allows the use of the bait, because in the short term before the run is reduced by overfishing, it may increase the catch. An increased catch raises the value of the fishery which is based upon a calculation of 'so many thousands of pounds' per fish.

Even worse than the prawn is the lob worm. I have used worms and caught salmon, but am not proud of my fish-hungry years. The worm is more deadly than the prawn. In this book this is the only time I have written that overused word *deadly*. It is cruel, not merely to the worm, but to the salmon which is allowed to swallow worm and hook and, being given time before the strike, is caught in the back of the throat or even in the stomach. A gravid hen fish caught in the throat cannot be returned undamaged to the river.

Prawn fishing

Bait

It is difficult to obtain fresh prawns and shrimps straight from the sea, but they must be sought. In August, fishmongers in fishing ports and small children with prawning nets are sources, and summer is the only season when prawns may be obtained. If you wish to fish the prawn in May, they will be last season's and come from the freezer.

Purchase 2 or 3 lb, take them home and cook until just pink, but not soft. However, prawns from inland fishmongers are usually soft, overcooked, stale and smelly. They break up when fished and are undesirable. A fresh specimen is required. To net a few prawns in the sea, take them to the river, cook them on the bank and mount them on the tackle with earthy fingers would be ideal.

To be practical, purchase and cook fresh prawns. Spread them on a towel, dry them with a hair-dryer, package them in half dozens of the same size and freeze. Large prawns are for cold water, small ones for the summer. Take them to the river in a wide-mouthed Thermos flask with ice in the bottom. Those which are unused at the end of the day may be taken back to the deep freeze.

The ice could have a life-saving use. My fishing partner on the river Test, Tony Allen, swallowed a wasp which stung him in the throat. We packed his mouth full of prawn ice to stop the swelling, and he was able to drive at once to the doctor.

Mounting the bait

The necessities for prawn fishing are a No 8 Partridge x1 or x3 outpoint treble hook, a Partridge T2 pin and some fine pink-coloured wire. For a shrimp, a No 10 treble is sufficient.

T2 pins have an eye at one end and a barb at the other. To suit both prawn and shrimp they are available in four lengths: $2\frac{1}{2}$, 2, $1\frac{1}{2}$ and 1 in. Fine pink wire may be obtained by unravelling electric flex. Pink-coloured cotton elastic thread is an alternative available from some tackle shops.

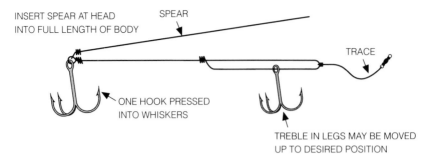

INSERT SPEAR AT HEAD
INTO FULL LENGTH OF BODY

SPEAR

TRACE

ONE HOOK PRESSED
INTO WHISKERS

TREBLE IN LEGS MAY BE MOVED
UP TO DESIRED POSITION

37 Prawn mount: the Tony Allen. When the spear has been inserted at the head and
one hook of the treble into the whiskers, the small hook hangs between the legs.
The whole is wrapped around with fine pink wire. The saw-like spear on the head
of the prawn, and the tail flaps, are broken off.

Break off the spear on the head of the prawn, for this spike may deter a
salmon from taking hold in the area where the hook is hidden in the whiskers.
Twist off the tail flaps; if left on they cause the bait to revolve and swim in an
unnatural manner. Press the T2 pin in under the tail and up through the body
to keep it straight. Thread the nylon of the trace through the eye of the pin,
knot on the treble with a tucked half blood and press one hook of the three
into the base of the head. The other two hook points should be camouflaged
by the whiskers. The nylon trace should lie under the belly between the legs
and the whole is then wrapped about with the thin pink wire. In wrapping, be
careful not to bind down the legs. Salmon are often circumspect in their
approach to the bait, appearing to sniff the prawn. This leads me to rub my
hands in earth or on the grass before setting up the bait.

Prawns may also be spun on a purchased spike with celluloid fins and a swivel
at the tail. I do not like prawn spinners; the action of a revolving prawn is
not natural.

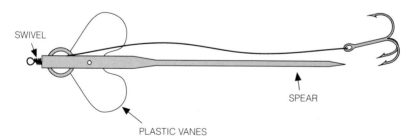

SWIVEL

SPEAR

PLASTIC VANES

38 Prawn spinning mount. The spear is inserted under the tail of the prawn and down
the interior of the body. The treble is at the head and the whole is wrapped about
with fine wire. The plastic vanes are at the tail.

Tackle

A 10 ft spinning rod, fixed-spool reel, 14 lb BS line and 12 lb BS trace are needed. The bait may be fished off a Paternoster or with a Wye weight at the line/trace junction. A short spinning rod is not suitable. A long rod enables an angler to keep the prawn in front of a visible fish close to the bank, whilst keeping low and out of sight himself. Some anglers use a long, stiff, double-handed fly rod.

Fishing the bait

One fishes either a pool, searching for a salmon, or for a visible fish. I like the Paternoster outfit, for one can feel the weight bump on the river bed and know the prawn is swimming at the level of the fish.

When covering a pool, cast out a short line, hold the rod in one hand and the line between the fingers of the other. The weight will sink and be felt to thump upon the river bed. Now, raise the rod for a moment, then drop. The weight will be lifted, swing a foot or two towards the bank and then bump down. All the time the line is 'handed', to feel a nibble or pluck. Increase the length of the cast by 1 or 2 yd until the pool is covered by a series of fan-shaped swings.

Plucks at the bait may be salmon or eels, or even escaped rainbow trout or large cannibal brown. Whether you are able to hook an interested salmon mouthing the bait out of sight depends, to an extent, on luck. It is probably advisable to allow the first tickle to take place without reacting. I usually strike quickly on the second touch or if there is a pull.

When the river is clear, fish may sometimes be seen resting on the bottom. Remain crouched whilst endeavouring to sway the prawn a few inches in

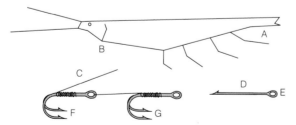

39 Shrimp mount. Wire C is whipped into the shank of hook F and inserted into the shrimp at point B. Shrimp pin D (Partridge D2) is inserted forward into the shrimp at A. The nylon trace from the rod passes through pin eye (E) and is tied to the eye of the hook (G).

Shrimp mount of two double fly hooks. The front hook is whipped to a short wire which has been thrust from the head to the tail of the shrimp. A T2 shrimp pin is inserted under the tail.

front of the nose of the fish. It is imperative that you are not seen. A few salmon take at once; others may watch the bait for several minutes before picking it up; some swim off in a scared manner, but return after 5 minutes or even half an hour. If the salmon is seen to engulf the bait, strike instantly, for a fish is able to blow out a prawn in a puff of water as quickly as you can strike. Do not allow the prawn or shrimp to wash down behind a visible fish, a prawn to the rear, out of sight and possibly up to mischief, will not be tolerated and the salmon will depart.

Shrimp fishing

The shrimp is an easily broken delicate bait which accounts for as many salmon as the prawn when fished as frequently. It should not be cooked, but used in its natural brown colour. It is easier to hook a salmon on a shrimp than on a prawn, for the whole bait is small enough to be enclosed in the mouth. I came across a novel method of mounting the shrimp in Northumberland. A T2 pin is inserted under the tail and up through the body. Two small double-fly hooks are made into a mount, one behind the other, the rear one being whipped to a short wire which is thrust into the head of the shrimp. The hooks are sufficiently close to each other for one to be under the head and the other beneath the legs of the shrimp. The trace is passed through the eye of the T2 pin and tied to the double hook closest to the tail. The shrimp is not bound with wire. The whole bait is shorter than the width of a salmon's mouth and cannot be taken without one hook coming into contact with the upper or lower jaw (see illustrations on page 181 and above).

Part 4

Sea trout fishing

17 Sea trout and fishing conditions

A sea trout is a migratory brown trout. Structurally it is identical to the brown trout and sea-trout milt will fertilize brown-trout eggs. In skin colour there is a slight difference: sea trout lack the red spots of a brown and have more black spots. In habit there is divergence: a sea trout spends one or more periods of its life at sea, whilst a brown trout lives solely in fresh water; brown trout feed in fresh water, but sea trout, after their first marine excursion, only do so intermittently, if at all. It is fortunate that sea trout, which may grow to considerable size, spawn in fresh water, where there are fewer predators than at sea, and feed in the sea, where there is more to eat than in fresh water.

The fish goes by many names: *peal* (in the south-west of England), *sewin* (in Wales), and *finnock* (small sea trout in Scotland). Gillies in Scotland refer to salmon as *fish*, and sea trout as *sea trout* (unless they are small when they are referred to as finnock); north of the border a sea trout is not called a 'fish'.

Identification of salmon and sea trout

Salmon and sea trout are sometimes killed illegally by mistake, due to incorrect identification, for their open seasons differ on many rivers. On the Camel in Cornwall you may fish for salmon until 15 December, but the sea-trout season closes on 30 September. On many rivers, salmon fishing also commences before the sea-trout season. They may be differentiated by three characteristics:

1 *The head* In salmon, with the mouth open, the back of the eye is level with the end of the maxillary. A sea-trout eye is wholly forward of the end of the maxillary. A sea-trout head appears shorter than the head of a salmon.

2 *The tail* School peal and finnock have forked tails. By the time a sea trout reaches 3–4 lb, and could be confused with a grilse, the trailing edge of the tail is square. The trailing edge of the tail of a grilse, and of two-sea-winter salmon, is concave. A very large sea trout has a convex tail.

3 *The scales* Count the scales in a line from the rear end of the adipose fin to the lateral line. A salmon has 9–12 scales, usually 11, and they are visibly larger than those of a sea trout, which has between 13 and 16, usually 14.

Head of hen salmon. The rear of the eye is in line with the end of the maxillary.

Head of large sea trout. Note the hunched head and the position of the eye, wholly forward of the maxillary.

Salmon tail. The tailer grips above the knob of gristle at the knife point. The thumb is on the lateral line, and forefinger by the adipose fin. The scales in a line from the rear of the adipose fin to the lateral line number 9–12. Note the concave end of the tail.

Tail of a large sea trout. The scales number 13–16. Note the convex end of the tail.

This 7 ¼ lb sea trout took a 1 in. Black Dart tube fly whilst
Lara Bingham was salmon fishing.

Life history of the sea trout

Sea trout cut their spawning redds in the headwaters of rivers, and sometimes
on the gravel shores of lochs, starting in November. The hen extrudes ova,
the cock milt, and the fertilized eggs are covered with gravel by the hen.
The time taken by eggs to hatch depends on the warmth of the water.
At temperatures varying between 38 and 43°F, the time ranges between 120
and 75 days, or thereabouts. The warmer the water, the shorter the
incubation. One might give an average of 3 months.

From the egg, an alevin emerges, sustained for a month by a sac of yolk
suspended beneath its chin. When the yolk has been absorbed it is known as a
fry, and starts to feed. Growth continues, the fishlet becoming known as a
parr. With the parr of salmon and brown trout, it shares the same water, food
and habits.

After 2 years, or probably 3, in spring, it migrates to sea as a silver fish about
8 in. in length and is known as a *smolt*. It does not travel the great distances
covered by salmon, but feeds near the coast. It is likely to return to the river in
July, August or September of the same year, at weights between 10 and 14 oz.
These returning shoals are known as *school peal* in the south-west of
England, and as *finnock* in Scotland. Schoolies may swim to the headwaters,
spawn and return to the sea during the winter or early spring, or they may go
back to sea without spawning.

On their return to salt water they continue feeding and usually come back to
the river in March, April, May and onwards at weights of about 2–2½ lb.
A second spawning may occur, and another return to sea.

These spawning and seaward migrations take place a number of times, but in steadily reducing numbers due to disease, accident, anglers, netting and being caught by marine and freshwater predators.

The numbers reaching weights above 4 lb form a minute proportion of the original alevins. In my life I have caught one peal of 5 ½ lb and several of 4 lb, but nothing larger. My daughter has caught one of 7 ¼ lb! This year I was able to photograph a peal of 10 ½ lb caught by a friend, a dedicated fisher who has taken 56 years to catch his peal of a life-time.

Feeding habits of sea trout in fresh water

I caught four school peal between dusk and 11 pm one night in August. They weighed between 12 and 14 oz. When cleaned the following morning I cut open their stomachs; all were empty. Last year, I opened up three schoolies; two had eaten and one was empty. Inside the feeders were nymphs, stonefly creepers, various unidentifiables, a wasp, half a bee and a beetle. Other than the occasional speck of something, the stomachs of larger peal, those above 2 lb, have been empty. Although there are rare exceptions, I consider that large peal do not feed, but small ones sometimes take advantage of an opportunity. A statement that sea trout of all ages, after their first marine visit, do not feed regularly in fresh water is supportable by examination of gut contents.

Thus, as with salmon, sea trout start to lose condition as soon as they enter the river from the sea. The flesh loses fat and firmness, being consumed for energy requirements and the development of ova and milt. A September peal, caught many miles above the estuary, makes a soft tasteless meal.

Night vision of sea trout

Sea trout may be caught by day on the fly in a loch, infrequently in daylight by spinning in a river, and mainly by chance in high water on the fly. So much for the day. The most productive and exciting river fishing is by fly at night. Many sea-trout flies used in the dark have silver bodies and a black wing, whilst some are entirely black. I am often asked how peal see a black fly at night. Of course, it is never entirely dark. In June and July the sky may be too light for good fishing. Black is the colour which creates the greatest contrast with the water *spacelight* near the surface, spacelight being the colour perception imparted to fish by light being scattered beneath the surface by water molecules and impurities.

Loch Maree for sea trout.

One of the most successful flies I fish at night is a tube, the Silver Stoat's Tail. This has a body of flat silver tinsel and two tufts of black hair for the wing. We know the reason for the success of black: contrast. There has, in addition, to be an explanation for the dominance of silver as the body colour of many sea-trout flies. I believe the answer lies in the reflection of light, from both the silver tinsel body of the fly (as from the silver flanks of little fish on which sea trout feed at sea), and the silver 'mirror' inside the eye of the fish.

The eye of a fish makes greater use of available light in low light conditions than the eye of a human being due to the presence of a mirror called the *tapetum*. This mirror is comprised of a layer of iridocyte cells, packed with crystals of silver-coloured guanine, and lies behind the retina. Light enters the eye, passes through the light-sensitive cells of the retina, hits the mirror and is passed back again to the retina. The light is thus used twice. Such a system could produce intolerable levels of light inside the eye by day, for the fish is unable to control the amount of light entering the eye through the pupil, as human beings can by the contraction of the iris. Instead, in a fish, the tapetum is blacked-out by day by a pigment which disperses at night and in conditions of low light.

Fishing conditions
Monthly catches

Very small numbers of sea trout are taken by rods in March, but the catch increases in April, with markedly greater numbers landed in May and June. In the south-west of England, peal taken in these early months are of a good size, being 2–4 lb in weight, with one or two specimens in, or above, the 6 lb class.

July sees an enormous leap in catches, due to the entry of shoals of school peal, and this continues through August. In September there is a reduction to about half the number of the preceding month. The runs in these 3 months, which bring the season to a close, are comprised of many school peal weighing under 1 lb, with smaller numbers of heavier entrants making a second or third return to the river.

The month-by-month rod catches of the 18 rivers in south-west England where peal were caught in 1991 were:

March	5	August	1114
April	54	September	590
May	361	October	20 (from the three rivers which
June	514		remained open)
July	1284		

This illustration of the timing of sea-trout entries, although for the south-west, is a guide to timing elsewhere in the British Isles. It is not sensible to take a fishing holiday on a Scottish sea-trout loch before the end of June or beginning of July.

The 3 lb 2 oz sea trout which took a 2½ in. Yellow Belly Devon Minnow on 1 April 1992. Note the sea lice above the tail.

Success on a salmon-fishing holiday, booked months in advance, depends largely on rainfall. If you arrive at a 'fly-only' river during prolonged drought, the keeper may send you off to fish for trout, salmon fishing being at a standstill. This is not the case with sea trout, which will enter and run up a river during drought – and be caught! During the 3 years from 1990–1992, we have suffered drought in early summer and yet, promptly in the first week of June, I have seen the first shoals of school peal. They are determined to conquer low-water conditions, even to the extent of flapping over shallows. This 'flapping' is beyond my comprehension. At night, standing in the river in my thigh boots, with the water above the knees, several times a season, the peal may be heard splattering through the shallows and yet there is plenty of water in the main channel.

Finding sea-trout lies

Much may be discovered by day with the aid of polarized spectacles. Go to the river in summer in low water, in the morning when the flow is clear, in sunlight and when there is little wind to ruffle the surface. You will see your quarry: grey shapes on the river bed, motionless, singly and in groups. Sometimes one becomes irritated and goes for a short cruise, setting off with the flash of a silver flank which reveals his presence.

Do not imagine that where you see them will be the only places from which they may be plucked at night. Sea trout move about in the dark, changing stations and occupying lies where they are not seen by day. In one of my pools a peal is never observed just above the tail where the water breaks into the next stickle, but it is a hot spot for a good fish at night.

My personal assessment is that sea trout like river pools to be at least 5 or 6 ft deep on the outside bend, overhung on that side by trees or bushes and shallowing-out towards the tail. By day they tend to take cover in these deep and shaded places, and may be caught there at night, but many move after dusk to the tail of the pool. If I analysed my season's catch, it would probably show that 10 per cent came from the heads of pools, 30 per cent from the middle lies, and 60 per cent from close to the run-off.

The water immediately above a weir is productive in high water for salmon and in low water for sea trout. A friend, who takes more peal than most, stands on the stonework of a weir, cast his fly upstream in the dark, and hauls the peal down.

I cannot write with enthusiasm about stickles or rough water. Some anglers say they take sea trout in hot weather in such places in the evening, the fish going there for additional oxygen. This has happened to me once or twice, but not regularly, although I have taken single peal from time to time on dry fly in rough water whilst fishing for trout by day.

18 Fly-fishing tackle and artificial flies

In Chapter 17 is recorded a 10½ lb sea trout, which is about the most testing size anyone is likely to land in their life. It was killed on a 9 ft trout rod, floating fly line and a home-made leader tapered to an 8 lb BS point. This outfit is the same as many anglers would use to fish for brown and rainbow trout in still waters.

If one has a set of equipment for river trout, still-water trout and river sea trout, and we all have tackle-collecting inclinations, slight differences should be apparent.

Rods

For some years I fished the fly at night on a 9 ft Hardy carbon Farnborough No 1, a stiffish rod which takes a No 7 or No 8 line. It was designed for distance casting on reservoirs and thus has a tip action and throws a tight loop of line. It killed many sea trout, but peal have soft mouths and I believe I lost a few, due to the hook being pulled through the soft flesh. When playing peal in the dark, particularly when they jumped, the lack of a more gentle response to accommodate the stress caused some worry.

This year the Farnborough was kept going on the still waters, but replaced at night by a 9½ ft Normark Gold Medallion, rated for a No 7 or No 8 line. Although of the same rating as the Farnborough, it has a more gentle action, bending through to the butt when playing a fish. The minimum sensible length of rod for night fly fishing is 9 ft, the ideal length between 9½ and 10 ft, and the maximum about 10½ ft. It should be remembered that the majority of sea trout are ¾–3 lb in weight. To fish in summer, when many school peal are in the catch, with a rod of 10½ ft, calls for a greater than necessary effort.

Bruce & Walker 10½ ft, single-handed, tubular-carbon Salmon & Sea-Trout rod with matt finish. The butt extension behind the Hardy St John reel may be removed.

Fly lines

One rarely casts a long way at night, and no great length of line is false cast outside the rod tip. It will be recalled from Parts 1 and 2 that, to balance a rod rated at AFTM No 7/8, a No 7 line would be used for long casting where a greater length of line than the average 30 ft is false cast outside the rod tip. A No 8 line balances that rod better if less than 30 ft of line is false cast. Sea-trout fishing at night is usually a close-range sport, peal rarely being sought beyond a distance of 15 yd. Thus, if a rod is rated at No 6/7, use the No 7 or, if rated at No 7/8, fish with the No 8.

The profile should be double taper and the colour white, cream, ice blue or yellow. A light-coloured floating line shows up on dark water and points to the position of the fly as it swims across the pool and to the whereabouts of a sea trout which has been hooked.

A white line flashes in the sky by day, but this does not scare fish in the dark. No doubt they can see a white line as it floats on the water; so also would they see a dark line against the sky. But an angler cannot see a dark line and thus cannot readily locate the fly or the position of a hooked peal.

I usually use a floating line. To some extent this is due to the trouble of changing the line at night or taking two rods. There are two or three places on my beat where peal lie deep enough for a Wet Cel 2 to be used without the fly catching on the river bed. I rarely find the time to fish them. As indicated, 60 per cent of my catches are in the tails of pools and there the fly would catch on the river-bed rocks with a sinking-line, and sometimes does so with a floater. Fishing at night is more tiring than by day. Three hours is enough – just enough to cover the best places.

Another reason for concentrating on the floater or sometimes a sink-tip line is that, by inclination, my peal fishing takes place from June until early September. In those weeks the water is warm and sea trout will lift to take a fly. Do not imagine, when all goes quiet in the small hours, that peal may then only be caught on the sinking line. That is not so. Fish may cease jumping, there may be no plucks or pulls for half an hour, but, at 2 am, a 3 lb peal may come to the fly fished just beneath the surface.

Further down the river, in the deep tidal pool where night fishing starts in the cold waters of April, sinking lines are used with success.

Reels

The reel should be at least 3⅝ in. in diameter, and with sufficient backing beneath the line to ensure the drum is full. An exposed spool rim is advisable for sensitive braking by finger pressure. The check may be of the noise-clicking or silent variety. If fishing on a single bank beat, the click will warn someone approaching on the far bank that the pool is being fished. He may then, if considerate, go elsewhere. I like a silent reel. Silence, finely tuned hearing, touch and the development of sensitive vision in the dark enable us to be aware of the night-life of the river.

Leaders

A salmon fly is usually cast downstream or down and across the river. As the current at once straightens out both line and nylon, a tapered leader is not a necessity. Sea-trout fishing in a river is by casting upstream, up and across, down, and down and across. One casts in all directions, and with or against the wind. A tapered leader with a thick butt ensures good turn-over, and the extension of the fly.

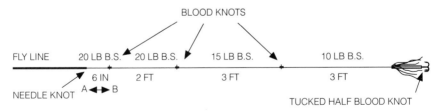

40 Home-made leader for night sea-trout fishing. Section A–B is permanently inserted into the fly line by a needle knot. The leader is replaced by cutting at point B. If the fly line terminates in a braided loop connector, a blood-bight loop would be tied in the end of the leader at point B.

My leaders are home-made in three sections:

Butt 2 ft of 20 lb BS Aqua monofilament.
Middle 3 ft of 15 lb BS Maxima Chameleon.
Point 3 ft of 10 lb BS Maxima Chameleon.

The short butt is joined by a blood knot to 6 in. of the same 20 lb BS Aqua nylon, needle-knotted into the end of the fly line. Aqua is cheap and thicker than most nylons for the rated strength and makes a good extension to the fly line. The whole leader is 8½ ft in length, slightly less than the length of the rod. If one uses a long leader to make short casts there may be insufficient weight of line outside the rod tip to balance the rod.

The line/leader joint must be by needle knot unless a braided loop connector is used. If this is the case, the butt of the leader would be 2½ ft in length, terminating in a blood-bight loop. The reason for these arrangements is to enable the line/leader joint to be wound through the top ring of the rod when netting a fish. This is essential at night, particularly if wading, for the distance between the rod tip and the peal on the surface of the water is short.

Flies

In wet-fly trout fishing, and salmon on the fly, I have suggested that a large fly be used in cold, turbid or spate conditions. A small fly is better when the water is warm, clear and low. The same applies to sea trout at night.

It is reasonable to assume that sea trout are sensitive to vibrations created by lures moving at a different speed than the flowing water. The heavier the flow of water, the greater the size of fly required to create a noticeable vibration. It may be that, in turbid, fast-flowing conditions, a peal first becomes aware of a fly by the disturbance it causes in the water. Then, moving closer to investigate, it sees the lure. Based on this supposition I use relatively fat tube flies with a No 10 treble hook if there is plenty of water and smaller thinner flies, sometimes single hooked, in clear, low-water conditions. None of these night flies are small, if by small one means the No 10 and No 12 singles used for daylight loch fishing. These traditionals have been used without much success.

Patterns of wet fly

There are five wet-fly patterns in my night-time box. They inspire me with confidence if fished in appropriate conditions. Each is a child of my fingers.

Alexandra tube

It is not productive to fish at night for sea trout in a full spate; this, my largest fly, is used as a spate falls away. The Alex tube is fat, sets up a slight disturbance, and the peacock herl wing, 2 in. in length, reaches beyond the treble hook.

Tube 1 in. Veniard Type B Slipstream, socketed

Hook No 12 Partridge CS8 black outpoint treble is designed for sea trout. It has a large eye to aid knot tying in the dark and the long shank of 9/16 in. extends well beyond the tube to catch the 'tail nippers'.

Tag Scarlet floss.

Body Flat silver tinsel.

Head Black varnish.

Wing Peacock herl.

Silk Black Naples.

Silver Stoat's Tail tube

For use in lower water than the Alexandra, it has brought me notable success by moonlight. The colours are entirely black and silver.

Tube 1 in. Veniard Type B Slipstream, socketed.

Hook No 12 Partridge CS8.

Body Flat silver tinsel.

Head Black varnish.

Wing Two tufts of stoat's tail, one on each side, to reach at least to the end of the tube.

Silk Black Naples.

Teal & Silver

A good fly for low clear water on light nights. There is no need to add the blue throat hackle of the Teal & Silver Blue.

Hook Partridge Code 01 Single Wilson No 8.

Body Flat silver tinsel.

Rib Fine oval silver wire.

Wing Teal flank feathers.

Silk Black Naples.

Black Lure

A fly for dark nights and low clear water. Single-hooked flies are more
suitable for beginners than those with treble hooks – there are fewer tangles!

Hook Partridge Code 01 Single Wilson No 8.

Body Black floss.

Rib No 14 oval silver tinsel.

Throat Black cock hackle.

Wing Two black cock hackles.

Silk Black Naples.

Night Prowler

When fishing in the dark, act as stealthily as a thief stealing fish from the
river. The Night Prowler fills the swag bag on my belt. The fly defeats the
pluckers and nippers whose activity peaks on nights when rain is imminent.
A foray will be described in Chapter 19.

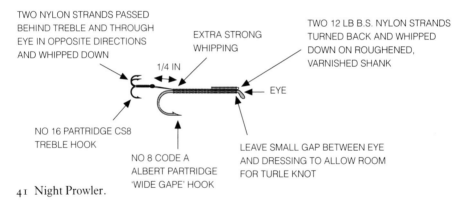

41 Night Prowler.

The prime feature of this fly is the No 16 Partridge cs8, black flying treble.
This is whipped to nylon behind the short shank, Code A, No 8 Albert
Partridge 'Wide Gape', down-eye single hook. The combination must be
made up before the fly can be dressed.

Place the single hook in the vice and roughen the shank with sandpaper.
Varnish the shank.

Take the treble, pass 12 lb BS nylon through the eye and around the back of
the treble, then pass it back through the eye in the opposite direction.
Whip the two nylon strands on to the treble shank. Offer the treble up to the
single hook, with the treble eye level with the bend of the single.

Whip the two strands of nylon down along the length of the single hook, starting opposite the hook point and finishing just behind the eye. Turn the two nylon strands to the rear and whip down over the first whipping to half the length of the shank. Cut off the nylon ends. A flexible gap of ¼ in. should be allowed between the eye of the treble and the rear of the whipping on the shank of the single hook.

Body Flat silver tinsel on single shank, red paint on the shank of the treble.

Cheeks Two short jungle cock feathers.

Head Black varnish.

Wing Six strands of peacock herl to extend just beyond the treble.

Silk Black Naples.

Jungle cock may be purchased legally from Fisherman's Feathers, who obtain them from home-bred birds.

I rarely fish the dragging dry fly at night for sea trout, but the method and flies will be discussed in Chapter 19.

Other equipment

Torches

I am not at all convinced that an occasional shaft of light disturbs sea trout. A friend takes peal close to a main road from which car headlights flash on to the water, but the risk of flashing torches is not worth taking.

Two torches accompany me whilst wading, enabling flies to be changed without the disturbance of leaving the river. The smallest takes two LR6 batteries and is pencil-shaped, with a flexible swan neck and a clip the size and shape of half a clothes peg. This is attached to a breast-high loop on my waistcoat or to the neck of my sweater. This small, close light enables flies to be changed without unclipping the torch.

The second torch is larger, takes two R20S/HP2P batteries, is ex-WD and carries the Code DT-198/S. The head of this lamp is at right angles to the body, which has a clip for attachment to my belt. In the base are various coloured filters, originally, I suppose, for signalling, of which I fit the red. This light enables me to knock sea trout on the head, remove the hook and place them in my belt bag. Before using either of these lights, turn your back on the lie being flashed.

A third torch is flat and takes a single 1289 battery. It is used to light the way along the river and, held between the teeth, enables tackle repairs and alterations to be made on the bank.

Left: Night equipment (clockwise from the top): 2½ lb peal, Jungle Formula midge repellent, whisky decanter, scissors on string, Hardy Marquis reel, priest on cord, glass of Scotch, red-filter ex-WD torch; fly box in centre.

Right: Changing the fly in the light of a swan-necked torch.

Miscellaneous

You must apply midge cream or be driven from the river on warm muggy nights – and those are the best for fishing! Don't forget your Orvis 'Hang-All Belt Loop' for net and fish-bag suspension.

Take a white, plastic shopping bag, easily located in the dark, to hold sea trout on the bank; if left lying uncovered on the grass they will be attacked by slugs. A 35 mm film-spool holder with a damp cloth impregnated with sink mix should be in your pocket, together with spare leaders and a spool of 10 lb BS nylon to replace leader points.

A priest secured by a cord around my neck is thrust into my right trouser pocket. Scissors are also held in this manner, to hang at waistcoat level.

A game bag is useful to contain a flask of coffee, spare sweater, coat in case it rains and a bin bag to keep all dry. In my car there is permanently a zip-bag of spare clothes in case I sit down in the river. As to clothes, it is comfortable to fish in sweater and waistcoat, but make sure these are of a dull colour. If you intend to fish the downstream, dragging dry fly, include a bottle of Supafloat and a tin of solid Mucilin. The flies for this method of fishing will be discussed in Chapter 19.

19 Fly fishing at night

Preparation – daylight survey

Even if you know your water intimately a daylight reconnaissance is
worthwhile to establish the presence and whereabouts of sea trout. If one is a
stranger to the water it is essential, not only to note the presence of fish but for
your safety. It is foolish to wade in the dark without either a staff or detailed
knowledge of the river bed. One or the other. Even if you take a staff, you
ought to survey the beat in daylight. On my own river I do not use a staff
because I know the exact position of holes and ledges. Even so, the handle of
a folding net can be used as a depth probe (see photograph on page 200).
The length of the handle is such that, with my hand at the hinge, the river is
about to lap over the top of my thigh boots if the water touches my fingers.
Move slowly at night. Shuffle your boots along the bottom, feeling with your
feet. Not only is this safer than taking long steps, it creates less disturbance,
by gently displacing water rather than thrusting it aside.

Barbed wire fences will tear thigh boots in the dark. Cover the wire with fertilizer bags.

Clearing branches to allow room for the back cast when wading the river in the dark.

Probing ahead for depth with a net shaft. If the fingers touch the water, the river will flow over the tops of the waders.

Take a fly rod with you on this daylight inspection. Select three or four places from which to fish, wade to them if necessary, and cast. Now is the time to establish whether there is room behind for the back cast, whether the fly will reach a particular lie, and how line and fly are treated by the current as they are swept across the pool. Cast whilst you can see.

I am often asked how to establish in the dark whether the fly is going to hit the far bank in a small river. The weight of line false cast outside the rod tip tells me – that is the result of experience. If the river is strange, go by day, stand at the place from which you will cast and establish the length of line required. This may be done by counting the number of arm's-length pulls from the reel which are needed to withdraw the necessary length of line. Twelve pulls will extend about 15 yd to land the fly beside that rock – and so on. If it is safe to withdraw 12 pulls, you would not commence by casting that distance because nearby sea trout would not see the fly, but be covered solely by the line. It is a length which you would gradually extend.

Whilst in the river, check the manner of your casting. Disruption is caused by leader tangles. Avoid them. Cast with an aerial ellipse in the flight of the line. In other words, separate forward and back casts in order that the fly, in passing overhead, does not touch the line or catch on the line/leader junction. When casting, take the back cast away to right or left and bring the forward movement straight over your head. Sooner or later you will develop the ability to take the back cast away to the right and left of your body in order to avoid obstructions to the rear on left or right.

By day, develop techniques which establish that the fly is not tangled and that there are no wind knots in the leader. The first system is the 'plop'. In one direction or another, at night, there is always a shaft or patch of light on the water. Cast to this; if the fly creates a visible 'plop' as it hits the water at the end of the leader, you know it has not caught on fly line or leader.

Check for wind knots every 15 minutes and ensure that the nylon is not caught in the treble hook behind a tube fly. Do not attempt to do this by lifting the point of the rod to dangle the fly at face level or the line and leader will wrap themselves around the rod. Instead, lower the rod to a horizontal position at right angles to the current. Draw in line until you can see that just 1 ft is extended outside the rod tip; you will be able to pick out the white line against the black water. Now, with one hand, grip the rod half way along its length, run the other hand out to the tip and down the line and leader to the fly. Your fingers, feeling along the leader, will recognize the section junction knots and arrive at the fly, checking that all is well. If there are wind knots, replace leader or point. After making repairs, wipe the nylon again with sink mix. The daylight survey with polarized spectacles, after mid-May when the river has usually fallen in level and cleared, reveals fish. In May and early June one sees either single large peal or one or two together. In July shoals of schoolies may be seen; go that night for they may depart up-river tomorrow.

Fishing Conditions

Weather and the moon

There are always peal in my beat in July and August. As one cannot fish every night, only the most propitious are chosen.

The night should be warm. Warmth is retained by cloud. A cloudy night is best. If there are no clouds, a southerly breeze from the Continent, or warm westerly off the Atlantic, will ensure that the air is warmer than the water. A cold, dry north-easter is undesirable. When standing in the river, fishless in the dark, with cold hands, dip your fingers in the water. If the water seems as warm as milk squeezed straight from the cow, in contrast to your frosted fingers, you might as well go home. The air must remain warm for good results.

I am not greatly concerned by the presence or absence of the moon, only by its position. Fish with the moon in your face; you may be dazzled but you will not be silhouetted. My fishing is mainly from the west bank.

A full moon rises in the east, facing me, swings across the sky and dips into the west. If the moon has tracked across a starlit sky and, in the small hours, is settling to your rear, consider your position. Now is the time to cut your silhouette by wading below a bank, kneeling, or keeping trees or bushes to the rear.

An ideal night is when there is a full moon behind clouds, a warm drizzle and no wind. Dispersed light from the clouds illuminates the river, midges abound and fresh sea trout have arrived on a high spring tide. The closer your water to the sea, the more the tide should be taken into account. At full and new moons the tides are at their highest and peal come in with the flood to continue up the river. We are 4 miles above the sea; if a spate coincides with a full moon, peal sometimes carry sea lice as far as our section of the river.

Fishing

Arrival at the river

Walk to the water at least half an hour before the night arrives. Pull on thigh boots, chest waders or gum boots, as required. Protect head, neck, hands and wrists with midge cream. Set up rod, reel and leader. Choose a fly according to the prevailing conditions and knot it to the leader point. If the fly is single-hooked, and this includes the Night Prowler, use a two-turn Turle knot; if a tube fly, the treble is attached with a tucked half blood. Rub down the leader with sink mix and place it in the river to soak, with the rod balanced on the bank or a rock. If this attention is given to the nylon it will sink below the surface of the water at your first cast. If the leader is not de-greased and soaked, you may fish for the first 15 minutes with the leader, and the section junction knots, creating V-wakes on the water. Those early casts on a virgin pool must be given every chance.

Now, sit beside the water, to watch and wait for the light to go. Sea trout leap as the night arrives; straight up they go – glistening shafts of wet silver. Some anglers say they start to fish when the colours of wild flowers can no longer be distinguished. The Irish wait to see three bats. Not being Irish I cannot distinguish one bat from another, and fear the third may be the first come by a second time. Anyway, I wait until the far bank cannot be seen in detail and the desire to start can no longer be contained. Then, retrieving the rod, hooking fish bag and net to the belt loop, I steal, shadow-like, into the water.

Touch, pluck, pull and take

Start by casting a short line downstream, then slightly across and down, then across. In this way the fly covers the water before the line. If your first cast is made straight out at right angles to the bank, it will be swept down by the current and the line will cover and scare peal between you and the fly. Whilst the lure is swept around by the current, keep the rod point within 1 or 2 in. of the water and in line with the position of the fly. The line should be under the forefinger of the hand on the rod butt. You are in direct contact with the fly. Any touch or pull will be felt. You are sensitive to the slightest interest, even the touches of bats. That bats flick at a floating fly line there is no doubt; the movement on the water surface attracts them. These tiny messages are exciting until you are able to distinguish them from the tweaks of investigating fish.

Now there is a pluck, the briefest of connections. Cast again to the same place. Let the fly swing over the same patch. Nothing. Then a second touch. Just a touch – no more. These are indications of one, two or a group of peal. Continue casting to the same place. Don't move or extend the line. If there are no more communications after 10 minutes of further effort, increase the length of the cast, or take two or three steps down river. Suddenly the rod bends to a delicate pull; you are into a peal which splashes as the hook takes hold. These fish almost always splash and thrash at that exhilarating moment. Raise the rod at once to form a shock-absorbing spring, strip in line over the forefinger and then recover it on to the reel.

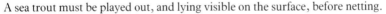

A sea trout must be played out, and lying visible on the surface, before netting.

Do not leave yards of slack line floating downstream on the water; it is a hazard as you play the fish and when the time arrives for netting.

Sea trout usually thrash and sometimes jump as soon as they are hooked. This may be followed by an upstream run which takes them above your position. That is good, for they have to fight current and rod pressure. If 15 yds or more of line are stripped from the reel on this run and the fish then turns about and comes downstream, you must wind fast to keep in touch. Don't let the line go slack. When a sea trout leaps, after the first startling splash-about, I drop the rod point whilst it is in the air. As pointed out in Part 2, whether to drop and slacken momentarily or keep the line taut is the subject of controversy. I drop, then come up tight as soon as the fish hits the water.

In time, the fish settles down in your vicinity. Now is the moment to unclip the net, flick it up to extend and lock the ring in the open position, and tuck it under your left upper arm. Your hands are still free. As soon as the fish turns on its side, net it. You can always see fish, on their sides. However dark the night, you will see a faint blur of lightness and, on a moonlit night, there shines a bar of silver.

When the fish is in the net, tuck the butt of the rod down inside one of your thigh boots. Now withdraw the priest from the trouser pocket and hit the fish on the back of the head whilst it is still in the net. Return the priest to the pocket.

If the peal has been taken on a single-hooked fly you will probably be able to free the hook and drop the fish into the bag at your waist.

Four school peal. The net and Heineken fish bag which the author suspends from his belt whilst wading.

If a treble is involved, or the Night Prowler, a hook will probably be caught in the meshes of the net. The peal is safe because you have thumped it on the head. Now is the time to use the red-filter torch, but first turn your back on the areas where peal lie. Hooks can usually be released without going to the bank. If a new fly has to be fitted, this may be knotted to the leader in the light of the swan-necked torch.

The Night Prowler is superb at catching both fish and net meshes. At one time I gave up using the fly due to the trouble with nets. This season I started again, netting large fish and picking the small ones out by hand or by stranding them on a sandy beach. It is not difficult to secure a peal with the hand, even at night, but the fish must be played out and still upon the water. Grip by the thumb and first two fingers, from above, just behind the gills. You have to be careful with the priest or you will thump your own knuckles.

Having cast down, down and across, and straight across, cast upstream. Search the area above your stand, retrieving line faster than it is washed back by the water. Many are the fish I have hooked on upstream throws, and the take is hard and fast. But upstream lacks the delicacy of downstream, in which every physical sense is concentrated on the fly.

Sea trout are mysterious creatures. Sometimes they are suicidal in their desire to take the fly. Go again the following night and nothing will persuade them, even though they leap and splash in the usual fruitful places. Before rain their plucks and pulls are infuriating. How can they avoid the treble hook whilst

To unhook sea trout, one sometimes has to wade to the bank.

Washing-out a sea trout prior to wrapping in polythene and freezing.

momentarily bending the rod? I don't know, but I do know that the Night Prowler has brought many a mocking leaper and plucker to the net.

Recently, in one pool, I had two pulls to the Alex tube, two splashes and a straight rod. Disheartened I moved upstream and caught a bat on the back cast. The bat sank to earth like a windless kite on a slack string. Released and thrown into the air, it disappeared. If one method fails, try another. On went the Prowler and out came a 2½ lb peal. Back to the first pool to relieve the other two fish of freedom.

Then there are the nights when nothing stirs. You cast for half an hour from the same position, searching the water to left, right and all about without encouragement. Don't give up. In some respects, the moods of peal resemble the feeding periods of trout. On a reservoir you will notice intervals when nothing stirs, then fish are taken to right and left and over the other side. Excitement activates the scene for half an hour, then the rise fades and the surface settles. Similarly on the night river; peal have their active hours, usually as soon as the light has gone, but sometimes later. Keep fishing, for in the darkest hours the heaviest denizens move.

The dragging dry fly

On the chalk streams, in the trout waters of Halford and Skues, the downstream dragger is cast from the fellowship of dry-fly men. Why? Because, I suggest, the method works too well. The damp mayfly, half submerged, but dry enough to count as dry, and washed down to create a wake beneath the bridge, is not the way of things. You would be blackballed, or, if already one of the elect, ejected from the company. We all have our moments of weakening resolve – give them full rein at night.

The downstream-dragging, wake-creating, bumbly surface lure takes fish. Select a fat dry fly, a greased Muddler or a deer-hair sedge or mayfly. Immerse in Supafloat, dry then add a smear of solid Mucilin and knot to the 10 lb BS point of the sea-trout leader. Grease the butt and centre sections of the leader, but not the 3 yd point. Choose a stand where the water is compressed to flow at a good speed to your front. Cast out and let the current sweep the lure across the surface of the river, creating a V-wake as it swings to hang downstream. Excitement is in the air. Try the method. Skill will be achieved and another string added to your bow, but the results will be patchy. The sub-surface lure is a more reliable way.

20 Fishing by day

It is a long way from Devon and the south of England to the sea-trout lochs of Scotland, yet the journey is worthwhile. Provided that there is a breeze or stiff wind ruffling the water, sea trout can be caught by day from a boat. You may rely upon it if they are there.

You would be ill-advised to make such a journey, or even drive 20 miles, to fish a river for sea trout in daylight unless there is high water. Even in spate conditions the game is rarely worthwhile. So, river at night, loch by day.

I would accept the chance to fish a Scottish loch for sea trout in July or August with alacrity; and a major Scottish salmon river with the mental reservation that the results could be superb or dismal; however, I would not fish a West Coast, salmon spate river at all if I had to drive 500 miles, because the chance of arriving at the right moment is slim. Staying at home, the local spate river may be fished for salmon when the water is right.

Realistically, daytime sea-trout fishing is seldom worthwhile in high water, except for a few short hours which may be separated by several weeks; it is even less so in low water, unless fishing worm or maggot. Deliberately, these live baits have been omitted from this book, in order to conserve fish. Worm has been banned from the river Test and maggot from Testwood pool; these baits kill too many fish.

Wet-fly fishing in coloured water

It is educational to climb a tree above a smooth pool holding a shoal of peal. Ask a friend to cast a dry fly on a 5x leader to the hindmost of the shoal, with the line outside its window of vision. Nothing startling will happen, but the shoal will fade away. 5x is the finest nylon I use for trout, except for small brown on moorland streams, yet it frightens peal. Dry fly on a smooth pool by day is largely a waste of time.

Let the situation change, rain fall in the hills, the river level rise and prospects improve. Not much, but there is a chance, and you never know the size of sea trout which may come your way.

Go to the river with the same equipment that is put to use at night. Station yourself at the tail of the pool where the water shallows to a depth of about 4 ft. Be sure the flow is not so coloured that you cannot see the river bed at that depth. The right moment for this fishing can be short-lived. It is unlikely to be a full day; a morning or afternoon is possible; 2 hours more likely. The vital ingredient is the colour of the water rather than volume. Once the whisky shade fades to gin, the time has passed.

Start to cast the No 8 Black Lure upstream and across, stripping in line over the forefinger. Peal may chase and take this lure with verve. There is not the delicacy of the night stalk – senses tingling, fingers feeling the line – instead, the movement of fish may be seen. Now try 'down and across' into the fastest shallow places just above the line where the water breaks into the next stickle.

By day, in high water, I do not have as much faith as at night in the lie just above the run-off; it seems that peal have to work too hard to stay there. Instead, they move forward to lie 1 or 2 yd upstream, where the river is deeper. That is why your main effort should be directed into the upstream cast. The very tail of the pool, just above the lip, is the low-water hot spot at night.

Few anglers pay attention to sea-trout fishing in the conditions just described. Instead they go for salmon. A falling summer river with a tinge of colour is an invitation to have a go at grilse. Sea trout, too, are taken on a salmon fly. Just by chance and good luck; rarely by intention. For reasons I do not understand, peal which take a salmon fly are usually large. It cannot be because the fly is larger; often it is not, for peal flies may be longer than small salmon patterns. Size of fly has little to do with size of fish. Yet, my daughter has had a peal of 7 lb and a friend one of 8 ½ lb; others of 4 lb have come my way. I have not taken many of small weight except for one of about 1 lb. I shall not forget that fish of long ago. It was in my low-water Hairy Mary years, the 1950s, the bachelor seasons. It took a No 6 and was placed in my riverside tent for supper. I went away and continued after salmon, but the peal was gone by suppertime. Perhaps the culprit was a mink; I have known one drag a salmon 10 yd to hide it in the bracken.

Dry-fly fishing in the stickles

Two weeks ago I asked a skilled game-fisher, doyen of the salmon and peal men, whether he caught sea trout by day with dry trout flies on the river. 'Yes', he replied with enthusiasm. He is always in good heart, ready to go,

and his rods have little rest. 'How many in the last two seasons?' Still smiling
at the recollection of those startling moments when the Blue Upright enticed
sea trout instead of 6 in. brown, he offered, 'Two or three'. That is the size of
it: daytime upstream dry fly on broken water will take an occasional fish.
That his victims weighed over 2 lb each does not suggest a reliable pursuit.
Such catches are a bonus; startling memorable events.

Spinning

There is little reward for spinning for sea trout in low water. Even the
upstream cast and fast retrive, using a small Mepp Aglia, will only achieve an
occasional peal. That it is exciting in summer is true. Shoals of schoolies may
be seen and cast to by the overshooting upstream throw. They chase and follow
the bait, but rarely take. At the final moment, as the lure approaches the
bank, even if you are out of sight upon your knees, they turn and swim away.

In high water it is different. The results may be startling in summer for
quantity, and notable for quality in spring. Our first sea trout in the 1992
season was caught on 1 April, 4 miles above the tide. It weighed 3 lb 2 oz and
had sea lice near the tail. We were not fishing for peal. I was teaching Bob to
spin for salmon in high water with a 2½ in. Yellow Belly Devon Minnow,
and he caught this fish. His peal took the largest most visible Devon minnow
we use, but that is the way in spring. Large sea trout take such baits in March
and April. My diary notes that the air temperature was 50°F, the water 45°F,
and the river level two-thirds up the gauge. Conditions were just right.

It is not unusual, at that time of year, to take hefty sea trout whilst spinning
for salmon – but note the by-laws. The sea-trout season may start days or
weeks after salmon fishing. Make sure you can distinguish between an 8 lb
sea trout and a salmon of the same size. To keep such a superb fish is
tempting; you could plead ignorance – and be suspect for evermore.

I do not spin specifically for sea trout in high water in summer, but take them
when after salmon. Some years ago a drought held up the salmon run for
over 4 months. When the rains came in the first week of September, salmon
and sea trout rushed upstream to jump the weirs at the rate of one every 2
minutes. With normal salmon spinning gear, the 8½ ft rod and Mitchell 300
fixed spool reel, we went to the river. Chucking a No 4 gold Mepp Aglia
upstream we took one salmon and four peal, to a total weight of nearly 18 lb.

In coloured, warm, summer water, not necessarily high, peal will take
artificial baits thrown upstream. The up-and-across cast is also good with a
large bait but, if you throw downriver, a small spoon in more attractive.

To sum up: I do not go to the river with the sole purpose of spinning for sea trout, but take them when after salmon; little is taken in low clear water; the catch may be good if there is colour in the flow, even at low levels.

Boat fishing

Boats and boatmen

A wooden clinker-built boat with an outboard motor and oars on thole pins is better than a light fibreglass one with rowlocks. Oars slide through rowlocks, which may themselves fall into the water. If rowlocks are fitted, tie them to the boat and, in either vessel, take a spare oar. Large waves can blow up in wide waters; life jackets should be taken and the boat should have built-in buoyancy. Thigh boots should not be worn; you cannot swim in waders. Gum boots enable one to enter and leave a boat with dry feet, and a pair of waterproof overtrousers keep dry your stern and knees. Cushions are a comfort. A deflated motor-scooter inner tube is easy to stow in the car; inflated it is both cushion and bouyancy aid.

Most desirable of all is a skilled and knowledgeable boatman. The bed of a loch is not uniform: there are deep, fishless, underwater ravines, well-populated shallow banks, promontories, bays and islands. The local boatman knows them all. He understands the dangers, where to shelter in a storm and when it would be wise to go home in anticipation of a gale. He is the key which opens the door to success.

Tackle for boat fishing

Fish sitting down on a thwart or on a board placed across the gunwales if you need a little extra height. Do not cast standing up or you may be pitched over the side in rough weather. Due to this low position, and the need to trickle droppers across the surface, a long rod is necessary. Casting is with or across the wind; in consequence a stiff rod, throwing a narrow loop of fast-moving heavy line, is out of place. Fish with a long, lightweight, single-handed rod casting a No 7 floating line. Bruce & Walker manufacture six models of Merlin tubular carbon rods between 11 and 12 ft in length, taking lines between AFTM No 4 and No 8.

The House of Hardy make many rods in suitable lengths, including their 11ft Drifter, designed for wet-fly fishing from a boat with a No 7 line.

The net should be large enough to hold both salmon and sea trout, for both fish are found in many lochs. The Gye is not suitable, for the net has to be

Use a large net.

held out from the boat and fish and net lifted; the aluminium shaft of a Gye will bend. Hardy's produce the fibreglass-framed Superlite net which will float if dropped overboard. It is capacious, the removable shaft also acts as a wading staff and the Y-shaped arms may be removed for storage in the car. The arms fit into sockets in the shaft; there is no risk of the net failing to open because it is open all the time.

The leader should be not less than 9 ft, and preferably 10 ft, in length. The breaking strain of the point ought to be chosen in relation to the weight of fly to be cast and the expected size of fish. The maximum wet-fly hook is likely to be a No 8, which is well balanced by a 1x leader tapered to a 7 lb BS point. Leeda Platil tapered wet-fly casts are 9 ft in length with two droppers, and the 1x rating is sufficient to deal with heavy sea trout and 5 lb grilse.

Home-made leaders in three sections are suitable and less expensive.
Using Maxima Chameleon, make them as follows:

Butt 3 yd of 20 lb BS.
Middle 3 yd of 15 lb BS.
Point 3 yd of 8 lb BS.

Droppers may be added as described in Chapter 2, using a spool of 10 lb BS
nylon. It is wise to slightly increase the strength of a dropper beyond the 8 lb
BS used for the point section. A dropper constantly waggles when cast and
fished; this will gradually weaken the nylon where it joins the main leader.
The butt should be joined by a blood knot to 6 in. of 20 lb BS monofilament
needle-knotted into the point of the fly line, or by a braided loop.

There will be three single-hooked flies on your leader in sizes ranging from
No 8 to No 12. Carry these lures: Peter Ross on the point; Mallard & Claret
on the first dropper; Black Pennell on the bob. Swap their positions about if
you wish; substitute a Butcher from time to time; try an Alexandra or a Zulu
on the bob. However, a wider choice is unlikely to add to the basket in the
boat. Having limited yourself to these six well-proven traditionals, your
boatman will have a favourite of his own in his pocket. Knot it to the prime
position on the point, or in any place on the leader that he suggests. Local
favourites are the result of trial and error on that water; use his pattern if it is
offered.

The fishing

It is usual to fish with a companion, with the boatman in the centre. He will
hold the boat broadside on and progress will be made by a downwind drift.
You are thus always casting with the wind, which is quite different from
trying to cast against the wind from the shore. In the latter case, you have to
continue the power of the forward cast until the rod tip almost touches the
water, aiming out parallel to the surface to cut beneath the opposing wind,
line being extended by two or three false casts.

There should be little or no false casting in boat fishing; it is unnecessary and
sometimes dangerous when three persons are in close proximity. None of us
like a hook in the back of the neck. Consider the position: you are closer to
fish in a boat than when on shore; you have a long length of line already
outside the tip of the 11 ft rod; the wind will assist the forward cast. so, after a
retrieve, cast forward and high, aim for the hills and stop the rod point 6 ft
above the water; the wind will carry out the line.

Now, the retrieve, the key to loch-fishing success. You have extended 20 yd of line. The recovery must be faster than on shore, for the boat is drifting towards the flies. As your team of lures is drawn closer, raise the rod, scuttle the bob across the surface and up into the air; the first dropper follows in its turn, skipping on the waves, and then you lift out the point fly slowly and go into the back cast. Slow retrieves are of little use. It is no good inching-in the line as one might a midge pupa on a reservoir – the boat will overshoot the pupa and sea trout don't feed! Finnock and sea trout are attracted by movement. Let each fly in turn create a wake.

There are no rules on the speed at which one should strike. Some fish just attach themselves; others roll into view with open mouths; some just swirl. If advice is offered it might be to match your response to the size of fish, if that may be discerned: fast for finnock; slow for large sea trout.

Dapping

You have to be skilled to fish wet fly from a boat and take more than other boats. When dapping, much depends upon the beat you have been allocated, the boatman's knowledge of the water and your ability to control the strike. After an hour or two a beginner is capable. Dapping does not present the

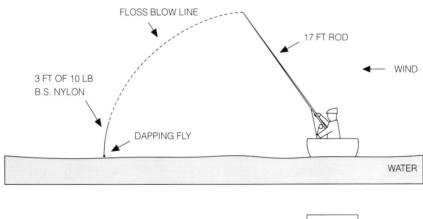

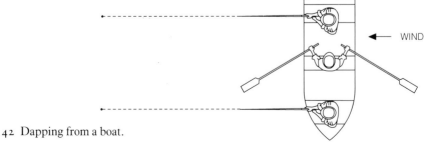

42 Dapping from a boat.

challenge of fishing with skill, but it does put fish in the boat and grant a rest from endless casting. Necessities are a long light rod, often loaned by the fishery or hotel. Mitchell now produce two telescopic dapping rods, marketed at low prices. The shorter is 14¼ ft in length and of five sections; the longer is 17 ft in six sections. They have a green, non-flash finish and metal re-inforced joints.

The reel should be filled with 100 yd of 20 lb BS monofilament, and 20 yd of nylon floss line. You may have to put an old fly line beneath the backing to fill the spool. To the end of the floss attach 1 yd of 10 lb BS Maxima and a fat, buzzy, well-waterproofed fly. The name of the fly and the colour do not matter – any large hairy fly well soaked in Supafloat will suffice. Red Palmer, Loch Ordie, Fore & Aft and Black Pennell are suitable.

A reasonable breeze is required to waft out the fly. This should be tripped across the surface without the nylon touching the water. With rod held high the fly searches the water from right to left and left to right. That is all, except for the strike, which should be slow rather than rapid. Allow his tail time to wave goodbye!

Glossary

Adipose fin Small fin on the back of a game fish between the dorsal fin and the tail.

AFTM Scale Defines the weight of a fly line.

Alevin Fishlet with yolk sac which hatches from an ovum.

Aquifer Chalk stratum underlying the hills and valley of a chalk stream.

Arlesley bomb Weight incorporating a swivel (used as part of Paternoster system of fishing a bait).

Backing An additional length of strong thin line joined to, and beneath, the fly line on a fly reel.

Backing-up Method of fishing a salmon fly in a fast-moving curve from the tail to the head of a river pool.

Baggot Hen salmon swollen with eggs which it is unable to extrude.

Bail arm Part of a fixed spool reel which gathers and winds the line onto the spool.

Bank (in boat fishing) Area of shallow water in a loch.

Bank (of a river) Looking downstream, the right bank is to your right, the left bank to your left.

Blow line (Floss line) Undressed fluffy line blown out by the wind from the tip of a long rod, to carry the fly over and onto the water when dapping from a boat.

Burn Small Scottish stream.

Butt (of leader) Thickest part of a tapered leader where it joins the fly line.

Butt (of rod) Handle end of a rod.

Caddis Another name for a sedge fly.

Chironomid Midge.

Collar Short length of thick monofilament attached to the end of a fly line and to which the leader is joined.

Crane fly Daddy-long-legs

Dangle (on the) Position of fly, or taking salmon, when straight downstream of the angler.

Dropper Second or third fly fished on a leader above the point fly. The top dropper is sometimes called a 'bob'.

Dun First aerial stage of flies of the order Ephemeroptera.

Finnock A small Scottish sea trout.

Fish In Scotland refers to a salmon rather than a sea trout or trout.

Flight (hook mount) Treble hook, wire (sometimes nylon) and swivel passing through hollow centre of Devon Minnow.

Floss line *see* Blow line.

Fry Small young fish (after the alevin stage).

Gaff Pointed barbless hook on a shaft for landing salmon.

Gape Defines the length of gap between the point and shank of a hook.

Gillie A person who should have detailed knowledge of a river or loch and who is employed to assist an angler.

Gravid Descriptive of a hen fish with well-developed roe.

Grilse A 'one sea-winter' salmon.

Gye net Large salmon or sea-trout net carried on the back.

Hackle Neck feather used in dressing flies; cock bird for dry flies, hen for wet flies.

Halford, F.M. (1844–1914) The doyen of dry-fly angling.

Hatch *see* Sluice.

Herling A small sea trout.

Kelt Spawned fish.

Kype Upward hook on lower jaw of cock fish.

Leader (historically called a 'cast') The length of nylon joining the fly line to the fly.

Ledger *see* Paternoster.

Lie Place where fish pause or rest in a river.

Lure Wide term embracing spinning baits, artifical flies, plugs etc.

Marrow spoon Narrow spoon used to withdraw the stomach contents of a dead trout for examination.

Mend To move the fly line on the water, after the initial cast, by switching upstream to decrease the speed of passage of a fly across the river to the angler's bank.

Mepp A revolving spoon bait.

Neck (of a river pool) Narrow entrance where the river runs into a pool.

Nymph Underwater stage in the life-cycle of some insects.

'On the fin' Position of feeding river trout close to the water surface and waiting to take passing, floating, natural flies.

Otter Device to release baits caught on the river bed.

Ova Eggs of a fish.

Parr Small fish in the early stage of its life-cycle.

Paternoster (Ledger) Method of fishing an artificial or natural bait slowly and close to the river bed.

Peal West Country term for a sea trout.

Peal sling Quick-release harness by which a Gye net is carried on the angler's back.

Piling Sheets or staves of wood or metal used to reinforce the bank of a river.

Plug An artificial vaned bait, usually fish-shaped, sometimes jointed, which moves about in a wiggly manner when retrieved by a spinning reel.

Point fly The fly at the end of a leader.

Priest Short truncheon with which to kill fish by hitting them on the head (administering the last rites).

Pupa Immature stage of some flies.

Rapala Type of plug bait.

Redd Depression cut in gravel or small stones by fish in river bed, into which the female deposits the ova, which are fertilized by the milt of the cock fish.

Run-off The downstream, tail end of a river pool.

School peal West Country term for small sea trout on their first return to the river in summer from the sea.

Scissors (to be hooked in the) Description of the point of the angle between the upper and lower jaws of a fish.

Sea lice Suckered lice found on the flanks and backs of salmon and sea trout when they enter the river from the sea.

Sea trout Migratory brown trout.

Sewin Welsh term for a sea trout.

Shoot (to) When false casting, and making the final throw, the extra line which passes out through the rod rings to obtain additional distance.

Skate (skid) A fly crossing the river, or drawn over the loch or lake surface, creating a wake.

Skues, George E.M. (1858–1949) Innovator of fishing the upstream nymph.

Sluice (hatch) Boards which may be raised or lowered to control the depth or flow of a river, usually a chalk stream, above which there is sometimes a fish lie.

Smolt An immature salmon or sea trout migrating down river in spring to make its first entry to the sea.

Spate Rise and fall of water level in a river following rain.

Spinner General term for revolving artifical baits.

Spinner (natural fly) Second aerial and egg-laying stage of flies of the order Ephemeroptera (sometimes called a 'spent').

Split cane Rod of hexagonal cross-section formed of six-faced strips of cane, bonded or wrapped together with silk.

Spoon A type of artificial bait, sometimes revolving.

Spring tide High tide occuring at full and new moons.

Stale fish A salmon or sea trout which has returned from the sea and been in fresh water for some weeks, commonest in the autumn.

Stickle Shallow section of a river between two pools.

Tailer Wire noose to land salmon. It grips the fish at the 'wrist' just above the tail.

Toby Type of long-spoon bait.

Trace About 3 ft of nylon, sometimes wire, between the swivel at the end of the line from a spinning reel and a natural or artificial bait.

Walk-up Method of persuading a salmon to move upstream by gentle pressure and follow the angler as he walks up the river bank towards the head of a pool.

Wye weight Weight used in salmon and sea-trout fishing by artifical or natural bait and consisting of a loop at one end, for line attachment, and a swivel at the other to which the trace is attached.

Wind knot Knot formed unintentionally in the leader whilst casting. The knot weakens the leader, which must be replaced or the knot removed.

Game-fishing instructors and schools

Register of Experienced Fly Fishing Instructors and Schools
Chairman: Charles Bingham, West Down, Warrens Cross, Whitchurch, Tavistock, Devon, PL19 9LD. Telephone 0822 613899.
Secretary: Richard Slocock, Wessex Fly Fishing, Southover, Tolpuddle, Dorchester, Dorset, DT2 7HF. Telephone 0305 848460.

This organization insists on a comprehensive Standard of Facilities and Code of Customer Care for member Schools and Approved Instructors. These facilities are regularly inspected. The following are members:

REFFIS Approved Instructors
Charles Bingham: salmon, sea-trout, river and still water trout. Address as above.

Simon Cooper: river and still water trout.
Fishing Breaks Ltd., 16 Bickerton Road, Upper Holloway, London N19 5JR.
Telephone 071 281 6737.

Roddy Rae: salmon, sea-trout, river and still water trout. Half Stone Sporting Agency, 6 Hescane Park, Cheriton Bishop, Exeter, Devon, EX6 6JP.
Telephone 0647 24643.

*Derek Herbert: salmon, sea-trout and river trout.
Parkburn Guest House, Grantown on Spey, Morayshire PH26 3EN.
Telephone 0479 3116.

*Brian Morris: salmon, river and still water trout.
Elite School of Game Angling Ltd., Ivy Cottage, Kingswood, Hereford.
Telephone 05444 230604.

*James Pembroke and Sean Roche: trout, sea-trout and salmon.
JMM Killorglin Ltd, Ardlahas, Killorglin, Co. Kerry, Eire.
Telephone 010 535 66 61 393.

*Pat O'Reilly: salmon, sea-trout, river and still water trout.
West Wales School of Flyfishing, Ffoshelyg, Lancych, Boncath, Dyfed, SA37 0LJ.
Telephone 023977 678.

*Richard Slocock: salmon, river and still water trout.
Address as above.

*Graham Ward: still water trout.
East Anglia Sporting Services, 22 Twyford Gardens, Bishop's Stortford,
Hertfordshire, CM23 3EH. Telephone 0279 659914.

*Also as REFFIS Approved School.

Game fishing instruction may also be arranged through the following:

Association of Professional Game Angling Instructors
Secretary: Michael Evans, Little Saxbys Farm, Cowden, Kent, TN8 7DX.
Telephone 0342 850765.

Farlow's of Pall Mall, 5 Pall Mall, London SW1Y 5NP. Telephone 071 839 2423.

House of Hardy, 61 Pall Mall, London SW1Y 5JA. Telephone 071 839 5515.

Orvis Co., Bridge House, High Street, Stockbridge, Hampshire, SO20 6HB.
Telephone 0264 810017.

The Rod Box, London Road, Kings Worthy, Winchester, Hampshire, SO23 7QN.
Telephone 0962 883600.

Game-fishing books

Bingham, C. (1988) *Salmon and Sea Trout Fishing*. Batsford.

Bingham, C. (1989) *The Game Fishing Year*. Batsford.

Bingham, C. (1990) *The River Test – portrait of an English chalk stream*. H. F. & G. Witherby.

Bingham, C. (1993) *Chalk Stream Salmon and Trout Fishing*. Swan Hill Press.

Bingham, C. *Salmon Fishing in Small Rivers*. In preparation.

Clarke, B. & Goddard, J. (1980) *The Trout and the Fly*. Ernest Benn.

Cooper, J. A. (1980) *The Great Salmon Rivers of Scotland*. H. F. & G. Witherby.

Falkus, H. (1975) *Sea Trout Fishing*. H. F. & G. Witherby.

Falkus, H. (1984) *Salmon Fishing*. H. F. & G. Witherby.

Goddard, J. (1966) *Trout Fly Recognition*. A. & C. Black.

Harmsworth, T. *Where to Fish*. Published biennially.

Mills, D. & Graesser, N. (1981) *The Salmon Rivers of Scotland*. Cassell.

Oglesby, A. (1971) *Salmon*. Queen Anne Press.

Oglesby, A. (1986) *Fly Fishing For Salmon and Sea Trout*. Crowood Press.

Pearson, A. (1984) *Reservoir Trout Fishing*. Crowood Press.

Taverner, E. (1929) *Trout Fishing from all Angles*. Seeley Service.

Taverner, E. & Scott, J. (1972) *Salmon Fishing*. Seeley Service.

*Scott, J. (193?) *Greased Line Fishing*. Seeley Service.

Veniard, J. (1952) *Fly Dresser's Guide*. A. & C. Black.

Veniard, J. (1964) *Further Guide to Fly Dressing*. A. & C. Black.

Weaver, M. (1991) *The Pursuit of Wild Trout*. Merlin Unwin Books.

Wilkinson, R. (1990) *The Trout and Sea Trout Rivers of Scotland*. Swan Hill Press.

*Probably compiled in about 1939, this book is about Arthur Wood, one of the originators of greased-line fly fishing for salmon. The scene is mainly the Aberdeenshire Dee.

Tackle suppliers

Bruce & Walker Ltd
Huntingdon Road, Upwood, Cambridgeshire. Telephone 0487-813764

*Farlow's of Pall Mall
5 Pall Mall, London, SW1Y 5NP. Telephone 071-839-2423

*House of Hardy
61 Pall Mall, London, SW1Y 5JA. Telephone 071-839-5515

Leeda Group Ltd
16–17 Padget's Lane, South Moons Moat, Redditch, Worcestershire, B98 0RA.
Telephone 0527-29030

*Orvis Co.
Bridge House, High Street, Stockbridge, Hampshire, SO20 6HB.
Telephone 0264-810017.
27 Sackville Street, London, W1X 1DA. Telephone 071-494-2660

Partridge of Redditch Ltd
Mount Pleasant, Redditch, Worcestershire, B97 4JE. Telephone 0527-541380

*The Rod Box
London Road, Kings Worthy, Winchester, Hampshire, SO23 7QN.
Telephone 0962-883600

Normark Sport Ltd
Pottery Road, Bovey Tracey, Devon, TQ13 9DS. Telephone 0626-832889

*Retail shop.

Index

Page numbers in *italic* refer to illustrations.